THE LIMITS

—— OF THE ——

LOST CAUSE

THE LIMITS

— OF THE —

LOST CAUSE

ESSAYS ON CIVIL WAR MEMORY

GAINES M. FOSTER

LOUISIANA STATE UNIVERSITY PRESS

BATON ROUGE

Published by Louisiana State University Press
lsupress.org

Manufactured in the United States of America
First printing

Designer: Michelle A. Neustrom
Typefaces: Whitman, text; Korolev Compressed, display
Printer and binder: Sheridan Books, Inc.

Jacket illustration: Postcard advertisement for *The Birth of a Nation*, 1917. Ku Klux Klan Collection,
Special Collections, Stuart A. Rose Library, Emory University.

Some of these essays have appeared previously in print, as follows: "Woodward and Southern
Identity," *Southern Review* 21 (April 1985): 351–60; "Guilt over Slavery: A Historiographical Analysis,"
Journal of Southern History 56, no. 4 (November 1990): 665–94; "Coming to Terms with Defeat: Post-
Vietnam America and the Post–Civil War South," *Virginia Quarterly Review* 66 (Winter 1990): 17–35;
"What's Not in a Name: The Naming of the American Civil War," *Journal of the Civil War Era* 8, no. 3
(September 2018): 416–54, reprinted here with permission from the University of North Carolina
Press. A different version of essay 8 appeared as "Today's Battle over the Confederate Flag Has
Nothing to Do with the Civil War," *Zócalo Public Square,* online, October 23, 2018.

The graphs were created by Mary Lee Eggart.

LIBRARY OF CONGRESS CATALOGING-IN-PUBLICATION DATA

Names: Foster, Gaines M., author.
Title: The limits of the Lost Cause : essays on Civil War memory / Gaines M. Foster.
Description: Baton Rouge : Louisiana State University Press, [2024] | Includes bibliographical
    references and index.
Identifiers: LCCN 2023035251 (print) | LCCN 2023035252 (ebook) | ISBN 978-0-8071-7138-7 (cloth)
    | ISBN 978-0-8071-8196-6 (pdf) | ISBN 9780807181959 (epub)
Subjects: LCSH: Lost Cause mythology. | Lost Cause mythology—Historiography. | African
    Americans—Social conditions. | United States—History—Civil War, 1861–1865—Influence.
    | Southern States—History—20th century. | Southern States—History—19th century. |
    United States—Social conditions. | United States—Race relations. | LCGFT: Essays.
Classification: LCC F215 .F6944 2024 (print) | LCC F215 (ebook) | DDC
    973.7/14—dc23/eng/20231025
LC record available at https://lccn.loc.gov/2023035251
LC ebook record available at https://lccn.loc.gov/2023035252

To my teachers

CONTENTS

PREFACE

NTIL I BEGAN WORKING on this book, I had never appreciated how much my scholarship mirrored my personality. Friends will readily agree that I am a bit of a contrarian—some might well leave off the "a bit." In any given conversation, I am likely to disagree or challenge someone's observations or plans; I just cannot seem to stop myself. When I compiled the essays published together here, I realized that my scholarship on the Lost Cause manifests the same tendency—to offer a contrary interpretation at any given opportunity. My early essays on the Lost Cause challenged the then reigning view of C. Vann Woodward that defeat and guilt shaped southern identity. Then, much later, as I returned to the topic of Civil War memory, I found myself questioning what seemed the new orthodoxy, that the South was still fighting the Civil War, a phrase that not only appeared in scholars' books but also surfaced repeatedly in public discussion. I do not see it that way, either.

The essays that follow are therefore a contrarian's take on the white South's memory of the Civil War, commonly called the Lost Cause. Although the Lost Cause played an important role in creating the modern South, it did not preclude white southerners from accepting reunion and embracing sectional reconciliation; indeed, it facilitated it. In part because of white southerners' resulting nationalism, in the years after 1915, the Lost Cause played a less important and direct role in shaping their behavior than it had before. In the first half of the twentieth century, the politicians they elected even made significant contributions to enlarging the national government's power—a role hardly in harmony with a region seeking to maintain its independence. The image of a South still fighting the Civil War, although alluring, obscures more than it explains.

The first three essays here date from long ago, 1985 and 1990, appeared in different journals, and in various ways explore Woodward's view of a southern identity shaped by defeat and guilt, although they also tried to speak to Americans' early struggles to understand the loss of the Vietnam War. I have kept them as they appeared when first published, although I have made minor stylistic changes and in one case have added a note to acknowledge a little of the relevant scholarship that has appeared since their publication. And with all three, I have added a brief headnote to provide context for the essays.

The fourth essay was also published elsewhere, but much later, in 2018, and a different version of the final essay on the Confederate flag appeared online at around the same time. The remaining essays appear here for the first time. Together, these essays make a case for sectional reconciliation and argue that it is important to remember the limits of the influence of the Lost Cause in the years since World War I. A rather extensive introduction puts these contrarian essays in their historiographical context.

ACKNOWLEDGMENTS

WHEN A FRIEND SUGGESTED I compile a collection of essays, it seemed such an easy way to publish a book, but as it turned out, more than half of the essays are new, and the process was not nearly so easy as I thought. Even acknowledging the aid without which this volume would not exist proves hard, since I am not sure I remember everyone who helped me with the early essays. I will start by apologizing to anyone I leave out. But I am happy to have the opportunity to thank some who have assisted me for so long.

The Department of History at Louisiana State University has been a wonderful home for many reasons, including the presence of great colleagues who are always willing to help me improve my work. While writing the older essays, the late Charles Royster and Anne Loveland proved very helpful, as did Bill Cooper. Paul Paskoff offered astute advice, as he has done on much that I have written. A newer colleague, Aaron Sheehan-Dean, provided sound guidance on a couple of the essays, even while serving as an excellent chair. Jerry Kennedy, at LSU but not in history, made suggestions on the essay about Thomas Dixon and W. D. Griffith.

John Shelton Reed kindly read the essay where I quoted him a few times, and old friends Peter Coclanis and Lacy Ford read an essay or two as well and offered useful advice. Fitzhugh Brundage read them all, a couple of them twice, and made invaluable suggestions. Over the years, Charles Eagles, too, read them all. On each occasion, he offered incredibly astute suggestions to tighten their arguments and worked hard to improve my prose.

Mary Lee Eggart crafted the graphs, and Kevin Duffy graciously produced some of the illustrations. I am also much indebted to Todd Manza for his careful, skillful copyediting. Rand Dotson at Louisiana State University Press encouraged the project early, proved perhaps too patient in awaiting its delivery, and then provided both sound advice on the manuscript and helped in so many ways an editor probably should not have to do. I am grateful for it all. As I am for Catherine Kadair's help with the final version and shepherding it through the press.

My greatest debt remains to my wife, Mary Mikell. She did not read the earliest essay—we had just started dating at the time—but she did read the rest, and she always improved them, especially by arguing for clarity. She has also, lo these many years now, put up with me, even as she helps so many people and works hard to improve our community, which is why I dedicated my last book to her.

This time I wanted to acknowledge another important influence. Since I have been teaching, every once in a while a student has come by or emailed to tell me how much they have enjoyed or have gotten out of my course, which, as is true of any teacher, means a great deal to me. Far too slowly, it dawned on me that as a student I had never been so thoughtful. Over the years, I have managed to thank some of my teachers, however belatedly, and the dedication of this book to them is further acknowledgment of how much their courses and they have meant to me. I particularly want to single out for thanks a few who helped me become a historian: Shirley Wilcox and Tom Crane at my high school in Florence, South Carolina; Lewis Jones and Phillip Racine at Wofford College; and Joel Williamson and Don Mathews at graduate school in Chapel Hill.

I should add, of course, that the kind folks who read the essays are not responsible for their remaining faults, just as my teachers cannot be blamed for how I turned out.

THE LIMITS

—— OF THE ——

LOST CAUSE

CONTEXT...BY WAY OF INTRODUCTION

O N JANUARY 6, 2021, A MAN carried a Confederate battle flag into the United States Capitol, and a picture of him with his flag became an iconic image of the attempt to stop the electoral count. A few other members of the mob that day also flew Confederate flags, although many more waved American flags or banners in support of Donald Trump. Nevertheless, the presence of the Confederate flags drew a great deal of comment and condemnation. The events that January came in the context of renewed debates over the flag and Confederate monuments following the massacre of the Emanuel Nine in Charleston, South Carolina, in 2015; protests in Charlottesville, Virginia, over the removal of its Robert E. Lee monument in 2017; and attacks on the statues along Richmond's Monument Avenue following the murder of George Floyd in 2020. Many pundits and others commented that even 155 years after Appomattox, Americans were still fighting the Civil War. At the very least, these events raised questions about how Americans remember the Civil War and how that memory functions in the early twenty-first century. The study of Civil War memory, long an interest of historians, has become even more important for the public. All the essays in this volume address, in one fashion or another, the white South's memory of the Civil War, most often called the Lost Cause. Putting these essays into some context requires an introduction that briefly defines what historians mean by memory and a survey of the historical literature on Civil War memory, particularly the Lost Cause.[1]

THE HISTORY PROFESSION'S CURRENT fascination with how Americans remember the Civil War constitutes part of its larger focus on historical memory. European historians first developed the concept of historical memory before

World War II, but it became common in United States historiography much later. In 1991, Michael Kammen published *Mystic Chords of Memory,* which provided an overview of how America's historical memory has changed over time, and the following year John Bodnar's *Remaking America* appeared. Since then, a host of books have analyzed the memory of various events. Even many traditional histories or biographies add a final chapter or two on the memory of their subject.[2]

With so much scholarship on the topic, a general working definition of what historians mean by memory has emerged. Historians have made almost no use of the vast literature in psychology on brain function and individual memory, because what historians mean by memory is what they term "collective" or "communal" memory, the stories about past events that society as a whole accepts and how it then commemorates those events. Memories, historians also assume, are socially constructed, as they think so much of identity and culture are. In other words, people and institutions shape the stories, the memory. Historians also contend that memory is tied to power; governments and political and cultural elites construct what Bodnar terms official memory. Other segments of or groups in society often counter with what he calls vernacular memories, which challenge official memory. Out of the interaction of official and vernacular memories, Bodnar concludes, public memory emerges. Historians therefore attribute a third characteristic to memory. Along with being collective and constructed, historians see memory as contested.[3]

With the possible exception of the Holocaust or World War I, historians have probably applied these conceptions of memory more to the Civil War than to any other historical event. Yet that scholarship, as with most topics, has never formed a collective understanding of Americans' memory of the war or its power. An initial study of Civil War memory stressed that sectional reconciliation had occurred by 1900 and that North and South shared a common purpose and beliefs. The confrontations between segregationists and the civil rights movement, however, rendered the topic more relevant and led to the first stage in the study of Civil War memory.

From the 1960s through the 1980s, historians most often focused on the Lost Cause and the creation of a distinctive southern identity. The most influential interpretation of that identity was C. Vann Woodward's argument that it developed out of defeat, guilt, and poverty. Studies of the Lost Cause continued, and in the late 1990s and early 2000s, the study of Civil War memory entered a second stage. The new literature emphasizes, as never before, the power and importance of a distinctive African American memory that contests the public memory of the war. Many of the newer studies also question the extent of sectional reconciliation. Both South and North, they conclude, harbored their resentments, held fast to their views, and, especially in the case of white southerners, sought to preserve their old ways. In the phrase that has become so popular, some historians—and more pundits—go on to claim that the South was, and is, still fighting the Civil War.

THE CASE FOR POST–CIVIL WAR sectional reconciliation received perhaps its earliest and most unequivocal presentation in 1937. That year, Harvard professor Paul H. Buck won a Pulitzer Prize for *The Road to Reunion, 1865–1900.* Buck never referred to memory, and his study had much to say about politics and economics, but it also surveyed writing about the war and what Buck called the "veteran mind," all of which stressed how both sides had abandoned their hatreds. Like some later historians, he perceived that reconciliation involved a mutual acceptance of the denial of African American rights, but unlike them, Buck thought that denial inevitable and acceptable. One chapter was titled "The Negro Problem Always Ye Have With You." The next praised "The New Patriotism" and began, "Thirty years after Appomattox there remained no fundamental conflict between the aspirations of North and South."[4]

In 1954, one of Buck's students, Thomas J. Pressly, in *Americans Interpret Their Civil War,* argued that both North and South held to their views of the war through the 1880s. Then, at the turn of the century, the first generation of professional historians—and much of Pressly's book discussed the writings of professional historians, not public memory—espoused a "spirit of nationalism and sectional reconciliation." By the 1930s, though, historians had begun to develop dramatically different interpretations of the causes of the war. Pressly ended his account with the observation that "in the middle of the twentieth century" disagreements "among historians over the meaning of the Civil War experience was matched . . . by sharp controversy in the arena of politics over issues related to those of Civil War days." Writing a preface to a new edition nine years later, he saw even more clearly parallels between the issues of the 1850s and the war and contemporary disputes over segregation. He predicted that disagreements over how to interpret the Civil War would only increase.[5]

Pressly certainly proved correct. In the 1950s and 1960s, the war's centennial and, far more, the civil rights movement made the Civil War a more prominent topic of public discussion than it had been in a long time. Civil rights activists' demand for long-delayed full citizenship and equality for African Americans offered an implicit and often explicit challenge to the public memory of the war, which tended to ignore the implications of emancipation. More important, the movement attacked and eventually succeeded in overturning the legal basis of the system of rigid racial repression that had been established in the 1890s. Most white southerners fought hard to prevent racial change, and segregationists often evoked the war's memory and the Lost Cause's symbols in their effort.[6]

As the modern battle progressed, what might be termed the first stage in historians' exploration of Civil War memory developed, although the concept itself only became common later. Although they did not use the term, two of the South's most influential intellectuals analyzed the memory of the war. In 1958, historian C. Vann Woodward suggested that defeat, guilt, and poverty had shaped southern identity and made the South a distinctive region within the nation. Woodward sought to discourage the white South from making racism the source of its identity and therefore continue to fight desegregation. Two years later, the essay in which he first couched that argument appeared in his book entitled *The Burden of Southern History*; the cover of its Vintage paperback edition featured a tree with the leaves made up of a Confederate battle flag. He dedicated this volume to his friend, the novelist and poet Robert Penn Warren.[7]

At about the same time, Warren, too, was wrestling with the war's meaning. In a brief "meditation," *The Legacy of the Civil War*, published in 1961, Warren maintained that the North and South remembered the war in starkly different ways. He explored the North's "Treasury of Virtue"—its sense of righteous innocence based on the fact that it had preserved the Union and ended slavery—and the South's "Great Alibi"—its contention that defeat and its destructiveness explained and excused the South's failings. Unlike most about whom he wrote, Warren lamented the war's failure to achieve racial equality, and despite some celebration of the sacrifice of the soldiers, he considered the war itself a tragedy. Most of all he stressed the importance of the memory of the war, particularly in the South. He called the war the nation's only "'felt' history" and argued that only when Lee surrendered "was the Confederacy born; or to state matters another way, in the moment of death the Confederacy entered upon its immortality." Although each offered different descriptions of memory, Woodward and Warren agreed on the war's continuing hold on the white South.[8]

Given the segregationists' use of Confederate symbolism in the 1950s and 1960s and Woodward's and Warren's stress on the Civil War's persistent influence on white southerners, by the 1970s historians began to focus more attention on the Lost Cause. In 1973, Rollin G. Osterweis published an analysis of the Lost Cause, which he termed a legend or myth and attributed to the South's proclivity for romanticism. He also portrayed the Lost Cause as persistent and powerful, a power "displayed in the resistance of Southerners to liberal social change in America, during the third quarter of the twentieth century." In 1978, Thomas L. Connelly published *The Marble Man*, a critical interpretation of both Robert E. Lee and his image in American society, followed three years later by *God and General Longstreet: The Lost Cause and the Southern Mind*, coauthored with Barbara L. Bellows. In between Connelly's two studies, Charles Reagan Wilson's influential *Baptized in Blood: The Religion of the Lost Cause, 1865–1920* appeared.

These studies of the Lost Cause argued that it created a distinctive society—in Connelly and Bellows, a folk society, and in Wilson a religious one. Wilson interpreted the Lost Cause as a civil religion, a conceptualization still widely accepted. In places, both echoed Woodward. Connelly and Bellows described the South's "awareness of defeat, alienation from the national experience, and a sense of separation from American ideals"; Wilson argued that the Lost Cause "had emphasized suffering, failure, and defeat." Wilson added that the South's participation in World War I brought a sense of vindication and acceptance of American ideals, but, he added, the disillusionment that followed that war fostered a renewed alienation, although one not so thorough as it had once been. Connelly and Bellows saw the South's distinctive vision persisting into the twentieth century but argued that it found expression not in the Lost Cause per se but in country music. Elvis Presley replaced Robert E. Lee as its central figure.[9]

My own attempt to interpret the meaning and influence of the Lost Cause, *Ghosts of the Confederacy*, appeared soon thereafter, in 1987. Like other early studies, it does not use the term "memory" but refers instead to "tradition." "Memory" would have been better, but I started out to study not memory but the South's response to defeat, and I do not think I had heard of the use of the term in the scholarship. *Ghosts of the Confederacy* concludes that white southerners first mourned their defeat, attempting to come to terms with it, before they gradually began to celebrate the Confederacy. Defeat left southerners defensive and Confederate soldiers worried about their honor and manhood. These and other "scars of defeat," as the book characterized those feelings, contributed to the emergence of the Lost Cause and its celebration of the Confederacy. That celebration in part sought to heal the scars, to reassure the veterans of their honor and to provide a sense of vindication for the region. The Lost Cause and its rituals, at their height between 1890 and 1913, made states' rights, not slavery, the Confederates' cause. It glorified its leaders Lee, Stonewall Jackson, and Jefferson Davis and praised the honor, heroism, and fighting skills of Confederate soldiers.[10]

In the process, the stories and rituals of the Lost Cause promoted, indeed ritually enacted, a vision of a hierarchical social order, one based on a rigid gender, class, and racial structure. The Lost Cause stressed how women remained loyal to "their" men and how faithful slaves were not only loyal to their masters but also happiest as slaves. Most of all, it celebrated loyal common soldiers who dutifully followed Lee, Jackson, and other Confederate generals. Confederate monuments offered a model and celebration of that loyal common man, someone who would unquestioningly follow aristocratic leaders and fight to preserve the existing order. Erin L. Thompson, in her 2022 *Smashing Statues*, offers a similar view of the monument's function of promoting obedience to the southern elite and provides a skillful interpretation of the meaning of the lone stone soldiers scattered across the southern landscape.[11]

The Confederate celebration's version of history and its rituals not only contributed to the emergence of a hierarchical society but also helped ease the region's transition into a more modern, interdependent society and nation. Too often, studies of the Lost Cause ignore the fact that the celebration of the Civil War formed part of a broader interest in and celebration of history that provided a sense of continuity in the midst of dramatic social and structural changes of the late nineteenth century, changes that affected not only the South. Nina Silber's *The Romance of Reunion* shows how in the North these social and economic forces contributed to the emergence of a gendered view of reunion and reconciliation, symbolized by the marriage of a northern man and southern woman. As Thomas J. Brown has shown, the North too put up Civil War monuments and celebrated the war. The development of Civil War memory in the North, though, has not garnered the scholarly attention the Lost Cause has enjoyed. Late nineteenth-century Americans, ill at ease in a modernizing society, did not limit their interest in the past to the Civil War. They also celebrated the American Revolution and created a mythic West, to offer only two examples.[12]

Ghosts of the Confederacy finds that significant sectional reconciliation occurred within the modern South. It argues that reconciliation depended on both sides acknowledging the other's honor and heroism, focusing on the battlefield, and ignoring the issues of the war. With the white South's sense of vindication established, the acceptance of the social changes, and reconciliation with the nation, not to mention the passing of the war's veterans, the social and cultural functions of the Lost Cause became less needed, and after 1915 or so, it did less to shape southern behavior. *Ghosts of the Confederacy* suggests that the Lost Cause did not offer a battle plan for a continuing Civil War, it only provided powerful symbols that could and would be employed in a host of other, later causes.

Shortly after *Ghosts of the Confederacy* came out, Charles Royster published *The Destructive War*, often overlooked by scholars of Civil War memory. Looking closely at the careers of William T. Sherman and Stonewall Jackson, the book explores Americans' experience of the war and attempts to understand its meaning. Royster also offers important insights into why and how Americans thought about the war over the course of the late nineteenth century. They wrote, talked about, and celebrated it, he argues, primarily as a means to comprehend and justify the war itself and its extensive and deadly violence. They needed to understand that experience in a way that both brought order out of its chaos and justified the war's terrible costs. They did not seek to continue the fight.

"After the war," Royster writes, white southerners "commemorated wartime courage and praised secessionists' integrity of conscience," but "they did not perpetuate the ideal of Confederate independence. They separated the memory of the fighting from the purpose of the war and often neglected both." They "treated the Confederacy's four-year claim to independence as an anomaly in American history and in Southern life." Royster adds that the "combination of respect and neglect in Southerners' treatment of the Confederate past made the memory of the war extraordinarily malleable. It could be invoked in support of disparate, competing concerns originating not in fidelity to the motives for secession but in divergent plans for the South in the late nineteenth century and the twentieth century."[13]

Royster's book appeared just as public interest in Civil War memory, which may have waned during the years after the victories of the civil rights movement, revived. In 1987, the NAACP started its campaign against the Confederate flag, which led, particularly in the 1990s and early 2000s, to intense public disputes over its official use in several southern states. In 1988, historian James McPherson won a Pulitzer Prize and a place on the bestseller list for his *Battle Cry of Freedom*, a history of the Civil War that made slavery and emancipation central to the war. Two years later, Ken Burns's *The Civil War* became public television's most watched series at the time. The documentary portrayed slavery as the cause of the war and did not shrink from its brutality and costs; it included many photographs of dead bodies. Yet with its haunting violin music, focus on the battles, and the prominence of interviews with a virtual Lost Cause champion, novelist Shelby Foote, it did not fully escape romanticizing the war. Three years later, in 1993, the movie *Gettysburg*, based loosely on Michael Shaara's *The Killer Angels*, offered an even more traditional focus on the battlefield. Shaara's novel, which did not ignore the role of slavery in the war but focused on the leaders, strategies, and heroics at the battle of Gettysburg, had come out in 1974. It won a Pulitzer Prize but at the time had only modest sales. Following the movie, its sales skyrocketed. In the 1990s, Americans seemed more interested in the Civil War than at any time since the 1960s.[14]

Toward the end of the decade, that growing popular interest in the Civil War attracted the attention of journalist Tony Horwitz, who himself found the war fascinating, in part because his father had. Touring the South, Horwitz visited various Confederate historical sites and memorials and talked with white southerners still obsessed with the war, particularly members of the Sons and Daughters of the Confederacy and Civil War reenactors. Based on his tour, he published *Confederates in the Attic* in 1998. Some readers may have found his subjects and even his subject amusing, particularly after reading his hilarious descriptions of hard-core reenactors. Horwitz, though, wrestled with the implications of "the South's obsession with the War." He concluded, "For many Southerners I'd met, remembrance of the War had become a talisman against modernity, an emotional lever for their reactionary politics," and noted that the "issues at stake in the Civil War—race in particular—remained raw and unresolved, as did the broad question the conflict posed. Would America remain one nation? . . . The whole notion of a common people united by common principles—even a common language—seemed more open to question than at any period of my lifetime." The book's subtitle was *Dispatches from the Unfinished Civil War*. Horwitz's views anticipated the scholarship soon to come, which would emphasize the role of race in the Lost Cause and say much about an "unfinished" Civil War.[15]

Around the time of Horwitz's book, scholars began to publish more studies of Civil War memory than ever before—and more than can be treated here. Another important book that focuses on race, by art historian Kirk Savage, appeared the year before Horwitz's. A study of the "history of slavery and its violent end," *Standing Soldiers, Kneeling Slaves,* analyzes monuments both to emancipation and to Confederate soldiers. It concludes that, in them, the "nation was recast more powerfully than ever before in the mold of the ordinary white man, leaving the black body once again on the margins."[16]

In 2001, David W. Blight published *Race and Reunion*. It developed many of the themes in the second stage of Civil War memory studies, and very quickly it became and remains the most influential study of the topic. It begins by quoting Warren on the war as America's only felt history, and throughout, it treats Civil War memory as central to understanding America. Although Blight stresses sectional reconciliation and never uses the image of an unfinished war, he makes much the same point. "As long as we have a politics of race in America," he writes in his introduction, "we will have a politics of Civil War memory."[17]

Nevertheless, Blight concludes that by World War I, the white North and South had not only reunited but also agreed on what he termed a "reconciliationist" memory of the war. It celebrated the glories of the battlefield, praised the service and heroism of soldiers on both sides, and ignored the issues of the war, especially slavery and emancipation. Blight never dismisses the importance of the preservation of the Union, but he emphasizes that reunion came at the cost of equality for African Americans. In perhaps his major contribution, Blight carefully—and passionately; there is never any doubt about where his sympathies lie—explains the early development by African Americans and a few of their white allies of what he labels an "emancipationist" memory of the war, one that contested the dominant reconciliationist memory. The emancipationist memory made ending slavery, not preserving the Union, central to the war, and emancipation its major accomplishment. Therefore, northern victory and African Americans', especially Black soldiers', contributions to winning the war demanded that Americans embrace full citizenship and equality for African Americans.

Blight does not ignore the white South's memory. Like many before him, he argues that white southerners adamantly proclaimed they fought to preserve states' rights, not slavery. More than previous students of the Lost Cause, though, Blight makes the defense of slavery, the white South's victory in Reconstruction, and the preservation of white supremacy central features of the white South's memory of the war. He sometimes refers to it as the Lost Cause, but he labels it the white supremacist memory. The works that followed Blight's book, many published between 2002 and 2005 and therefore begun before his book appeared, also emphasize the role of white supremacy in the Lost Cause and the existence of an African American–contested memory of the war. But they challenge his account of reconciliation, and some make his implicit case for an unfinished war explicit.

The year after *Race and Reunion*, in 2002, David Goldfield did just that in *Still Fighting the Civil War*. He, too, writes of the importance of a distinct African American memory, one that after World War II gave strength and force to the civil rights movement. He focuses more, though, on the white South's view of history. Like Wilson, he stresses the influence of religion, and like Woodward, he makes history central to southern identity. Unlike Woodward, though, Goldfield finds that white southerners learned little from the past but instead crafted an interpretation that served the cause of white, male supremacy. Goldfield then traces through the twentieth century white males' attempts to maintain their supremacy; that is what he means by the South still fighting the Civil War. Goldfield's title, especially, evokes the idea of a continuing Civil War—and the phrase all but took on a life of its own.[18]

After Blight's and Goldfield's books appeared, studies of Civil War memory only increased. Other new works expanded on two of Blight's major interpretive points—the centrality of race to white southerners' memory of the Civil War and the importance and power of a contrasting and contesting African American memory. Karen L. Cox's 2003 *Dixie's Daughters,* a history of the United Daughters of the Confederacy, demonstrates the importance of women in perpetuating the Lost Cause, something Blight does not stress. Like Blight, though, she portrays white supremacy as important in the Lost Cause. W. Fitzhugh Brundage's 2005 *The Southern Past,* too, stresses the role of women and, perhaps more strongly than Blight or Cox, puts the Lost Cause into the context of a pervasive white supremacy. Brundage also analyzes how Civil War memory was woven into a larger and longer memory that incorporated many other aspects of the South's past, thereby making the Lost Cause less central and persistent than in Blight's conception. No study, perhaps, makes the relationship between the Lost Cause and race more direct than Adam H. Domby's *The False Cause.* Published much later, in 2020, it had its origins in Domby's discovery of a manuscript copy of a speech delivered at the dedication of the University of North Carolina's Confederate monument, in which the speaker gave an account of his savage beating of a Black woman right after the war. Domby then makes much of that story in his ensuing book.[19]

Brundage and other scholars also further develop Blight's emphasis on the power and continuing influence of a dissenting African American vision of the past. Early African American celebrations of the war, Brundage shows, displayed a respectful Black community and demonstrated African American manhood, always an important part of the emancipationist memory. Later commemorations, which were less public spectacles after white elites reasserted their control over public life, interpreted the war as God's punishment for the sin of slavery and recalled that institution's horrors. William A. Blair's 2004 *Cities of the Dead* chronicles a battle in Virginia among Unionist (at least during Reconstruction), Confederate, and African American memories of the Civil War. Blair's account of African American commemorations shows that by the 1890s, a division emerged between those who wanted to avoid mentioning the slave past and those who wanted to celebrate emancipation and the progress African Americans had achieved. Both agreed on tying the commemoration to a call for national action against racism. These and other studies tend to reinforce Blight's close identification of the Lost Cause with white supremacy and expand his analysis of an emancipationist memory that contested the dominant public memory.[20]

Blight's case for sectional reconciliation, however, came under increasing challenge. Well into the twentieth century, Benjamin G. Cloyd explains, veterans' accounts of the horrors experienced in Civil War prisons forestalled sectional reconciliation. John R. Neff, too, argues against reconciliation, in his history of Civil War cemeteries. In a study of veterans of the Army of the Cumberland, Robert Hunt finds persistent hostility toward their former Confederate foes, as does Barbara A. Gannon, in her work on Black and white veterans in the Grand Army of the Republic. Gannon and Hunt also make the case that most Union veterans remained hostile to their Confederate counterparts, and even as they stressed their achievement in preserving the Union, they acknowledged slavery as a cause of the war and took credit for emancipation.[21]

The most thoroughgoing challenge to Blight's emphasis on reconciliation came in Caroline E. Janney's *Remembering the Civil War*, published in 2013. Janney acknowledges reunion but differentiates it from reconciliation, a distinction Blight did not draw. She then maintains that reconciliation was limited, if it occurred at all. Union and Confederate veterans both remained bitter toward their former foes and kept the issues of the war alive. Northerners still saw Confederates as traitors who fought to preserve slavery, and Janney contends that even many white southerners admitted that slavery had contributed to the outbreak of the war. Like Cox and others, Janney stresses the role of women, particularly white women in the South who shaped a powerful Lost Cause, which she also associates closely with white supremacy. Because of the women's efforts, if any memory came to dominate the nation by the late 1930s, it was the Lost Cause. M. Keith Harris's *Across the Bloody Chasm,* published the year after Janney's book, also stresses continuing hostilities.[22]

Taking the study of Civil War memory further in time than most historians have, Nina Silber, who had earlier written of reconciliation in the 1890s, discovers divergent memories in the 1930s. In an earlier essay, she challenges much of the literature on reunion and reconciliation and calls for a focus instead on "the imagined reconstitution of the nation." In her 2018 book on the 1930s, she shows how "different groups derived different lessons from" the Civil War and explains how Civil War memory could both push people apart and be used to bring them together, particularly with the coming of World War II. Yet the title of the book, and the final chapter, place the emphasis on continued conflict: *This War Ain't Over: Fighting the Civil War in New Deal America.*[23]

Historians who reject the idea of sectional reconciliation do not inevitably argue for a continuing Civil War, but certainly the idea that white southerners cherished their hostility for the North encourages the conclusion that the South is still fighting the Civil War. In the twenty-first century, when controversies arise, especially when they involve race, many are quick to place them in the context of a continuing Civil War. Indeed, the idea of the South still fighting the Civil War has become common. In 2015, David Blight made his implicit case for a continuing Civil War explicit. He published in the *Atlantic* an article entitled "The Civil War Isn't Over," in which he primarily wrote, as he had earlier, of the nation's failure to achieve full equality for African Americans and of the continued public opposition to that goal. The question of equality was "at the heart of the war," he writes, and in that sense "not only is the Civil War not over; it can still be lost." At the end of the essay, he returned to the theme: "As Americans disturbingly learn, generation after generation, many have never fully accepted the verdict of Appomattox."[24]

Three years after Blight's essay appeared, and after President Trump's election, Rebecca Solnit, the American correspondent for the *Guardian,* made much the same case, considerably less subtly, in a piece entitled "The American Civil War Didn't End. And Trump Is a Confederate President." In 2022, historian Jeremi Suri published a book that primarily offered a history of Reconstruction but, using the man pictured with a Confederate flag in the Capitol, also linked the January 6 attack with the Confederacy and the Lost Cause. Suri begins his book, "Worries about a new civil war in America are misplaced: the Civil War never fully ended." Commentator Steve Phillips also argues that it has not ended. His 2022 *How We Win the Civil War* more closely identified attempts to preserve white supremacy with the continuation of the Civil War, terming proponents of white supremacy Confederates and their tactics a "Confederate battle plan."[25]

THE ESSAYS THAT FOLLOW challenge both the older view of a South chastened by defeat and the newer emphasis on a South still fighting the Civil War. Their arguments emerge out of the interpretation first developed in *Ghosts of the Confederacy.* Given the scholarship that followed it, two aspects of its interpretation, though, merit comment, if not correction. *Ghosts of the Confederacy* has been criticized for various failings, but perhaps most often for not making women, especially the United Daughters of the Confederacy, central to the creation and perpetuation of the Lost Cause. It does stress the role of veterans in the years from 1890 to 1907, but it also finds that women's influence dominated both right after the war and after 1907. No doubt it could have done more to emphasize the central role women played in the twentieth century, and done more to show how, for some, their vision of the Lost Cause contributed to their role in reform movements. Nor does *Ghosts of the Confederacy* identify the Lost Cause as closely with white supremacy as recent works have done, although it does argue that the Lost Cause bolstered it. In part, the book did not do more to emphasize racism because in my research I found fewer explicit appeals to racism during the rituals of the Lost Cause than I anticipated. More important, the book put the Lost Cause's role in supporting white supremacy in the context of the creation of a hierarchical society based not just on race but also on gender and class. Nevertheless, it could have done more to stress the role of the Lost Cause in promoting racism, and certainly it should have emphasized that reconciliation came at the cost of African American rights.[26]

With those caveats, the fundamental perspective in *Ghosts of the Confederacy* continues to shape my arguments in the essays that follow. They do not offer a history of Civil War memory or even the white South's memory of the war. Each essay stands alone and explores different aspects of Civil War memory. The first three, rather old now, challenge the even older interpretation that defeat and guilt shaped southern identity. One uses the Lost Cause to question Woodward's contention that defeat shaped southern identity; the second offers a historiographical analysis of the development of the guilt thesis, which again touches on Woodward's description of southern identity. A third uses the Lost Cause to better understand America's initial response to defeat in Vietnam.

The remaining essays, all but one published here for the first time, are influenced by my response to the second stage in the development of the literature on Civil War memory, with its doubts that sectional reconciliation ever occurred, emphasis on the persisting power of the Lost Cause, and contention that the South is still fighting the Civil War. One explores how changing names for the Civil War revealed the extent, and limits, of sectional reconciliation. Another analyzes the use of the fiery cross and the Confederate flag in the novels of Thomas Dixon and in W. D. Griffith's movie *The Birth of a Nation*. Both Dixon and Griffith advocated sectional reconciliation, and both promoted the fiery cross as a racist symbol tied not to the Confederacy but to a white Protestant nationalism. An essay on Robert E. Lee, both the man and the memory of him, "The Marble Man," traces how the Marble Man promoted sectional reconciliation at the cost of ignoring the racism of the real Lee and the Confederacy. Another essay develops a case for the South's important role in the expansion of federal power, which hardly fits the idea of a South that rejected reunion and continued to fight the Civil War. A final essay examines recent disputes over the official use of the Confederate flag and finds that, though Civil War memory still plays a role, support for the flag has much more to do with unabashed white supremacy, white fears that the government does too much to help African Americans, and the current cultural and political divide. Together these final five essays make a case for sectional reconciliation, question the idea of the South still fighting the Civil War, and suggest that the racism inherent in the Lost Cause may now be better understood in the context of American attitudes on race and a more recent white Protestant nationalism than as a manifestation of a white southern identity rooted in the Lost Cause.

NOTES

1. Such a brief introduction cannot incorporate the incredible number of books and articles that have explored Civil War memory. A few more appear in the notes to the essays that follow. Several historiographical essays on the topic exist. Among the more recent are Caroline E. Janney, "The Civil War in Public Memory," in *The Cambridge History of the American Civil War*, vol. 3: *Affairs of the People*, ed. Aaron Sheehan-Dean (New York: Cambridge University Press, 2019), 481–505; Nina Silber, "Reunion and Reconciliation, Reviewed and Reconsidered," *Journal of American History* 103 (June 2016): 59–83; Matthew J. Grow, "The Shadow of the Civil War: A Historiography of Civil War Memory," *American Nineteenth Century History* 4 (Summer 2003): 77–103. Also not discussed here are two helpful syntheses of Civil War memory, Robert J. Cook, *Civil War Memories: Contesting the Past in the United States Since 1865* (Baltimore: Johns Hopkins University Press, 2017); and Barbara A. Gannon, *Americans Remember Their Civil War* (Santa Barbara, Calif.: Praeger, 2017).

2. Michael Kammen, *Mystic Chords of Memory: The Transformation of Tradition in American Culture* (New York: Alfred A. Knopf, 1991); John Bodnar, *Remaking America: Public Memory, Commemoration, and Patriotism in the Twentieth Century* (Princeton, N.J.: Princeton University Press, 1992).

3. For more on historians' conception of memory, see W. Fitzhugh Brundage, "No Deed but Memory," in *Where These Memories Grow: History, Memory, and Southern Identity*, ed. Brundage (Chapel Hill: University of North Carolina Press, 2000), 1–28. For a challenge to the emphasis on collective memory, see Silber, "Reunion and Reconciliation," 79.

4. Paul H. Buck, *The Road to Reunion, 1865–1900* (Boston, Mass.: Little, Brown, 1937), 236, 283, 298.

5. Thomas J. Pressly, *Americans Interpret Their Civil War, with a New Introduction* (1954; New York: Free Press, 1962), 221, 360.

6. Robert J. Cook, *Troubled Commemoration: The American Civil War Centennial, 1961–1965* (Baton Rouge: Louisiana State University Press, 2007); Jon Wiener, "Civil War, Cold War, Civil Rights: The Civil War Centennial in Context, 1960–1965," in *The Memory of the Civil War in American Culture,* ed. Alice Fahs and Joan Waugh (Chapel Hill: University of North Carolina Press, 2004), 237–57.

7. C. Vann Woodward, *The Burden of Southern History* (New York: Vintage, 1960).

8. Robert Penn Warren, *The Legacy of the Civil War: Meditations on the Centennial* (1961; New York: Vintage, 1964), 4, 15, 75.

9. Rollin G. Osterweis, *The Myth of the Lost Cause, 1865–1900* (Hamden, Conn.: Anchor, 1973), xi; Thomas L. Connelly, *The Marble Man: Robert E. Lee and His Image in American Society* (New York: Alfred A. Knopf, 1977); Thomas L. Connelly and Barbara L. Bellows, *God and General Longstreet: The Lost Cause and the Southern Mind* (Baton Rouge: Louisiana State University Press, 1982), 137; Charles Reagan Wilson, *Baptized in Blood: The Religion of the Lost Cause, 1865–1920* (Athens: University of George Press, 1980), 178.

10. Gaines M. Foster, *Ghosts of the Confederacy: Defeat, the Lost Cause, and the Emergence of the New South, 1865–1913* (New York: Oxford University Press, 1987).

11. Erin L. Thompson, *Smashing Statues: The Rise and Fall of America's Public Monuments* (New York: W. W. Norton, 2022), 34–51.

12. Nina Silber, *The Romance of Reunion: Northerners and the South, 1865–1900* (Chapel Hill: University of North Carolina Press, 1993); Thomas J. Brown, *Civil War Monuments and the Militarization of America* (Chapel Hill: University of North Carolina Press, 2019). Along with Silber's and Brown's, several of the books discussed later in this introduction and in the essays that follow do look at both the North and the South. Brian Matthew Jordan, *Marching Home: Union Veterans and Their Unending Civil War* (New York: Liveright, 2014), focuses on northern veterans; and James Marten, *Sing Not War: The Lives of Union and Confederate Veterans in Gilded Age America* (Chapel Hill: University of North Carolina Press, 2011), also has much on the North. Gannon, *Americans Remember Their Civil War,* has a very good analysis of what she calls the "Union Cause," along with a discussion of additional works on northern memory.

13. Charles Royster, *The Destructive War: William Tecumseh Sherman, Stonewall Jackson, and the Americans* (New York: Alfred A. Knopf, 1991), 156–57.

14. James M. McPherson, *The Battle Cry of Freedom: The Civil War Era* (New York: Oxford University Press, 1988); Phil Leigh, "Making 'Killer Angels,'" *New York Times,* June 28, 2013, https://arch ive.nytimes.com/opinionator.blogs.nytimes.com/2013/06/28/making-killer-angels. On the NACCP and fights over the flag, see John M. Coski, *The Confederate Battle Flag: America's Most Embattled Emblem* (Cambridge, Mass.: Harvard University Press, 2005), 237–71.

15. Tony Horwitz, *Confederates in the Attic: Dispatches from the Unfinished Civil War* (New York: Pantheon, 1998), 384, 386.

16. Kirk Savage, *Standing Soldiers, Kneeling Slaves: Race, War, and Monument in Nineteenth-Century America* (Princeton, N.J.: Princeton University Press, 1997), 3, 210. For some of the import-

ant books on the Lost Cause that appeared around this time, see LeeAnn Whites, *The Civil War as Crisis of Gender, Augusta, Georgia, 1860–1890* (Athens: University of Georgia Press, 1995); Gary W. Gallagher and Alan T. Nolan, eds., *The Myth of the Lost Cause and Civil War History* (Bloomington: Indiana University Press, 2000); Gallagher, *Lee and His Army in Confederate History* (Chapel Hill: University of North Carolina Press, 2001).

17. David W. Blight, *Race and Reunion: The Civil War in American Memory* (Cambridge, Mass.: Harvard University Press, 2001), 4.

18. David Goldfield, *Still Fighting the Civil War: The American South and Southern History* (Baton Rouge: Louisiana State University Press, 2002).

19. Karen L. Cox, *Dixie's Daughters: The United Daughters of the Confederacy and the Preservation of Confederate Culture* (Gainesville: University Press of Florida, 2003); W. Fitzhugh Brundage, *The Southern Past: A Clash of Race and Memory* (Cambridge, Mass.: Harvard University Press, 2005); Adam H. Domby, *The False Cause: Fraud, Fabrication, and White Supremacy in Confederate Memory* (Charlottesville: University of Virginia Press, 2020).

20. Brundage, *Southern Past*; William A. Blair, *Cities of the Dead: Contesting the Memory of the Civil War in the South, 1865–1914* (Chapel Hill: University of North Carolina Press, 2004). Both Kathleen Ann Clark and Mitch Kachun discuss the African American memory of the war in larger contexts—in Clark's case, the context of other commemorations, and in Kachun's, of a longer history of celebrations. Clark, *Defining Moments: African American Commemoration and Political Culture in the South, 1863–1913* (Chapel Hill: University of North Carolina Press, 2005); Kachun, *Festivals of Freedom: Memory and Meaning in African American Emancipation Celebrations, 1808–1915* (Amherst: University of Massachusetts Press, 2003).

21. Benjamin G. Cloyd, *Haunted by Atrocity: Civil War Prisons in American Memory* (Baton Rouge: Louisiana State University Press, 2010); John R. Neff, *Honoring the Civil War Dead: Commemoration and the Problem of Reconciliation* (Lawrence: University Press of Kansas, 2005); Robert Hunt, *The Good Men Who Won the War: Army of the Cumberland Veterans and Emancipationist Memory* (Tuscaloosa: University of Alabama Press, 2010); Barbara A. Gannon, *The Won Cause: Black and White Comradeship in the Grand Army of the Republic* (Chapel Hill: University of North Carolina Press, 2011).

22. Caroline E. Janney, *Remembering the Civil War: Reunion and the Limits of Reconciliation* (Chapel Hill: University of North Carolina Press, 2013); M. Keith Harris, *Across the Bloody Chasm: The Culture of Commemoration Among Civil War Veterans* (Baton Rouge: Louisiana State University Press, 2014).

23. Silber, "Reunion and Reconciliation," 78; Silber, *Romance of Reunion*; Nina Silber, *This War Ain't Over: Fighting the Civil War in New Deal America* (Chapel Hill: University of North Carolina Press, 2018), 8.

24. David W. Blight, "The Civil War Isn't Over," *Atlantic*, April 8, 2015, https://www.theatlantic.com/politics/archive/2015/04/the-civil-war-isnt-over/389847.

25. Rebecca Solnit, "The American Civil War Didn't End. And Trump Is a Confederate President," *Guardian*, November 4, 2018, https://www.theatlantic.com/politics/archive/2015/04/the-civil-war-isnt-over/389847; Jeremi Uri, *Civil War by Other Means: America's Long and Unfinished Fight for Democracy* (New York: Public Affairs, 2022), 1; Steve Phillips, *How We Win the Civil War: Securing a Multiracial Democracy and Ending White Supremacy for Good* (New York: New Press, 2022).

26. For examples of female reformers employing the Lost Cause in behalf of an expanded role for women, see Anastatia Sims, *The Power of Femininity in the New South: Women's Organizations and Politics in North Carolina, 1880–1930* (Columbia: University of South Carolina Press, 1997); W. Fitzhugh Brundage, "White Women and the Politics of History and Memory in the New South, 1860–1920," in *Jumpin' Jim Crow: Southern Politics from the Civil War to Civil Rights*, ed. Jane Daily, Glenda Elizabeth Gilmore, and Bryan Simon (Princeton, N.J.: Princeton University Press, 2000), 115–39.

– 1 –

WOODWARD AND SOUTHERN IDENTITY

From the 1950s through at least the 1980s, C. Vann Woodward, a native of Arkansas who spent much of his career in the History Department at Yale University, was the most influential historian of the South. In the 1950s, he published Origins of the New South, *a widely read and cited history of the years from 1877 to 1913, and* The Strange Career of Jim Crow, *an even more influential explanation of the origins of segregation in the 1890s. A liberal who promoted racial change, Woodward sought to define southern identity on the basis of something other than racism. In the essays analyzed below, Woodward wrote of the South's distinctive experience of poverty, guilt, and defeat. In the late 1960s and 1970s, white, liberal southerners shared Woodward's commitment to racial change and hope of finding some basis for southern identity other than racism. Woodward's essays, republished in 1960 in a collection titled* The Burden of Southern History, *became very influential. The book appeared in three editions; the last came out in 1993, with an updated version published in 2008. Early studies of the Lost Cause echoed Woodward's emphasis on a South shaped by defeat.*

They yelled for the old, crippled, aged-ridden [sic] soldiers; for the flags riddled with shot, powder-burnt, moth-eaten, but grand in the sublimity of defeat, and it must be borne in mind that every shout was for the living and dead of a cause long since buried. . . . I well remember a lad not six years old who stood near me on that memorable occasion and whose absolute abandon of enthusiasm attracted the attention of all around. An old gentleman approached him and began to question him, but the boy found time to reply only between yells. The dialogue was something like this: "What is your name?"

"———, Ya'hoo!" "What are you?" "A Confederate, ya-hoo!" "Who was the greatest man on earth?" "General Lee—ya-hoo!" The old gentleman smiled, saying, "The boy has learned his lessons well," but the boy was still yelling.

—FROM A NORTHERNER'S ACCOUNT
OF A CONFEDERATE VETERANS' PARADE IN 1896

R ARELY HAD DEFEAT and guilt proved so appealing. In 1960, historian C. Vann Woodward published a collection of essays, *The Burden of Southern History*, which examined certain aspects of the South's "distinctive heritage." Woodward quoted historian Arnold Toynbee on how, as a young boy at the Diamond Jubilee procession in England, he had believed that he and his country "are on top of the World, and we have arrived at this peak to stay there— forever! There is, of course, a thing called history, but history is something unpleasant that happens to other people." If he "had been a small boy in New York in 1897," Toynbee added, he would have "felt the same." But if he had been "a small boy in 1897 in the Southern part of the United States, I should not have felt the same; I should then have known from my parents that history has happened to my people in my part of the world."

Woodward, who had also used Toynbee's observations as an epigraph for his earlier *Origins of the New South, 1877–1913*, concurred. This peculiar sense of the past, Woodward explained, emerged from the region's experience of defeat, poverty, frustration, and guilt. The rest of the United States, on the other hand, seemed blinded by what Reinhold Niebuhr in *The Irony of American History* described as illusions of innocence and virtue. More readily than other Americans, Woodward argued, white southerners therefore should have developed "a special awareness of the ironic incongruities between moral purpose and pragmatic result, of the way in which laudable aims of idealists could be perverted to sordid purposes, and of the readiness with which high-minded ideals can be forgotten."

In the 1960s, the Vietnam War, for many a tragic example of the dangers of American innocence, led Woodward to doubt whether southerners had developed such an awareness. The South had offered no warning about the perils of Vietnam. In fact, during much of the war a Texan served as president, a Georgian as secretary of state, and a South Carolinian as commander of American

C. Vann Woodward, photographed in 1989 at Robert Penn Warren's Connecticut farm.
(Curt Richter, platinum-palladium print, National Portrait Gallery,
Smithsonian Institution, Washington, D.C. © Curt Richter.
Used with permission of Curt Richter.)

forces in Vietnam. The white South supported United States intervention in the conflict with at least as much enthusiasm as, and possibly more than, the rest of the nation. In Spartanburg, South Carolina, in 1971, an audience at an all-night gospel sing even stood for the singing of "The Battle Hymn of the Republic," the hated war hymn of the Yankee armies and virtual anthem of American innocence, because it had been dedicated to "our boys in Vietnam." Four years later, when the United States made what some considered a dishonorable peace, one veteran wanted to return to Vietnam to continue the fight under a Confederate flag.

Southern response to Vietnam, in sum, had revealed no special regional perspective on American innocence. White southerners appeared no more cognizant of the possibility of failure, no more aware that good intentions could have bad results, than northerners or westerners. In a second edition of *The Burden,* published in 1968, Woodward speculated that one should not have expected the South to learn from its history or southern politicians to not adopt American myths when in the national arena. Roughly a decade later, Woodward reiterated his conclusion that the South had not embraced his vision of its past. The heritage of defeat, frustration, and guilt, he admitted in the essay "The Aging of America," found expression only in a "few" of the South's "brilliant writers." Most southerners accepted national myths and therefore failed to serve the nation and themselves. "It is doubtful," Woodward concluded, with a hint that he still did not want to abandon his vision of a southern identity, "that the defeated South was ever able to make its heritage of adversity contribute substantially to its maturity and wisdom save among a few individuals."

Within a few years, however, the notion of a distinctive southern view of the past crept back into Woodward's writings. In 1980, he asserted that Jimmy Carter's role in the post-Watergate era "seemed to confirm rather than expose the old American (but not Southern) heresies of exceptionalism. These included the dream of a special destiny, a faith in collective innocence, and immunity from the evils of history and from the guilt of wielding power." That same year, in a review of a book on Lyndon Johnson, Woodward argued that the notion that America "could police the world and offer it a moral example at the same time" was not something "that Johnson picked up on the banks of the Pedernales or Rusk along the Chattahoochee." Other historians in the 1980s, too, still clung to the vision of a white South ennobled and educated by its historical experience. Woodward's observations on southern identity had an obvious appeal for southerners. Yet long before Vietnam, the Spanish-American War demonstrated that the South had not been "able to make its heritage of adversity contribute substantially to its maturity and wisdom."

THE LACK OF MATURITY and wisdom, or in other words the failure of the white South to perceive the ironies of its past so clearly or interpret its experience so wisely as its brilliant writers did and as Woodward wanted it to, rested in the South's interpretation of its defeat in the Civil War. If ever there was a moment when white southerners should have appreciated Woodward's observation that nothing about its history "was conducive to the theory that the South was the darling of divine providence," it came at Appomattox. Having fought a war which their ministers assured them had been God's cause, the Confederates suffered overwhelming defeat. Southerners had to wonder why God had deserted them. A very few offered the obvious answer: God had punished them for the sin of slavery or—in a variation offered more often—for abuse of the godly institution of slavery. Others agreed that the South had displeased God but argued that it had done so through sins of dance, drink, or various other failings of personal holiness. Their accounts of these sins, however, sounded less like the fiery jeremiads of Cotton Mather than the casual comment of Claude Rains at the end of *Casablanca*: "Round up the usual suspects."

Most white southerners, even some who lamented the South's sins, turned to their faith not for judgment but for solace. They read in their Bibles and heard from their preachers the promise of God's consolation. They reminded themselves that "all things work together for good to them that love God," and this scriptural promise came to underlie the South's interpretation of history. God, most southerners believed, allowed their defeat only to ensure a greater triumph in the future. The loss of the war, in other words, did not shatter southerners' faith that the South was the darling of divine providence. They considered defeat only a detour on the way to the South's fulfillment of God's will, not a denial of divine mission.

Even if bolstered by faith in their continued status among God's chosen, white southerners still had to face the accusations of the conquering North. Northern churches demanded a confession of the sin of slaveholding and northern congressmen demanded an admission of the evils of secession. Although rendered defensive by the onslaught, the former Confederates admitted neither moral nor political sins. Queried by a visiting Yankee about his fears of divine judgment, one feisty southerner looked perplexed and replied that the South expected God to punish the North for its abuse of southerners. He spoke for many. Southerners, most of whom were Protestants who believed in the necessity of the admission of sin, confessed little. More important, they did not publicly enunciate any feelings of guilt over the South's role in the war. In the decades after Appomattox, in fact, individual Confederates and southern periodicals reviewed the alleged sins of morality and politics and proclaimed the South guiltless. White southerners considered slavery a moral and humane institution. Secession, they believed, was a reasonable and legal response to northern violations of the Constitution.

While southerners easily banished any feelings of guilt, they still faced the frustration of defeat—the failure to achieve independence and preserve slavery. Yet even the sense of frustration and failure rapidly diminished. By the late 1880s, the issues of the war no longer seemed terribly important. Most southerners had accepted reunion, and almost no one harbored a desire for independence. The South had replaced slavery with a system of racial separation and exploitation that proved almost as effective, though not so romantic, as slavery. Many southerners still idealized the old ways or bewailed lost wealth, of course, but most had adapted to the new order. As a result, southerners as a group no longer felt so acutely frustrated by the results of defeat, even though former Confederates still carried painful memories.

The disgrace of corporate and personal failure on the field of battle proved to be one of the more painful memories. In the first years after Appomattox, some of the former Confederates claimed that a reliance on such and such a strategy or a failure by some leader or another brought on defeat. A few even blamed the southern people as a whole for not supporting the cause with sufficient dedication. Before too long, however, a consensus emerged that the Confederates had not failed at all; they had only succumbed to the overpowering numbers and resources of the North. White southern soldiers, therefore, had no reason to be ashamed. They needed to feel no personal sense of failure but rather should proudly remember their contribution to one of the world's greatest armies.

By the end of the 1880s, white southerners had created a public memory of the war that incorporated little sense of guilt, defeat, or frustration. They believed that God had not abandoned the South in defeat but had only prepared it for a higher purpose. They considered the South blameless in pressing the war and heroic in fighting it. In the decades that followed, southerners conducted a public celebration of the war, a cultural ritual of vindication, based in this interpretation of the conflict. They erected in public squares monuments to the memory of the heroism of the soldiers, joined in joyous veterans' reunions, and cheered parades of the former Confederates. At these parades a young southern boy would not have felt the painfulness or the reality of the past. Rather, he would have learned the lessons of heroism inherent in his society's interpretation of the war and would have shouted for joy. He would have developed little appreciation for the ironies of history, and amid the revelry, he would not have paused to contemplate the way grand causes have of ending in failure.

When, during the 1890s, the United States began to discuss increased activism in the world, most white southerners therefore expressed little more awareness of the possible incongruence between moral purpose and results than the boy at the parade would have. In 1891, when an incident in New Orleans generated talk of war with Italy, one Georgia Confederate veteran wired the War Department for permission, in the event of war, "to raise a company of unterrified Georgia rebels to invade Rome disperse the mafia and plant the stars and stripes on the dome of St. Peters." He hardly sounded chastened by defeat. Four years later, the South's premier expansionist, John T. Morgan, extrapolated a defense of involvement abroad from the southern interpretation of God's will for a defeated South. "If, in the history of men," the Alabama senator wrote, "a nation has been 'set apart' and qualified by long suffering for the vicarious work of bettering the conditions of the world, that nation is the people of our Southern States. We have not suffered in vain, and we will not have to wait long for the revelation of the fact that we have supposed to redeem."

In 1898, as Morgan had expected, the United States did undertake a crusade to better the conditions of part of the world. Yet the Spanish-American War, in which Americans sought to be active agents for good in the world, resulted, in places, in tragic consequences. Southerners issued few warnings, and most enthusiastically joined the crusade. Before a group of Confederate veterans, John B. Gordon, one of the region's preeminent spokesmen, celebrated the sense of American mission. He claimed that "our boys are to bear, wrapped in the folds of the American flag, the light of American civilization and the boon of Republican liberty to the oppressed islands of both oceans; they are to place on a higher plane than ever before the influence of America in the councils of the nations, and are to command for their country a broader and more enduring respect for its prowess on land and sea throughout the world." His speech revealed no appreciation of the fact that great causes had tragic results and no awareness of any incongruities between moral purpose and result. At a memorial service in Boston the following year, Gordon's fellow Confederate general Joseph Wheeler joined Julia Ward Howe in singing "The Battle Hymn of the

Republic" in honor of the ongoing crusade abroad. Christian soldiers had once more marched off in innocence to trample out evil, and they came as readily from the South as the North.

When the aftermath of the crusade for Cuban freedom brought hard choices about imperialism, some white southerners did question national policy. Few critics, however, based their opposition on the wisdom gleaned from the South's history, unless it was the lesson that trying to govern dark-skinned peoples was unwise. No "southern position" emerged, and many southerners supported the taking of colonies. Young southerners enthusiastically participated in the most tragic consequence of this grand crusade, a nasty guerrilla war to suppress a nationalistic revolution in the Philippines. They helped quell the rebels with a rebel yell and displayed no apparent appreciation of the irony. In a letter, one even thanked a Confederate general for the example of the soldiers of the 1860s and expressed his hope that white southern troops in the Philippines had lived up to it. Like the boy at the parade, he had learned his lessons well. The white South's interpretation of the Civil War had not encouraged him to question his nation's purpose but rather had led him, like his counterpart from the North, to consider it part of a divine plan. The celebration of the Confederacy during the decade before he went off to war had not communicated an appreciation of tragedy or irony but instead had glorified loyalty and martial skills.

THE SOUTH'S INVOLVEMENT in the Spanish-American War and its aftermath should have rendered its reaction to Vietnam less surprising. In both instances, white southerners responded to the nation's foreign crusades much like other Americans and not as Woodward's vision would have suggested. They did so, in part, because the South's interpretation of the Civil War contained less sense of the tragic, less acknowledgment of guilt, and less awareness of defeat and frustration than did Woodward's. His hope that white southerners would challenge American innocence rested on the assumption of a special southern sense of history, yet the South's interpretation of the Civil War had helped make its view of the past less special than Woodward believed. As Richard H. King has proposed, Woodward's argument owed more to the critical consciousness of the 1930s—the work of William Faulkner, Robert Penn Warren, and other intellectuals—than to the traditional southern interpretation of the past. It was not just their influence that guided Woodward, though, and the forces shaping his vision may suggest something about the burden of southern historians.

Woodward's frequent and insightful use of an ironical approach has obscured the fact that *The Burden of Southern History* incorporated two different visions of what the past is and how it can speak to the present. "The Irony of Southern History," originally presented in 1952 and therefore the first of the major essays in which Woodward developed his interpretation, raised the idea of a special southern sense of the past, but the argument did not depend upon it. In the heart of the piece, Woodward held up the South's intolerant reaction to criticism of slavery in the 1830s to expose the dangers of the hysteria of the McCarthy era. Woodward then suggested that because of the peculiar nature of the southern experience, historians might find other instances in which the history of the region would protect against the nation's obliviousness to problems or evils. He expressed the hope that southern historians would be especially active in the task of exposing American innocence but pointedly admitted that any historian could use the South's past to do so. In this essay, Woodward in effect acted, and asked other historians to act, as a "moral critic," in John Higham's later phrase. Woodward had created a dialogue between the reality of the past and the needs of the present. The "lessons" of history emerged out of this dialogue, out of the process of studying history.

Five years later, Woodward developed what had been a minor theme in the first piece—the South's special experience of the past—into a major interpretation of southern identity. The South's experience with defeat, poverty, frustration, and guilt, Woodward argued in "The Search for Southern Identity," constituted a special heritage "that should prove of enduring worth" to the South and the nation. When Woodward published both essays in *The Burden of Southern History*, its introduction and title expanded the idea of the special heritage's worth, which was only touched upon in "The Search." The introduction referred to the collection as a study of a distinctive southern "character," a term that implied that Woodward described not just a possible identity but an existing perception. By explicitly labeling both "The Search" and "Irony" explorations of that character, he encouraged the reader to assume that all southerners shared an appreciation for the ironies of the southern past and the dangers of American innocence. Putting "burden," a word that did not appear anywhere in the text, in the title strongly reinforced the idea. Especially because of the dedication of the book to Robert Penn Warren, the word unintentionally evoked Warren's character Jack Burden and thereby suggested that southerners were not only troubled by their past but also called by it to act in history.

The emphasis on "identity," "character," and "burden" overpowered Woodward's usual cautious understatement and his specific emphasis on the conditional. Therefore, in 1960, when the book was published, Woodward offered a slightly different vision of the past than in the first of its essays, published nine years before. The South's experience had become less an external reality to be studied and more an internal perception to be exercised. The wisdom from the southern past did not emerge when the historian—whether southern or not—studied the history of the South as a moral critic, but rather existed within the southern heritage—if only southerners would exercise it.

The change probably had several sources. Surely the rising popularity of studies of national character and the increasing use of the term "identity" among historians during the 1950s influenced Woodward. Yet the subtle shift in emphasis may also have reflected Woodward's reaction to the civil rights struggle in the South. He responded both as a liberal reformer and a loyal southerner—two seemingly contradictory attitudes that had always characterized his work, as David Potter has shown. In the essay on southern identity, Woodward the liberal reformer continued the crusade to ease racial change that he had begun shortly before in *The Strange Career of Jim Crow*. That book attempted to remind white southerners that segregation had not existed forever, so that they would be encouraged to accept an alternative. Similarly, "The Search" offered a basis for southern identity other than white supremacy, so that southerners could more easily accept its end.

At the same time that Woodward wrote as a liberal reformer, he also wrote as a southern loyalist. "The Search" explicitly worried that in the midst of economic development and racial change, all sense of southern identity might disappear. Woodward feared that the "Southern heritage [had] become an old hunting jacket that one slips on comfortably at home but discards when he ventures abroad in favor of some more conventional or modish garb." Woodward's reformulation of southern identity in terms of the South's past offered a means to preserve a regional heritage no matter how much contemporary developments altered the region.

But Woodward also offered an identity that could be worn proudly in the

North. He seemed as worried by the increasing northern attacks on a benighted, racist South as he was by the economic transformation of the region. The year before he published "The Search," Woodward had commented in "The Disturbed Southerner," an article not republished in *Burden,* on the tendency of southerners, as a minority, to become defensive when attacked by northerners for the mistreatment of Black people. At about the same time Woodward himself displayed a certain defensiveness in a review of Carl Rowan's description of southern race relations, *Go South to Sorrow.* "Mr. Rowan is not the first who has gone South to sorrow, nor is this his first lamentation," Woodward remarked with uncharacteristic bite. "The South has long served as the wailing wall of the national conscience." Woodward's vision in *The Burden of Southern History* simply transformed the South from the wailing wall to the foundation of the national conscience. The South's moral failings and evil past became in Woodward's analysis a possible source of wisdom. Its character, forged in its special experience and understanding of the past, could offer an escape from American innocence.

In this positive identity, Woodward had unconsciously constructed a secular version of the postwar South's interpretation of the Civil War. Defensive under northern attack, white southerners had maintained that God had allowed defeat in order to prepare them for some greater purpose. Woodward's version of history also made defeat a source of mission. The experience of poverty, frustration, and defeat, Woodward argued, should have chastened and ennobled southerners. It had placed the South in a position to save—or better, had forged a southern character capable of saving—the nation from itself.

In offering such a vision, and in wanting to hold to it even after events in the 1960s made that difficult, Woodward demonstrated his loyalty to the South and his defensiveness when the region came under northern attack in the 1950s and 1960s. That so acute and severe a southern dissenter as Woodward wanted or needed to defend the South suggests that defensiveness has deeper roots in the southern heritage than an appreciation of irony or an absence of innocence. It certainly has been a greater burden for the southern historian.

The 1960s should have encouraged Woodward to lay down this burden. As the decade progressed, racial problems seemingly moved North; the South appeared less specially cursed. Americans should have come to realize that the guilt of slavery rested on both North and South, as Abraham Lincoln had pointed out in his second inaugural address, and that racism was truly an American, not just a southern, dilemma. In the wake of the moral confusion over the Vietnam War, Americans discovered guilt in the nation's history. Wallowing in guilt has its dangers, as Woodward has pointed out, but this rethinking of the past after Vietnam does suggest that in a nation that dispossessed the Indians, fought the war in the Philippines, and dropped the atomic bomb, the South has no monopoly on tragedy, irony, or evil.

If the South has no monopoly on evil, then its historians have no reason to be especially defensive. They should instead turn their attention to serving not as defenders but as moral critics of both the South and the nation. When they do, they can find no finer examples of the approach than Woodward's *Origins of the New South* or "The Irony of Southern History." Woodward has been a most astute observer of the South's history and a most able practitioner of the art of addressing the past to the needs of the present. In letting the South's past speak to the nation's present, as Woodward admitted in "Irony," the historian need not have a drawl. And, perhaps for the historian at least, southern identity should become simply an old hunting jacket, worn at home or among strangers.

— 2 —

GUILT OVER SLAVERY

In the twenty-first century, after a generation of histories that have stressed slavery's brutality, its role in the emergence of capitalism, and, as popularized by the 1619 Project, its centrality in the development of the United States, few if any historians still write of white southerners feeling guilty over slavery. An earlier generation of historians did, though, as discussed in the previous essay on Woodward's interpretation of southern identity. By the time Woodward wrote, most historians had abandoned the benign view of slavery so common in the profession's early years and instead stressed the cruelty and evil nature of enslavement. At the same time, unlike more recent scholars, they sought to distance Americans from slavery, treating it as an aberration, an institution in conflict with both the nation's political ideals and its religious beliefs. It was also a time when historians incorporated paradoxes and ambiguities into their interpretations and wrote of an American consensus, a shared sense of values, including the belief in democracy. In such an intellectual climate, many historians of the South wrote of the Americanness, not the distinctiveness, of the South. If antebellum white southerners shared American values yet still supported slavery, the idea that some white southerners felt guilty about it appealed to historians. Though far from universally accepted, the guilt thesis for a time became an important part of how historians interpreted the history of the South; understanding its origins and evaluating its arguments still merits attention.

T HE CONTENTION THAT WHITE southerners felt guilty about slavery, that in their heart of hearts they found it impossible to reconcile their peculiar institution with their democratic sentiments and evangelical faith, has long occupied an important place in the historiography of the South. Except for a seminal article by Charles G. Sellers Jr., however, historians have rarely offered a systematic examination of this guilt thesis. Most references to it appear in books or articles that focus on some larger issue and often cite Sellers and other secondary works to establish the existence of guilt. Only a few of these works rigorously examine the evidence of guilt or clearly define the concept itself. Most do not make it clear whether guilt was manifested in a religious or a psychological sense or constituted a conscious or a subconscious sense of moral failure or wrongdoing.

Despite this vagueness, historians have treated guilt as a powerful force, crediting it with shaping southern culture and influencing the white South's behavior in antebellum sectional conflicts, in the secession crisis, and in the conduct of the Civil War. Any concept put to such important historiographical uses deserves rigorous evaluation. Such an analysis begins with an understanding of the intellectual context out of which the guilt thesis emerged. It must also include an examination of the validity of the assumptions that underlie the thesis and of the evidence cited in its behalf.[1]

Before the Civil War some abolitionists suspected that white southerners did not fully believe in slavery, that they doubted its legitimacy and morality, and after Appomattox a few southerners admitted as much. But by the end of the nineteenth century, most white southerners looked back on slavery as a benign if not a beneficial institution. Few early, white academics in the South criticized it, and those who did never questioned the region's commitment to it. When the professionalization of history began in the early twentieth century, as John David Smith has convincingly demonstrated, "the vast majority of white students of slavery . . . pointed to slavery's overall benefits for the blacks," portrayed "slavery as a benign school in which blacks fared better than as freedmen," and "revived, refined, updated, and modified many of the same arguments espoused by antebellum and postbellum proslavery writers." Although challenged by white and Black neo-abolitionist historians, these proslavery historians "ultimately carried the day in the age of segregation."[2]

Central to proslavery historiography, of course, was the work of Ulrich B. Phillips, especially his *American Negro Slavery*. In it, Phillips described paternalistic slaveholders who conducted a "school for civilization" for savage but childlike Africans. His planters sometimes felt burdened by their charges' demands but experienced no guilt in holding them. Even during the American

Revolution—a time, many later historians believed, during which white southerners fretted over slavery—Phillips found little anxiety. A few Virginians, he admitted, were "disquieted" by slavery, but the vast majority of southerners never questioned the institution despite widespread discussion of liberty and equality. "The negroes of the rice coast were so outnumbering and so crude," explained Phillips, "that an agitation applying the doctrine of inherent liberty and equality to them could only have had the effect of discrediting the doctrine itself." The limited influence of "revolutionary doctrines" soon passed, and "self-interest" regained its "wonted supremacy"; after 1800, Phillips contended, a conservative trend led to the acceptance of proslavery beliefs and, eventually, to the Civil War. Phillips did describe slavery as "a thing of appreciable disrelish in many quarters" and "the slave trade, . . . whether foreign or domestic," as bearing a "permanent stigma," but he apparently never wrote about southerners feeling guilty. After all, if planters did Black people a favor, why should they feel guilty? For Phillips the demands of white supremacy and the logic of economic interest were so compelling that he seemed not even to consider the idea that whites would feel guilty over slavery.[3]

Unlike Phillips, his contemporary William E. Dodd acknowledged that during the revolutionary era democratic precepts and evangelical beliefs led many southerners to doubt the morality of slavery. But like Phillips, Dodd argued that by 1850 the South had succumbed to reaction and slaveholders had come to dominate society. In 1861, white southerners fought to realize a society based on a "social philosophy which began with the repudiation of the Declaration of Independence and ended with the explicit recognition of social inequality." In Dodd's view, antebellum white southerners never questioned slavery's incompatibility with America's democratic ideals because they had abandoned those ideals for a fixed, hierarchical social order. Dodd decried their abandonment of democracy, but as a progressive historian he expected southerners, like other people, to think and act out of economic interest. In the sectional battles, Dodd concluded, both North and South simply adopted positions dictated by their financial interests. He even equated slavery with the protective tariff: the former was "uglier in outward appearance" than the latter, but both involved "the exploitation of the weaker and more ignorant classes of society by the wealthier and more intelligent."[4]

Both Phillips and Dodd, in sum, portrayed antebellum white southerners as thoroughly committed to the institution of slavery. Their works, typical of their times, showed how both proslavery and progressive views discouraged historians from even considering whether southerners felt guilty over slavery. Historians who accepted the proslavery apologia would hardly expect slaveholders to have moral qualms about such a benevolent institution for controlling so depraved a people. Those who shared the progressives' suspicion of economic elites easily believed that southern slaveholders' ideals reflected their material interests. In the years when proslavery and progressive beliefs reigned among professional historians, few if any of them wrote of southern guilt over slavery.

The initial formulation of the guilt thesis came from outside the profession, from the writers of the Southern Renaissance. As Daniel J. Singal showed in his excellent analysis of the influence of modernist thought on southern intellectuals during the interwar years, many writers of the Southern Renaissance first questioned and then abandoned the region's "Cavalier myth," which, in part, constituted a literary equivalent of the proslavery interpretation. Not all of these writers attacked slavery, but certainly the modernist sensibility's emphasis, in Singal's words, on the "necessity of making contact with 'reality,' no matter how ugly or distasteful that reality might be," encouraged them to abandon old views on slavery. Perhaps more important for the development of the guilt thesis, the modernist sensibility encouraged writers to appreciate paradoxes, to explore contradictions, and "to plumb the nether regions of the psyche." This psychological perspective proved particularly central to two books Singal considered signs of the triumph of the modernist spirit, books that contained the first full, twentieth-century expositions of the guilt thesis: W. J. Cash's *The Mind of the South* and Lillian Smith's *Killers of the Dream*.[5]

In *The Mind of the South,* published in 1941, W. J. Cash described the Old South as "a society beset by the specters of defeat, of shame, of guilt—a society driven by the need to bolster its morale, to nerve its arm against waxing odds, to justify itself in its own eyes and in those of the world." Attributing its feelings of guilt to various factors, Cash emphasized that "in its secret heart," the South "always carried a powerful and uneasy sense of the essential rightness of the nineteenth century's position on slavery." To support his claim, Cash pointed out that evangelical sects had at first denounced slavery, that in Jefferson's time many white southerners had opposed it, and that the majority of early antislavery societies had been in the South. Other than this antislavery heritage, he offered little evidence to support his thesis, and considering the work's later influence, he made surprisingly little use of it. Cash argued that guilt helped shape the battle with the Yankee that, in turn, fostered the Cavalier myth, excessive sentimentality, and the "philosophy of caste" that characterized the mind of the Old South. But Cash did not clearly distinguish between the role of guilt and the sectional battles in creating the South's mentality.[6]

Eight years after Cash, another southern modernist, Lillian Smith, wrote *Killers of the Dream*, part memoir, part historical analysis, part impassioned plea for an end to segregation. Smith offered a psychological interpretation of southern racism that incorporated what later became some of the standard features of the guilt thesis. In slavery times, Smith argued, southerners responded with ferocity to northern abolitionists' attacks, in part because of a defensiveness rooted in their realization that their critics were "so obviously right." Trapped by their interest in slavery, white southerners tried to convince themselves that it was right "by making the black man 'different,' setting him outside God's law, reducing him to less than human." They failed, Smith implied, because they knew that Blacks were human, that slavery violated their own political and religious ideals, and that slavery and racism perverted their own humanity. Therefore "the lies and defenses and fabulous justifications did not keep [southerners] from feeling guilty," and here Smith anticipated the idea that guilt helped lead to defeat—"feeling it, they felt also a need to suffer, and like guilty people everywhere, they had to find 'enemies' to be punished by."[7]

Both Cash and Smith wrote not as dispassionate historians but out of a "rage to explain" the South, as Fred Hobson has put it. In other words, they wrote of their perceptions of southern distinctiveness—what made the South the South. That goal meant they spent little effort in providing evidence to support their historical arguments. Their grounding in the modernist perspective made it even less likely that they would do so. Modernists assumed that surface realities were misleading, sought explanations based on paradox or contradiction, and therefore rarely felt the need to offer definitive proofs. Hence, Cash and Smith readily discounted southern assertions of support for slavery without ever fully documenting their case for southern guilt.[8]

But at the time, Smith's book had little immediate influence on historians. Cash's book, which became an almost instant classic, had an immense impact on southern historiography, but at first its ideas about a guilty South did not take hold. The modernist sensibility still had not penetrated the mind of the southern historian, where the Cavalier myth and proslavery interpretation remained firmly entrenched. In the late 1930s, when C. Vann Woodward arrived at the University of North Carolina for graduate study, he found no "renaissance" in progress within the history department—"no surge of innovation and creativity," he recalled years later, "no rebirth of energy, no compelling new vision." Instead, at Chapel Hill and within the history profession generally, not only in the 1930s but well into the 1940s, Phillips remained "the most celebrated Southern historian of the time," and slavery continued to be seen as "a school for civilizing Africans" and "the plantation . . . an efficient training camp for future captains of industry." Even far to the north, in the old abolitionist seat of Boston, according to David Brion Davis, a graduate student at Harvard in the early 1950s, Phillips's remained the standard text on slavery.[9]

By the early 1950s, though, the proslavery apologia had come under increasing attack. W. E. B. Du Bois, John Hope Franklin, and other Black historians had long challenged it, but few whites had listened. In 1944, Richard Hofstadter, perhaps only coincidentally one of the first historians to display a modernist sensibility, delivered a severe critique of Phillips's work. Hofstadter and other whites had been influenced by changing intellectual assumptions about Black people and racism. Reflecting and accelerating this trend, in 1956, Kenneth M. Stampp wrote The Peculiar Institution, and it quickly replaced Phillips's American Negro Slavery as the authoritative account of slavery.[10]

Stampp abandoned the benign view of slavery as a school for civilization and instead showed it to be a harsh institution that sought, but never fully achieved, the degradation of the slave. Toward the end of the book, Stampp considered how slaveholders felt about keeping people in bondage. Having just damned slavery, he could hardly commend them for doing good, as proslavery historians had. Nor did he seem particularly comfortable saying that race overrode all considerations, as Phillips had, or assuming that masters simply followed their economic interest, as Dodd had. Both economic and racial interest contributed to the persistence of slavery, Stampp acknowledged, the former in the case of the slaveholders and the latter in the case of the nonslaveholders. But Stampp believed southerners ultimately needed a better justification for slavery: "The pathos in the life of every master lay in the fact that slavery had no philosophical defense worthy of the name—that it had nothing to commend it to posterity, except that it paid." In "the sterile rhetoric and special pleading of the proslavery argument," southerners sought not just to convert a world that had turned against slavery but to convince slaveholders themselves who suspected "that the world might be right." The slaveholders' "conscience was not clear," Stampp concluded, and "the feelings of most masters drove them to rationalize the system rather than escape it, and this is why they were such tragic figures," "trapped" in a "moral dilemma." Stampp did not say how aware the masters themselves were of this "moral dilemma," did not explicitly state that they experienced guilt. But although Stampp did not use the word "guilt," he had anticipated much of the argument of the historians who soon did.[11]

The same year that Stampp's book appeared, a series of lectures Bell I. Wiley had delivered in 1954 was published under the title *The Road to Appomattox*. In a brief passage, Wiley offered as one reason for southern defeat in the Civil War the "inordinate quarrelsomeness among Confederates," rooted in part in "a sense of guilt about slavery," which southerners realized conflicted with their egalitarian, humanitarian, and Christian ideals. Two years later, in 1958, C. Vann Woodward incorporated the idea of guilt into his influential article "The Search for Southern Identity." In it, Woodward, although he agreed with little else Cash wrote, argued that during the antebellum period the South tried desperately "to convince the world that" slavery "was actually a 'positive good,' but it failed even to convince itself. It writhed in the torments of its own conscience until it plunged into catastrophe to escape." Limited by the essay format, Woodward provided no evidence to support his contention; to that extent, he, like Wiley, really did little to develop the guilt thesis. But Woodward, whom Richard H. King has rightly included within the ranks of the Renaissance writers, appeared to make explicit what was implicit in the accounts of Cash and Smith—the idea that guilt helped make the South distinctive. Guilt, along with defeat and poverty, Woodward seemed to say, shaped the very nature of the South. Certainly, many of his readers reached that conclusion, and as a result, Woodward did much to popularize the idea of southern guilt.[12]

In 1960, Charles G. Sellers Jr. wrote "The Travail of Slavery," the first full exposition of the guilt thesis; it remains the most fully developed study of the topic and the one most carefully supported with various types of evidence. Sellers, though, used the word "guilt" only twice, neither time in a context important to his argument. He preferred to characterize the problem white southerners experienced as an "ambivalent attitude" or "inner turmoil" or "inner conflict." This "inner conflict" had its roots in the revolutionary generation's opposition to slavery. Like Dodd before him, Sellers argued that antislavery views persisted at least to the 1830s (and for many, beyond), when a "Great Reaction" closed the internal debate over slavery and committed the South to a rigorous defense of it. But unlike Dodd, Sellers contended that even after that Great Reaction, southerners cherished the Union and liberty, in its "universalist sense of the eighteenth-century Enlightenment," and believed the humanitarian teachings of evangelical Christianity. Both their political principles and religious convictions, therefore, condemned slavery even as their economic and racial interests kept them from abandoning it; hence an "inner conflict."

Sellers further attributed "the Southerner's ambivalent attitude toward slavery" to "his inability to regard the slave consistently as either person or property." Beset by such contradictions, Sellers concluded, "Southerners did not and could not rationally and deliberately choose slavery and its fruits over the values it warred against. Rather it was the very conflict of values, rendered intolerable by constant criticism premised on values Southerners shared, which drove them to seek a violent resolution." In 1861, this "fundamental moral anxiety" and a "fear" of racial assault, exacerbated by John Brown's raid, produced a "hysteria" in the South. That hysteria and a "paralysis of will" among conservatives allowed the Fire-Eaters to take the South into the Civil War, a cause that southerners "abandoned . . . with an alacrity which underscored the reluctance of their original commitment."[13]

Published in the year following Sellers's "Travail," Ralph E. Morrow's "The Proslavery Argument Revisited" explored similar themes. From a careful analysis of proslavery writings, Morrow concluded that the authors sought to convince southerners of the morality of slavery with "the conversion of northerners as merely extra dividends." White southerners, even slaveholders, needed to be convinced because their consciences, shaped by an antislavery tradition grounded in Jeffersonian liberalism and evangelical religion, told them slavery was wrong. Attempting to conquer "guilt and doubt," the proslavery writers only "helped to aggravate the condition they wanted to alleviate. The propaganda fusillade caught the South in a vicious circle. Agitation heightened fear and uncertainty that seemingly called for still more agitation. A trial by arms was not an illogical exit from this cycle, for the strength that supposedly came from righteousness could then be definitively asserted."[14]

In 1966, William W. Freehling employed the guilt thesis, and the word itself, far more often than Sellers or Morrow had, in interpreting the Nullification Crisis. Freehling maintained that conditions in Lowcountry South Carolina "might (for this is speculative) have intensified the guilt" planters there felt over slavery and "helped to make slavery at the South Carolina tidewater . . . peculiarly disturbing." This "acute guilt," along with other factors, spurred planters there (but not elsewhere in the South) to nullify the tariff of 1832, since doing so allowed them to attack abolitionists in Washington without openly addressing the issue that so deeply troubled them. In making his case for the slaveholders' sense of moral failing, Freehling followed Sellers's argument fairly closely but added Cash's observation that the disparity between plantation ideal and reality also generated guilt. Again, like Sellers, Freehling found that a "Great Reaction" followed the failure of nullification; South Carolinians then adopted the proslavery argument and tightened control over the slaves. By 1861, this reaction, Freehling added, had "probably eased the guilty consciences of many slaveholders."[15]

Kenneth M. Stampp, whose history of slavery had helped open the academic discussion of the notion of guilt over slavery, did not agree but rather argued that the burden of guilt persisted and helped explain why the South lost the Civil War. In a 1968 address, "The Southern Road to Appomattox," Stampp contended that Confederate defeat resulted from "the failure of political leadership, the absurd lengths to which state rights was carried, the reluctance of Southerners to accept the discipline that war demanded, and the internal conflicts among the Southern people." These failings, in Stampp's view, ultimately "point to a Confederate weakness that matched in importance its physical handicaps"—the "weakness of morale." Weak morale resulted not only from the failure of leaders to develop and sustain popular support for the cause but also from "the inherent frailty of the cause itself," since "except for the institution of slavery, the South had little to give it a clear national identity." Defeat offered white southerners a "reward: a way to rid themselves of the moral burden of slavery." Stampp supported his portrayal of extensive guilt among southerners by citing Cash, Wiley, and Sellers. He bolstered his case for the role of guilt in bringing about Confederate defeat by pointing not only to the Confederacy's failings but also to the absence of a resistance movement in occupied areas, the failure to resort to guerrilla warfare after Appomattox, and a ready acceptance of the end of slavery.[16]

Stampp's essay marked the end of the first phase of professional historians' interest in southern guilt. No doubt Stampp and other proponents embraced the thesis on the basis of their reading of the evidence from the Old South, but clearly a changing intellectual climate rendered these historians more open to Cash's arguments, whose influence they acknowledged, than their predecessors had been fifteen to twenty years earlier. The profession's abandonment of progressive historiography and the proslavery apologia helped make the mind of the slaveholder a more open question than it had ever been before. A new emphasis on consensus, which in much historical writing replaced the progressives' stress on conflict, probably rendered believable the idea that slaveholders found slavery just as distasteful as other Americans did. And certainly the growing pervasiveness of modernist notions left historians open to explanations that dismissed surface appearances and sought deeper psychological realities. Yet none of these historians openly acknowledged the influence of modernist thinkers, nor did they rely heavily on psychological or other social science literature on guilt, which, like Sherlock Holmes's dog that did not bark, may be the most important clue that these historians had incorporated modernist assumptions.[17]

Professional historians' interest in the guilt thesis developed between 1956 and 1968, the years of the civil rights movement and the Second Reconstruction, which suggests that social as well as intellectual developments played a role in the adoption of the guilt thesis. Obviously, changes in racial attitudes contributed to the abandonment of the proslavery interpretation. But rejecting it or embracing African American equality did not necessarily lead to an acceptance of the guilt thesis. Although a few later endorsed it, no Black historian contributed to the early development of the thesis. The same year that Stampp first wrote of morally troubled slaveholders, John Hope Franklin described them as martial and militant defenders of the institution. From the Black side of America's historic racial divide, the slaveholders' moral qualms apparently appeared less evident than they did from the white side. Among white historians, though, spreading acceptance of Black equality contributed to increasing criticism of slavery—and when white historians themselves condemned slavery, they found it more believable that white slaveholders would also have been troubled by the institution.[18]

Such changes, wrought in part by the civil rights movement, may well explain the greater receptivity to the guilt thesis in the 1960s than in the 1940s. But the context of the Second Reconstruction surely had a more complex influence on those who actually wrote of southern guilt. No recent change in their ideas about Black people led them to the guilt thesis; most, in fact, were pioneers in the quest for racial equality. They may well have seen the guilt thesis as a way to change other white southerners' attitudes and behavior and thereby ensure a better reconstruction of the South the second time around.

The work of C. Vann Woodward and Charles Sellers clearly suggested such a goal. At the time that he wrote of southern guilt, Woodward was very concerned about rising racial tensions in his native South. His earlier *The Strange Career of Jim Crow*, as many have pointed out, sought in part to encourage the white South to abandon its defense of segregation by revealing that system's recent origins and pointing out forgotten alternatives. Similarly, in "The Search for Southern Identity," Woodward seemed to offer an alternative to white supremacy as the defining characteristic of the South. Sellers made the racial crisis's influence on his work explicit, but unlike Woodward, he sought to minimize rather than to redirect arguments for a distinctive southern identity. Sellers published his essay in a collection he edited and entitled *The Southerner as American*. In its introduction, Sellers expressed the hope that the collection would encourage southerners to embrace their own Americanism and discourage them from repeating the mistakes of a century before. He echoed this theme at the end of "Travail," proclaiming that the Civil War freed southerners "to move again toward the realization of their essential natures as Southerners, liberals, Christians, and Americans."[19]

Just as the civil rights movement helped encourage new perspectives on the Old South among historians, so too did the women's movement in the late 1960s and early 1970s and a growing interest in the history of women. Sudie Duncan Sides and Anne Firor Scott suggested that many white southern women disliked slavery and doubted its morality. White female slaveholders, perhaps most clearly Mary Boykin Chesnut, perceived themselves to be oppressed in a slaveholding patriarchy, and that awareness created bonds with the slaves and a distinctly female view of slavery. This view, at least as argued by Sides and Scott, involved covert opposition to slavery rather than suppressed feelings of guilt. Perhaps because of the stress on opposition rather than guilt, arguments for a special female perspective based on sisterhood remained in something of a historiographical separate sphere. A few historians incorporated it into their discussions of guilt, but subsequent major discussions of the guilt thesis hardly mentioned it.[20]

In fact, apart from Donald G. Mathews and Ronald T. Takaki, few historians during the 1970s used any version of the guilt thesis. The decade's intellectual climate seemed inhospitable. The hopefulness of the early years of the Second Reconstruction gave way to despair over the prominence and persistence of racism in America. Still influenced by that and other cultural, political, and intellectual attitudes of the late 1960s, historians often believed the worst about Americans and emphasized conflicts over values and ideologies. Neither tendency encouraged them to see slaveholders as committed to common American ideals or convinced of the immorality of their acts. When historians dismissed the Radical Republicans as timid conservatives, they hardly seemed likely to defend slaveholders as troubled liberals.[21]

By the 1980s, these restraints had eased as yet another intellectual climate emerged, although historians who offered a radical critique of American society retained a stronghold within the profession. But neither their historiographical perspective nor any other dominated as the progressive or, later, the consensus view once had. Several historians revived the guilt thesis, but befitting an era of diversity, did so in different ways. Catherine Clinton argued, with more explicit reference to guilt than did Scott and Sides, that the plantation mistress resolved "the moral dilemmas of slavery through the displacement of guilt. To escape their own implication in the slave system, wives either blamed their husbands—the primary beneficiaries of that system—or the slaves themselves." Clarence Mohr mentioned women's special perspective on slavery, but in explaining the death of slavery in Civil War Georgia he stressed the role of religion in generating guilt among reformers who sought the gradual amelioration of slavery. In his analysis of southwestern ministers, David T. Bailey, too, made much of the religious sources of guilt. Two works, *The Ruling Race* and *Why the South Lost the Civil War*, testified to the continuing influence of Sellers and Stampp. However, neither book paid much attention to the role of political thought in generating guilt; both, like Mohr and Bailey, stressed the role of Evangelicalism. This shift in emphasis may have occurred in response to other historians who had done much to show slavery to be compatible with democratic and republican principles, or it may have reflected a new emphasis on Evangelicalism in the historiography of the South.[22]

In *The Ruling Race*, James Oakes described the Old South as a society shaped by planter capitalists who embraced "liberal democracy and free-market capitalism"; to that extent, his interpretation stressed the similarities between antebellum South and North. Oakes, like Sellers, also found significant anti-slavery sentiment in the South until 1830, which southerners then suppressed but never really abandoned. Oakes departed from Sellers, however, in giving little attention to the role of political ideals in generating slaveholders' guilt but instead emphasizing the part played by evangelical Protestantism. Evangelicalism, Oakes contended, "in its implicit egalitarianism and explicit rejection of materialism . . . questioned two of the fundamental tendencies of the slave system: the dehumanization of the bondsmen, and the grasping materialism of their owners." Behaving in ways that contradicted their "fundamental norms," evangelical slaveholders developed varying degrees of usually unexpressed, "deeply rooted psychological ambivalence." Oakes offered less evidence than Sellers had to support his assertions, but he did proffer a new argument—that evangelical slaveholders were obsessed with their damnation even as they and their slaves expected death to liberate the slaves. The planters' obsession revealed their "deeply troubled consciences." Their consciences, however, played no role in fomenting secession; Oakes explained that movement with none of Sellers's references to guilt and irrationality but rather as a rational revolt to preserve slavery.[23]

Nor did *Why the South Lost the Civil War* make guilt central to secession. Its authors, Richard E. Beringer, Herman Hattaway, Archer Jones, and William N. Still Jr., argued that, for the most part, southerners made a reluctant but rational decision to leave the Union. For many, the prospect of losing the resulting war seemed so disastrous that they blotted it from their minds and "managed to convince themselves—not merely to assert but truly to believe—of the inevitability of victory." But "probably," these authors continued, widespread guilt unconsciously compromised the initial determination of many Confederates and from the outset presaged the eventual defeat." Nevertheless, their argument—more so than Stampp's, whose it resembled—contended that the South could have won and did fight hard for a time. At the start of the war, the Confederates believed God directed their cause, but by 1865 battlefield losses made them wonder if He had abandoned and sought to punish them. Southerners then began to reconsider their decision for war, to experience "cognitive dissonance," and, especially after the Confederate decision for emancipation, to wonder about their true goals. In the midst of doubt, confusion, and fears of God's judgment, guilt became more intense and the evil of slavery more obvious. Consequently, morale was weakened, and the way was prepared for defeat.

The Confederacy succumbed because of the deficiencies of southern nationalism, which was rooted in many things, but perhaps most prominently in guilt over slavery. For the authors of *Why the South Lost the Civil War*, nothing testified to the preponderance of guilt and the weakness of nationalism more than the Confederates' failure to wage guerrilla war after Appomattox. Even as these historians expanded Stampp's explanation for Confederate defeat, they added little to the case for the existence of southern guilt. Writing an account avowedly based on the work of other historians, the authors relied on the work of Cash, Sellers, Wiley, and Oakes to establish its existence. Even more than Oakes, whose work they considered the best of the school, they emphasized the evangelical origins of guilt, almost ignoring Sellers's contention regarding the contradiction between slavery and southern conceptions of liberty.[24]

Why the South Lost the Civil War probably made guilt over slavery more central to southern history than had any previous book, but it built upon forty years of historiography. Two major strands come together in that historiography. The first grew out of the modernist perspective of the liberal wing of the southern literary renaissance. Cash, Smith, and Woodward, all of whom proved important in shaping or spreading the guilt thesis, worked within that tradition. They acknowledged the evil of slavery but dismissed southerners' apparent acceptance of the institution and laid bare the dark complexities of the slaveholders' psyche. Their slaveholders seemed peculiarly modern, living in existential tension, frustrated by guilt but with not a therapist in sight and only a punishing war to free them. Such an interpretation, like much of the work of the Southern Renaissance, rendered southerners a special people, scarred but somehow ennobled by their battle with guilt.

The second strand within the historiography emerged in the academics' discussion of southern guilt. Wiley and Morrow wrote early, influential accounts, but Stampp and Sellers, through both their work and their students at the University of California at Berkeley—Freehling, Bailey, and Oakes—proved central to its development. The Renaissance and academic strands were intertwined, of course, since the seminal works of the latter owed much to Cash. The two differed in a fundamental way, however. Where the Renaissance writers used the notion of guilt to help define southern distinctiveness, the academics—particularly Sellers, Stampp, and Oakes—wrote of common American values. To some extent, the difference reflected the Renaissance writers' emphasis on outcome, on what guilt meant for southerners, versus the academics' interest in origin, or why southerners felt guilty. Most academic historians who wrote of guilt over slavery assumed the essential sameness of the antebellum South and North. Those who found the Old South distinctive, on the other hand, tended to be suspicious of the guilt thesis.

A review of the historiography also suggests another factor that may well be more important than attitudes toward distinctiveness in influencing how historians interpreted the Old South and therefore responded to the guilt thesis: how much causative power they granted to such forces as racism and economic interest. Historians who believed that either factor fundamentally shapes an individual's thinking or a society's value system had little intellectual need for the guilt thesis. Those, like Stampp, who thought people acted on the basis of substantial philosophical or ideological principles, proved more open to the guilt thesis.

Such considerations, as well as the social and intellectual context of the Second Reconstruction, may help explain why the thesis appeared when it did or why certain scholars found it more plausible than others, but to appreciate the intellectual context of the guilt thesis is not to explain it away. Such factors have proved no more important in shaping the work of historians who argued on behalf of the guilt thesis than similar factors have in influencing the arguments of their opponents or other historians. Neither attitudes toward southern distinctiveness nor beliefs about the importance of racial or economic interest dictated conclusions about southern guilt; rather, both subtly shaped how historians interpreted the Old South or read signs of southern guilt.

The importance of questions of southern distinctiveness and views of human motivations, though, illustrate how complicated it can become to establish southern guilt feelings. The plausibility of the thesis ultimately rests on interrelated assumptions about the society of the Old South. Its defenders assume, first, that southerners openly criticized slavery from the revolutionary era until at least the 1830s, and therefore, in the late antebellum period, they knew they had repudiated their heritage. Second, defenders take for granted that southerners were committed to liberal or democratic political principles and evangelical Protestantism throughout the pre–Civil War period and that these beliefs naturally led them to doubt the rightness of slavery. Consequently, on some level, southerners experienced an internal value conflict. But have recent works on the Old South supported these assumptions?[25]

Almost all historians agree that revolutionary era southerners—particularly leaders like George Washington, Thomas Jefferson, and Henry and John Laurens—expressed antislavery sentiments and that the fledgling Methodist and Baptist Churches condemned the institution. William Freehling argued that Jefferson and the Founding Fathers not only opposed slavery but also restricted its expansion and thereby did all that they could to ensure its eventual extinction. Not all historians, however, take either the antislavery sentiments or accomplishments of the revolutionary generation as seriously as Freehling did.[26]

Robert McColley, for example, dismissed the pronouncements of the Virginia statesmen, since they "so rarely" sponsored any "positive" initiatives against slavery and "normally resisted" any "proposed by others." Their behavior made "still more doubtful the proposition that their constituents were agreeable to antislavery sentiments." Rather, McColley concluded, "indirect evidence" suggested that most "Virginia planters . . . were for all practical purposes proslavery." Other scholars added that southern leaders not only failed to suggest plans to end slavery but actively sought to preserve it. At the Constitutional Convention, according to Paul Finkelman, southern representatives did everything possible to protect the institution, and David Brion Davis added that they secured a "fixed bastion" for their region's power and a constitution that "gave slaveholders privileges and powers that exceeded the wildest dreams" of their counterparts in the British West Indies.[27]

Even historians who agreed on the existence of an antislavery heritage in the South differed among themselves as to when open opposition to the institution came to an end. Alison Goodyear Freehling, like the exponents of the guilt thesis, found that antislavery sentiment persisted, in Virginia at least, into the 1830s and beyond. In contrast, Duncan J. MacLeod contended that the "Great Reaction" occurred in the 1820s, and Winthrop D. Jordan discovered that intensified white racial fears led to a "hardening of slavery" in the early 1800s, following the revolution in Santo Domingo and Gabriel's rebellion in Virginia. Whether the timing of the reaction proves crucial to establishing the guilt thesis rests in large measure on how historians explain the influence of the South's antislavery heritage. If they argue that white southerners were influenced only by a vague historical awareness of revolutionary era attitudes, then the timing of the Great Reaction is of little importance.[28]

Both Sellers and Oakes, however, claim that the generation that guided the South in the 1840s and 1850s had matured under the influence of the "afterglow of Revolutionary liberalism," in Sellers's phrase. To argue for such a direct influence makes establishing when the Great Reaction occurred more significant. If it occurred before 1830, as MacLeod and Jordan claimed, then few of the Confederacy's leaders (who were generally in their forties) and almost none of its soldiers (many of whom were only eighteen) could have been influenced by it. Instead, most would have come of age in a society dominated by a proslavery consensus, would have heard all their lives of the rightness of slavery.[29]

On the other hand, a fuller explication of the influence of the antislavery tradition can also provide support for the guilt thesis. Some studies have suggested that secessionists tended to be slightly younger than unionists and that enthusiastic supporters of the Confederacy were often younger than less ardent patriots. If so, many factors, the conservatism of age and lingering ties to the Union among them, may explain the apparent relationship between age and enthusiasm for the Confederate cause. But so too could a stronger, more personal memory of an antislavery past and a consequently more intense experience of guilt.[30]

Of course, guilt could have emerged even if southerners had no personal or even corporate memory of revolutionary era condemnation of slavery. Moral anxieties could just as easily have been generated by outside attacks or from internal, even unspoken, awareness of the contradictions between southern values and slavery. In the years since Sellers's article, however, many historians have challenged the second and more crucial assumption of the guilt thesis, that southerners experienced a conflict between slavery and their faith in liberal democracy and evangelical Protestantism.[31]

Eugene D. Genovese has provided the most explicit, sustained, and comprehensive attack on the guilt thesis, employing a Marxian analysis that resembled the progressives' argument from economic interest. Not unlike Dodd,

Genovese maintained that the South initially accepted liberal and capitalistic principles and, during the revolutionary period, expressed nominally antislavery views. Long before the Civil War, though, an emerging planter class established its hegemony, developed a proslavery argument, and created a "world view that authentically reflected the position, aspirations, and ethos of the slaveholders as a class." Contradictions remained within the ideology of the planters and between their values and those of the outside market economy with which they had contact, but by the time of the Civil War, few doubts about slavery remained and few if any southerners felt guilty about holding slaves.[32]

In constructing this argument, and in later work with coauthor Elizabeth Fox-Genovese, Eugene Genovese implicitly but thoroughly dismissed the second basic assumption of the guilt thesis. In their view, neither the political nor the religious beliefs of southerners contradicted slavery. As a hierarchical society dominated by a planter aristocracy, the South did not embrace liberty or democracy. And southern religion upheld the morality of slavery. Southern slaveholders considered their bondspeople a Christian duty and burden, and the slaveholders' reading of the Bible reassured them that God sanctioned slavery and that slavery provided the basis for true community.[33]

Few historians have challenged the guilt thesis as boldly or explicitly as Genovese, but many have questioned whether southern political values and slavery conflicted. These scholars described white southerners as committed to the ideal of liberty, but unlike Sellers, they did not conclude that southerners perceived a conflict between that ideal and holding Blacks in bondage. In his exploration of the origins of slavery, Edmund S. Morgan reached just the opposite conclusion, positing a close connection between slavery and republicanism, which in his view was the political philosophy in which southern conceptions of liberty rested. Slavery helped create an identity of interests between planters and small slaveholders, reduced the fear of the unpropertied masses, and provided a splendid example of the results of the loss of liberty. Hence, according to Morgan, a republican love of liberty and slavery became intertwined. Like Morgan, Kenneth S. Greenberg, J. William Harris, Larry E. Tise, and Lacy K. Ford Jr. stressed the republican, not the democratic, origins of southern conceptions of liberty, and each concluded—through different arguments—that by the late antebellum period southerners had reconciled their love of liberty with their peculiar institution.[34]

Still other historians agreed with Sellers that the Old South was democratic but differed in their conclusions about the implications of that fact. George M. Fredrickson labeled the Old South a "*Herrenvolk* democracy," an extremely democratic society but one for whites only. Indeed, Fredrickson argued, democracy for whites rested on the denial of freedom to Blacks. William J. Cooper Jr. also argued that democracy always "reigned" in southern politics and that revolutionary era conceptions of liberty persisted, but he found that the South's love of liberty supported rather than threatened slavery. The presence of slaves made liberty more dear because slavery offered white southerners a fearful specter of what happened to those who lost their freedom. And in Cooper's view, liberty came to be defined in part as independence from outside interference, especially interference with the right to hold slaves. That the Old South had a democratic political order, a deep commitment to liberty, and a firm desire to defend slavery also received support in J. Mills Thornton's study of Alabama's antebellum politics. If these historians are correct in saying that southerners could and did consistently embrace both "liberty and slavery," to quote Cooper's succinct title, then one part of the guilt thesis's second basic assumption proves false.[35]

Although recent scholarship on southern politics has cast doubt on the idea that an inherent contradiction existed between white southerners' political values and slavery, recent work on religion in the Old South has proved somewhat more supportive of the other part of the second basic assumption of the guilt thesis, that evangelical Protestantism led southerners to have reservations about the institution. One historian has questioned the importance of evangelical Christianity in shaping southern morality. Bertram Wyatt-Brown postulated that "white Southerners adhered to a moral code that may be summarized as the rule of honor"; it predated slavery but nevertheless was "wholly compatible" with the institution in ways "that were not so apparent in the godly and commercial settlements of New England and Pennsylvania." The South, according to this view, operated from moral premises fundamentally different from those of the North and would have had no basis for feeling guilty over slavery.[36]

Other historians cast doubt on the idea that Christianity, even evangelical Christianity, naturally led to the conclusion that slaveholding was a sin. David Brion Davis's work reminded historians that for centuries Christianity and the institution of slavery had coexisted in at least tenuous peace. Forrest G.

Wood went much further, attacking Christianity as "fundamentally racist in its ideology, organization, and practice" and calling it "a cornerstone of modern slavery." Most historians proved more cautious than Wood but still concluded that churches rarely condemned slavery, and often supported it. Jon Butler showed how, in the colonial period, Anglican priests helped white southerners accept slavery and thereby prepared the South for the paternalism that developed later. Lacy K. Ford Jr. argued that, in Upcountry South Carolina during the 1780s and 1790s, Evangelicalism spread slowly until its "leaders muted their objections to slavery." Lester B. Scherer minimized the importance of antislavery thought in most early American churches. John R. McKivigan contended that even in the antebellum North, few denominations actually adopted "uncompromised abolitionist principles and programs," and most absolved "slaveholders of any individual guilt." In the South by the 1830s, H. Shelton Smith and Anne C. Loveland argued, evangelical churches and their members publicly supported slavery. Loveland added that some believers had reservations about the institution but never considered it fundamentally sinful. In different ways, both Larry Tise and Drew Gilpin Faust placed southern proslavery thought in a broader tradition of Christian benevolence. And Jack P. Maddex Jr. claimed that some white southern Christians embraced a "proslavery millennialism," believing that Christ's reign on earth would reform but would not end slavery. In sum, all of these historians supported the conclusion that southern religious beliefs did not necessarily stimulate doubts about the morality of slavery.[37]

Claims that Evangelicalism subverted slavery persisted among historians, however. James D. Essig credited eighteenth-century evangelicals with meaningful "opposition to human bondage," although he admitted that they had retreated from that position by the early nineteenth century. Even then, according to David T. Bailey, many southwestern clergy still felt guilty about slavery and assuaged their consciences through "missionary work among the slaves." His argument resembled that of Donald G. Mathews, who contended that, for political as much as for religious reasons, early southern evangelicals tried to end slavery but found that social and political realities prevented them from doing so. They therefore accommodated themselves to the institution, but many continued to harbor reservations that they revealed when they referred to slaves as a "burden." To ease these doubts, some helped promulgate a proslavery ideology, "characterized by singleness of purpose and arrogant assurance."

More white southern Christians embraced a "slaveholding ethic" that defended the morality of slavery but still revealed southerners' "ambivalence" and "guilt." Evangelicals were not tortured by their ambivalence and guilt, Mathews maintained, but channeled them into a mission to the slaves that ultimately supported slavery.[38]

In the three decades since Sellers wrote, scholarship on southern politics and religion has fundamentally challenged the basic assumptions of the guilt thesis. These studies again suggest that the causative power granted to the forces of racism and economic interest—or, for some scholars, class interest—heavily influences conclusions about southern society and southerners' attitudes toward slavery. Historians who emphasize one or both of these factors either reject the notion of the Old South as a liberal, democratic society or argue that the Old South's conception of liberty and democracy did not necessarily conflict with slavery. In similar fashion, historians contend that religious beliefs supported rather than threatened the existing economic and racial order. Their interpretations thereby undermine the plausibility of the guilt thesis. So too do recent findings that a proslavery consensus dominated the antebellum South. Even some who contend that white southerners felt guilty argue that they channeled their feelings into public support for slavery. If southerners heard constantly of slavery's righteousness, they—particularly the young ones—probably would have come to accept it, just as people in most societies accept the social order and reigning values. But, proponents of the guilt thesis would reply, not necessarily.

An analysis of the evidence offered in behalf of the guilt thesis, like that of the assumptions underlying it, offers no definitive proof for or against the thesis but does tend to reduce its plausibility. The best support for the guilt thesis, of course, would be explicit acknowledgment of guilt by southerners. Almost all historians concede that a few southerners felt guilty and said so. No one, not even defenders of the thesis, claim to have found very many of them. One of Cash's first critics on this point, Rollin G. Osterweis, maintained that in his own research on the Old South he had seen "no direct evidence of" a guilt complex and complained that "Cash gives none." But the absence of such evidence, Osterweis added sarcastically, meant "little in this realm of Freudian psychology." More than thirty years later, Oakes, a proponent of the thesis who read many planters' papers, admitted he found a "paucity of open expressions of remorse among slaveholders, either before or after the Civil War." That paucity, Oakes added seriously, "cannot be taken as evidence for the absence of guilt. For while remorse normally follows an avoidable misdeed, guilt is the product of a deeply rooted psychological ambivalence that impels the individual to behave in ways that violate fundamental norms even as they fulfill basic desires." Though Osterweis scoffed at such a conclusion, Oakes argued that in the case of so deep a psychological problem, historians should not expect to find open acknowledgment of guilt.[39]

In an evangelical culture, given to public or at least to private confession of sin, southerners with a conscious sense of failing to live up to religious ideals by holding slaves would have confessed that sin more readily than surviving evidence indicates. Minimizing the importance of the admitted absence of open confession has important implications for how proponents of the guilt thesis define the term "guilt." They have rarely explained whether they employ it in primarily a religious or a psychological sense. By not taking seriously the absence of open confession one would expect in a religious conception of guilt, however, they clearly indicate that they write of a psychological phenomenon—as, in their own ways, both Osterweis and Oakes acknowledged. Indeed, Oakes has put the matter most forthrightly: guilt started as a religious feeling but was so suppressed that it became a psychological problem. This interpretation better fits the evidence than one that conceives of guilt primarily in religious terms, but it still may not explain away the absence of open admission of remorse.

Another group of people caught in a moral dilemma, Vietnam veterans, offers a very rough standard of comparison. Of those who, in counseling, eventually evinced guilt over their actions in the war, psychologists have found that about a third easily and openly admitted their guilt feelings. Such a rate of open expression, if applied to antebellum southerners, would suggest that far more confession should be found, if indeed widespread guilt existed. Whether guilt is defined as a religious or a psychological phenomenon, the limited amount of direct evidence for it still reduces the thesis's plausibility, even if it does not disprove it.[40]

Proponents can still claim that doubts were so suppressed and southern society tolerated so little criticism of slavery that few dared to express their feelings even to themselves. They can also maintain that southerners were not even aware of their feelings of guilt—or, in other words, define guilt in subconscious terms. Since historians cannot put the slaveholders on the couch, they must instead look for signs of guilt in southern behavior. The advocates of the thesis have pointed out many such signs, but five predominate in the literature: manumission of slaves, a confusion in southern society over whether to treat slaves as persons or property, the stridency of the proslavery defense, southern attitudes toward the slave trade, and the South's response to defeat and emancipation in 1865.

Troubled about the morality of slavery, Sellers contended, southern slaveholders manumitted their slaves, even in the face of public hostility and legal prohibitions. Three thousand manumissions occurred in 1860, he added, or one for every 1,309 slaves. The percentage of slaveholders who felt a need to free a slave, however, would be a more telling statistic. Even if each of these three thousand enslaved people had been freed by a different slaveholder, the percentage of slaveholders who decided on manumission in 1860 was less than 1 percent, hardly an impressive figure. Some historians have questioned not the number but the motives of slaveholders who freed those they had enslaved. Ira Berlin, who closely examined manumissions in his study of antebellum free Blacks, admitted that a few slaveholders manumitted out of conscience but concluded that most freed only one or two of their slaves and acted out of "cold utility" rather than a need to "shed the sin of slavery." Slaveholders used manumission "as a mechanism of control," a "means of encouraging divisions among blacks" and of rewarding favorite slaves or those related to their enslavers. In his comparative study of slave societies, Orlando Patterson agreed that freeing slaves served to support slavery, not to relieve guilt. More important, Patterson showed that the South's "manumission rate was one of the lowest of all slave systems." If manumissions signaled guilt, then the South was one of the least guilty of all slave regimes.[41]

Patterson's work also put in slightly different perspective another factor cited as evidence of southern guilt. Sellers presented convincing evidence that southerners never really decided, even in their law codes, whether to treat slaves as persons or property. For Sellers, this reflected the slaveholders' own confusion, and ultimately their guilt. But as Patterson and David Brion Davis have shown, the inherent contradiction involved in treating a person as property always lay at the heart of slavery. Indeed, Patterson argued that a slave was "socially dead" but "remained nonetheless an element of society." He or she therefore lived on the margins, a person but not a person, or to use Patterson's anthropological term, the slave occupied a liminal status. In many ways, this liminal status represented just what Sellers described in the American South, a position somewhere between person and property. But for Patterson and Davis, rather than being a sign of guilt rooted in unique American values, the confusion between person and property was characteristic of all slave systems.[42]

The South's extreme defensiveness over slavery is also frequently cited as evidence of guilt. Despite few real internal or external threats to their institution, the argument goes, southerners responded to antislavery critics with a vehement, frenzied defense that arose out of their troubled consciences. Many historians have offered alternative interpretations of this seemingly irrational response, however. Genovese, building on observations by Georg W. F. Hegel, pointed out that the slaveholder placed supreme importance on his independence but realized, on some level, that that independence rested on his control and command of the enslaved, leaving him dependent on them. Questioning "either the morality or the practicality of slavery," Genovese continued, exposed "the root of the slaveholder's dependence in independence," threatened his self-image, and thus helped render southerners violent and defensive under northern attack. William Cooper developed a similar idea, albeit less metaphysically, in his observations on the importance of honor in the South. Southerners, Cooper argued, considered northern attacks on slavery not just political but personal affronts; indeed, they probably drew no distinction between the two. In their minds, to question the institution was to besmirch their social reputation and, in a culture based on honor, their image of themselves. Their value system dictated a vehement defense of the morality of slavery as well as of their own honor and impelled them to seek northern acknowledgment of both.[43]

Other historians attributed the intensity of the South's defense of slavery to the personal motives of individual proslavery ideologues. David Herbert Donald and Drew Gilpin Faust have suggested that proslavery apologists did not simply defend slavery but pursued goals of their own that had nothing to do with guilt. In Donald's view, proslavery writers were marginal, unhappy men, failures in life, who reacted against social changes and longed for a return to older days when their ancestors had dominated the South. In Faust's view, they were intellectuals in a society that recognized no legitimate social role for intellectuals and therefore sought through a defense of slavery to create one. Still other historians pointed to the rationality of the South's defense of slavery. Tise tacitly undermined claims of a peculiar southern irrationality by demonstrating the similarities between the South's proslavery argument and that of other slave societies. Peter Kolchin flatly stated that the South's "siege mentality" was "by no means paranoid, because the South was under attack." In different ways, each of these historians cast doubt on the argument that the South's response to criticism signaled its guilt.[44]

Where many historians have addressed the defensiveness of southerners, few have explored the South's refusal, even as an independent nation, to reopen the international slave trade—yet another factor cited in defense of the guilt thesis. In his history of the crusade to resume slave importation, Ronald Takaki argued that its proponents believed that if slavery was moral, then so was the international slave trade. They therefore campaigned to reopen it, in part, to force the South to declare in some sense its unequivocal support for the institution. Takaki's own account reveals that many factors other than attitudes about the morality of slavery, especially economic ones, influenced the decision not to resume importation of slaves. During the war, for example, southerners feared that doing so would doom chances of foreign recognition of the Confederacy. On the other hand, the fact remains that to defend slavery and yet to prohibit slave importation did constitute a contradiction, one that suggests at the very least that southerners did not embrace their proslavery ideology as fully as they claimed.[45]

Finally, proponents of the guilt thesis point to the Confederacy's timid and confused war effort and ready acceptance of defeat and emancipation as signs of guilt. Gerald F. Linderman, Reid Mitchell, and James I. Robertson Jr. have all recently published accounts of the thoughts of Civil War soldiers, yet none of these historians mentioned finding any evidence of guilt over slavery. Mitchell cautioned historians against denigrating Confederate commitment and sacrifice, as have many historians before him. James M. McPherson questioned whether morale sagged because of lack of dedication to the cause and to slavery or because of battlefield reverses. Even the authors of *Why the South Lost the Civil War* saw the loss of battles and morale as acting on each other. Neither their account nor Stampp's offered much evidence of a direct relation between flagging zeal and guilt over slavery, but as with the entire matter of guilt, the argument almost assumes the absence of evidence and thereby renders evaluation difficult.[46]

The contention about the South's failure to resort to guerrilla war after Appomattox, even though it willingly fought a terrorist campaign against Republican racial policies during Reconstruction, can be more easily evaluated. The South rejected irregular warfare for many reasons, not least of which was the fear of the disorder it would bring. Moreover, attributing the failure to fight on in 1865 to a lack of commitment to slavery, while dismissing the importance of the pursuit of the war through the previous four hard years, seems arbitrary. Clearly the South sacrificed far more between 1861 and 1865, in hopes of preserving slavery and achieving nationhood, than it did after 1865 in defending home rule and segregation. Likewise, there is little more consensus on southerners' response to emancipation than on their response to defeat. Where some proponents of the guilt thesis believe southerners greeted the end of slavery with relief, as if a moral burden had been lifted, James L. Roark, Leon F. Litwack, Dan T. Carter, and other scholars find at best a grudging acceptance of emancipation. Here, as on so many issues involved in the evaluation of the guilt thesis, no consensus seems likely to emerge and no shared standard of proof appears readily available.[47]

Indeed, a review of the major evidence cited on behalf of the guilt thesis—manumissions, the confusion of person and property, the vehemence of the proslavery defense, the failure to reopen the slave trade, and the response to defeat and emancipation—reveals no more definitive proof for or against the guilt thesis than does an analysis of the assumptions on which it rests. Rather, both suggest that, as in most important and interesting historiographical controversies, no definitive proof is possible. This is especially true in this case because historians have so little direct evidence on which to rely and instead must speculate on the subconscious or interpret complex and confusing signs. Often the question becomes not what happened or what was said but rather what was meant or what was revealed. Manumissions did occur, but in significant enough numbers to suggest widespread guilt? White southerners often referred to slavery as a "burden," Genovese and Mathews agree, but one interprets that as self-justification and the other as an expression of doubt.

In the face of such difficulties and disagreement, the best that historians can do is to evaluate the relative plausibility of the guilt thesis. To be sure, a few southerners felt guilty, but recent works of scholarship render increasingly implausible the notion that guilt permeated the culture of the Old South or shaped southern behavior. These works have done so by challenging the basic assumptions of the guilt thesis: that white southerners opposed slavery in the revolutionary period and that southern political and religious thought conflicted with slavery. In addition, they have offered alternative explanations for much of the behavior sometimes attributed to troubled consciences.

Just as surely, a review of the literature suggests a disparity between the confident, dogmatic tone of the South's proslavery ideology and the actual feelings of slaveholders. Even Phillips and Genovese found that slaveholders were at least disquieted about slavery, and certain signs, particularly the squeamishness about the slave trade, do suggest that doubts existed about the institution. Some of these doubts can be explained as unhappiness over certain practices within the slave system—failure to recognize marriages, for example—rather than as fundamental doubts about the institution itself, as Faust has recently argued. Other doubts, as Davis and Patterson have suggested, reflected the general social confusion inherent in the slaves' position in society, one that left them at the margins of society, neither inside nor outside of it, neither people nor property. Disquiet over such anomalies did not necessarily constitute opposition to or guilt about the system itself. It arose not from deep-seated conflict between American political and religious ideals and slavery but out of the very nature of the institution. It was neither a function of guilt nor something peculiarly southern or American but rather something characteristic of slavery.[48]

Attributing doubts and confusion to contradictions inherent in the institution of slavery explains southern behavior as well or better than the guilt thesis does. If white southerners really doubted the morality of slavery and welcomed its eventual end, why did they choose to secede and fight for it? Sellers, logically enough, attributed the decision to irrational factors, but few subsequent historians, adherents of the guilt thesis or others, have endorsed his argument. Moreover, it is hard to explain why, once southerners declared their independence, they fought for so long in a cause to which they had so little commitment. To consider the contradictions inherent in slavery, not in the southern conscience, makes it easier to see secession and the war as rational attempts to preserve slavery and to create a nation in which to do so. Yet it still allows for the fact that the contradictions could become more manifest or important in the throes of war, could thereby inhibit the creation of a true, viable southern nationalism, and ultimately, when combined with battlefield reverses, could sap morale.[49]

Attributing behavior usually interpreted as the result of guilt to contradictions within a slave system, therefore, does not eliminate the role of slavery in the collapse of Confederate nationalism. Nor does it necessitate a return to the simple arguments from self-interest inherent in progressive and proslavery historiography. Like the modernists' perspective, it allows for contradictions and paradoxes—renders slaveholders slightly less of one mind than the progressives or proslavery apologists did. But this approach does minimize the psychological turmoil with which southern modernists invested the Old South and reduces their sense of the region's uniqueness rooted in guilt. Paradoxically, it challenges the other strand in the historiography of the guilt thesis, the emphasis on the similarity between the Old South and the rest of the United States. Rather, as C. Vann Woodward proposed long ago in another context, it suggests, in this regard at least, that the South resembled not the North but the rest of the world—or, more accurately, the rest of the slaveholding world.[50]

Such a revision, though it undermines his argument, renders Sellers's title, "The Travail of Slavery," even more apt. Emphasizing contradictions inherent within slavery rather than guilt generated by American values acknowledges the difficulties and disquiet of the slave system—the travails of slavery. But such an emphasis also renders antebellum white southerners less self-tortured and more a people who, out of racism, greed, or simple moral inertia, ignored the contradictions in their not so peculiar institution and thereby helped to bring about their own defeat.

NOTES

1. Charles G. Sellers Jr., "The Travail of Slavery," in *The Southerner as American*, ed. Sellers (Chapel Hill: University of North Carolina Press, 1960), 40–71. My analysis makes no claim to be an exhaustive account of every work mentioning guilt over slavery but rather only an evaluation of major works. James M. McPherson offers an early review of the thesis itself; McPherson, "Slavery and Race," *Perspectives in American History* 3 (1969), 460–73. For a more comprehensive review of the literature on the antebellum South, see Drew Gilpin Faust, "The Peculiar South Revisited: White Society, Culture, and Politics in the Antebellum Period, 1800–1860," in *Interpreting Southern History: Historiographical Essays in Honor of Sanford W. Higginbotham*, ed. John B. Boles and Evelyn Thomas Nolen (Baton Rouge: Louisiana State University Press, 1987), 78–119.

2. Aileen S. Kraditor, *Means and Ends in American Abolitionism: Garrison and His Critics on Strategy and Tactics, 1834–1850* (New York: Pantheon, 1969), 260; John David Smith, *An Old Creed*

for the New South: Proslavery Ideology and Historiography, 1865–1918 (Westport, Conn.: Greenwood Press, 1985), 8–9; and Gaines M. Foster, *Ghosts of the Confederacy: Defeat, the Lost Cause, and the Emergence of the New South, 1865 to 1913* (New York: Oxford University Press, 1987), 23–24, 180–91.

3. Ulrich Bonnell Phillips, *American Negro Slavery: A Survey of the Supply, Employment, and Control of Negro Labor* (1918; Baton Rouge: Louisiana State University Press, 1966), 118, 125, 131. Phillips's views on the overriding importance of race became clear in "The Central Theme of Southern History," *American Historical Review* 34 (October 1928): 30–43.

4. William E. Dodd, *The Cotton Kingdom: A Chronicle of the Old South* (New Haven, Conn.: Yale University Press, 1919), 146 (first quotation); Dodd, *Expansion and Conflict* (Boston: Houghton Mifflin, 1915); and Dodd, *Statesmen of the Old South, Or From Radicalism to Conservative Revolt* (New York: Macmillan, 1911), 135 (second and third quotations).

5. Daniel Joseph Singal, *The War Within: From Victorian to Modernist Thought in the South, 1919–1945* (Chapel Hill: University of North Carolina Press, 1982), esp. 373–75, quotations on 8–9. For more on Cash and Smith as modernists, see Bruce Clayton, "A Southern Modernist: The Mind of W. J. Cash," in *The South Is Another Land: Essays on the Twentieth-Century South*, ed. Bruce Clayton and John A. Salmond (Westport, Conn.: Greenwood Press, 1987), 171–85; and Anne C. Loveland, *Lillian Smith, a Southerner Confronting the South: A Biography* (Baton Rouge: Louisiana State University Press, 1986).

6. W. J. Cash, *The Mind of the South* (New York: Alfred A. Knopf, 1941), 59–98 at 60–61, 87.

7. Lillian Smith, *Killers of the Dream* (New York: W. W. Norton, 1949), 53–55.

8. Fred Hobson, *Tell About the South: The Southern Rage to Explain* (Baton Rouge: Louisiana State University Press, 1983).

9. C. Vann Woodward, *Thinking Back: The Perils of Writing History* (Baton Rouge: Louisiana State University Press, 1986), 23–24; and David Brion Davis, "Slavery and the Post-World War II Historians," in Davis, *From Homicide to Slavery: Studies in American Culture* (New York: Oxford University Press, 1986), 188–89. See also Peter Novick, *That Noble Dream: The "Objectivity Question" and the American Historical Profession* (Cambridge: Cambridge University Press, 1988), 134. Cash's influence is clear, but historians did not at once accept his observations on guilt. Of nine contemporary reviews that I checked, only three mentioned the idea.

10. Davis, "Slavery," 189; Richard Hofstadter, "U. B. Phillips and the Plantation Legend," *Journal of Negro History* 29 (April 1944): 109–24; Daniel Joseph Singal, "Beyond Consensus: Richard Hofstadter and American Historiography," *American Historical Review* 89 (October 1984): 976–1004; Stanley M. Elkins, *Slavery: A Problem in American Institutional and Intellectual Life*, 2nd ed. (1959; Chicago: University of Chicago Press, 1968), 17–23.

11. Kenneth M. Stampp, *The Peculiar Institution: Slavery in the Ante-Bellum South* (New York: Vintage, 1956), 422–24, 430.

12. Bell I. Wiley, *The Road to Appomattox* (Memphis, Tenn.: Memphis State College Press, 1956), 102–5, quotation at 102; C. Vann Woodward, "The Search for Southern Identity," in Woodward, *The Burden of Southern History* (Baton Rouge: Louisiana State University Press, 1960), 3–25, quotation at 20–21; and Richard H. King, *A Southern Renaissance: The Cultural Awakening of the American South, 1930–1955* (New York: Oxford University Press, 1980), 256–77. For Woodward's interpretation of what he said, which differs from how he was read, see Woodward, *Thinking Back*,

116–19. About the same time, Robert Penn Warren came very close to endorsing the guilt thesis. See Warren, *The Legacy of the Civil War: Meditations on the Centennial* (New York: Alfred A. Knopf, 1961), 87–89, 96.

13. Sellers, "Travail of Slavery," 40–71, quotations at 40–41, 51, 56, 67, 69, 70–71.

14. Ralph E. Morrow, "The Proslavery Argument Revisited," *Mississippi Valley Historical Review* 48 (June 1961): 79–94, quotations at 81, 93–94.

15. William W. Freehling, *Prelude to Civil War: The Nullification Controversy in South Carolina, 1816–1836* (New York: Harper and Row, 1966), chapters 3 and 9, quotations at 72, 360.

16. Kenneth M. Stampp, "The Southern Road to Appomattox," in *The Imperiled Union: Essays on the Background of the Civil War* (New York: Oxford University Press, 1980), 246–69, quotations at 251, 255, 260.

17. On general trends in the profession, see John Higham, *History: Professional Scholarship in America* (Baltimore: Johns Hopkins University Press, 1983), 198–262. Earl E. Thorpe took a clinical and explicitly Freudian approach, but his work has had little or no influence on the guilt thesis. See Thorpe, *Eros and Freedom in Southern Life and Thought* (Durham, N.C.: Seaman Printing, 1967); and *The Old South: A Psychohistory* (Durham, N.C.: Seaman Printing, 1972). David W. Southern argued for the importance of Gunnar Myrdal's *An American Dilemma* (1944) for historians, and even suggested that it influenced Sellers. Certainly, the guilt theory's slaveholders faced a dilemma very much like the one sketched by Myrdal, but neither Sellers nor other authors of the guilt thesis cited *An American Dilemma*. See Southern, *Gunnar Myrdal and Black-White Relations: The Use and Abuse of "An American Dilemma," 1944–1969* (Baton Rouge: Louisiana State University Press, 1987), esp. 161, 167–68.

18. In addition to Thorpe, previously cited, see John W. Blassingame, "The Planter on the Couch: Earl Thorpe and the Psychodynamics of Slavery," *Journal of Negro History* 60 (April 1975): 320–31. For John Hope Franklin's description of slaveholders, see Franklin, *The Militant South, 1800–1861* (Cambridge, Mass.: Harvard University Press, 1956), chapter 5.

19. C. Vann Woodward, *The Strange Career of Jim Crow* (New York: Oxford University Press, 1955). For the controversy over *Jim Crow* and Woodward's own observations, see Woodward, *Thinking Back*, 81–99. For more on guilt and identity, see Hobson, *Tell About the South*, 11; Gaines M. Foster, "Woodward and Southern Identity," *Southern Review* 21 (April 1985): 351–60; and Sellers, *Southerner as American*, vix, 71.

20. Sudie Duncan Sides, "Women and Slaves: An Interpretation Based on the Writings of Southern Women" (PhD diss., University of North Carolina at Chapel Hill, 1969), 30–94; Sides, "Southern Women and Slavery, Part I," *History Today* 20 (January 1970): 54–60; Anne Firor Scott, *The Southern Lady: From Pedestal to Politics, 1830–1930* (Chicago: University of Chicago Press, 1970), 46–54; Scott, "Women's Perspective on the Patriarchy in the 1850s," *Journal of American History* 61 (June 1974): 52–64; C. Vann Woodward, ed., *Mary Chesnut's Civil War* (New Haven, Conn.: Yale University Press, 1981), xlvi–liii. On women and slavery, also see Blassingame, "Planter on the Couch"; Suzanne Lebsock, *The Free Women of Petersburg: Status and Culture in a Southern Town, 1784–1860* (New York: W. W. Norton, 1984), 136–41; Jean E. Friedman, *The Enclosed Garden: Women and Community in the Evangelical South, 1830–1900* (Chapel Hill: University of North Carolina Press, 1985), 87–90; James L. Roark, *Masters Without Slaves: Southern Planters in the Civil War and Reconstruction* (New York: W. W. Norton, 1977), 97; Donald G. Mathews, *Religion in the Old*

South (Chicago: University of Chicago Press, 1977), 79–80, 118, 184; and Elizabeth Fox-Genovese, *Within the Plantation Household: Black and White Women of the Old South* (Chapel Hill: University of North Carolina Press, 1988), 47–48, 334–71.

21. Mathews, *Religion in the Old South*; and Ronald T. Takaki, *A Pro-Slavery Crusade: The Agitation to Reopen the African Slave Trade* (New York: Free Press, 1971). On radicals as conservatives, see, for example, Michael Les Benedict, "Preserving the Constitution: The Conservative Basis of Radical Reconstruction," *Journal of American History* 61 (June 1974): 65–90.

22. Catherine Clinton, *The Plantation Mistress: Woman's World in the Old South* (New York: Pantheon, 1982), 180–98, quotation at 196; Clarence L. Mohr, *On the Threshold of Freedom: Masters and Slaves in Civil War Georgia* (Athens: University of Georgia Press, 1986), 235–71; David T. Bailey, *Shadow on the Church: Southwestern Evangelical Religion and the Issue of Slavery, 1783–1860* (Ithaca, N.Y.: Cornell University Press, 1985); James Oakes, *The Ruling Race: A History of American Slaveholders* (New York: Alfred A. Knopf, 1982); and Richard E. Beringer et al., *Why the South Lost the Civil War* (Athens: University of Georgia Press, 1986).

23. Oakes, *Ruling Race,* esp. 96–122, quotations at xii–xiii, 102–3, 111, 120. Oakes's more recent *Slavery and Freedom: An Interpretation of the Old South* (New York: Alfred A. Knopf, 1990) makes no mention of guilt.

24. Beringer et al., *Why the South Lost the Civil War,* esp. 336–67, quotations at 87, 89, 280.

25. My distinction between the two assumptions is somewhat arbitrary because democratic principles influenced revolutionary-era antislavery thought.

26. William W. Freehling, "The Founding Fathers and Slavery," *American Historical Review* 77 (February 1972): 81–93.

27. Robert McColley, *Slavery and Jeffersonian Virginia* (Urbana: University of Illinois Press, 1964), 124; Paul Finkelman, "Slavery and the Constitutional Convention: Making a Covenant with Death," in *Beyond Confederation: Origins of the Constitution and American National Identity,* ed. Richard Beeman, Stephen Botein, and Edward C. Carter II (Chapel Hill: University of North Carolina Press, 1987), 188–225; David Brion Davis, *The Problem of Slavery in the Age of Revolution, 1770–1823* (Ithaca, N.Y.: Cornell University Press, 1975), 107 (first quotation); and Davis, "American Slavery and the American Revolution," in *Slavery and Freedom in the Age of the American Revolution,* ed. Ira Berlin and Ronald Hoffman (Charlottesville: University of Virginia Press, 1983), 273 (second quotation). See also Donald L. Robinson, *Slavery in the Structure of American Politics, 1765–1820* (New York: Harcourt Brace Jovanovich, 1971); and Sylvia R. Frey, "Liberty, Equality, and Slavery: The Paradox of the American Revolution," in *The American Revolution: Its Character and Limits,* ed. Jack P. Greene (New York: New York University Press, 1987), 230–52.

28. Alison Goodyear Freehling, *Drift Toward Dissolution: The Virginia Slavery Debate of 1831– 1832* (Baton Rouge: Louisiana State University Press, 1982); Duncan J. MacLeod, *Slavery, Race and the American Revolution* (New York: Cambridge University Press, 1974), esp. 184; Winthrop D. Jordan, *White Over Black: American Attitudes Toward the Negro, 1550–1812* (Chapel Hill: University of North Carolina Press, 1968), 375–426, quotation at 403.

29. Sellers, "Travail of Slavery," 46; Oakes, *Ruling Race,* 117.

30. On the age of Civil War era soldiers, legislators, and other leaders, see Drew Gilpin Faust, "Christian Soldiers: The Meaning of Revivalism in the Confederate Army," *Journal of Southern History* 53 (February 1987), 69; Jon L. Wakelyn, "Background and Preparation of the Confederate

Leaders," in Wakelyn, *Biographical Dictionary of the Confederacy* (Westport, Conn.: Greenwood Press, 1977), 26–27; Ralph A. Wooster, *The Secession Conventions of the South* (Princeton, N.J.: Princeton University Press, 1962), 256; Thomas B. Alexander and Richard E. Beringer, *The Anatomy of the Confederate Congress: A Study of the Influences of Member Characteristics on Legislative Voting Behavior, 1861–1865* (Nashville, Tenn.: Vanderbilt University Press, 1972), 29–30.

31. Because of the focus here on the guilt thesis, and due to limitations of space, I have not examined the intellectual context that helped shape the work of the critics of the thesis.

32. Eugene D. Genovese, *The World the Slaveholders Made: Two Essays in Interpretation* (New York: Vintage, 1969), esp. 143–50, quotation at 99; Genovese, *The Political Economy of Slavery: Studies in the Economy and Society of the Slave South* (New York: Vintage, 1965), esp. 13–36; Genovese, *Roll, Jordan, Roll: The World the Slaves Made* (New York: Vintage, 1974), 3–158.

33. Eugene D. Genovese and Elizabeth Fox-Genovese, "The Religious Ideals of Southern Slave Society," *Georgia Historical Quarterly* 70 (Spring 1986): 1–16; Genovese and Fox-Genovese, "The Divine Sanction of Social Order: Religious Foundations of the Southern Slaveholders' World View," *Journal of the American Academy of Religion* 55 (Summer 1987): 211–33.

34. Edmund S. Morgan, *American Slavery—American Freedom: The Ordeal of Colonial Virginia* (New York: W. W. Norton, 1975), esp. 295–387; Morgan, "Slavery and Freedom: The American Paradox," *Journal of American History* 59 (June 1972): 5–29; Kenneth S. Greenberg, *Masters and Statesmen: The Political Culture of American Slavery* (Baltimore: Johns Hopkins University Press, 1985), 85–103; J. William Harris, *Plain Folk and Gentry in a Slave Society: White Liberty and Black Slavery in Augusta's Hinterlands* (Middletown, Conn.: Wesleyan University Press, 1985); Larry E. Tise, *Proslavery: A History of the Defense of Slavery in America, 1701–1840* (Athens: University of Georgia Press, 1987); Lacy K. Ford Jr., *Origins of Southern Radicalism: The South Carolina Upcountry, 1800–1860* (New York: Oxford University Press, 1988).

35. George M. Fredrickson, *The Black Image in the White Mind: The Debate on Afro-American Character and Destiny, 1817–1914* (New York: Harper and Row, 1971), 61–64; William J. Cooper Jr., *Liberty and Slavery: Southern Politics to 1860* (New York: Alfred A. Knopf, 1983); J. Mills Thornton III, *Politics and Power in a Slave Society: Alabama, 1800–1860* (Baton Rouge: Louisiana State University Press, 1978).

36. Bertram Wyatt-Brown, *Southern Honor: Ethics and Behavior in the Old South* (New York: Oxford University Press, 1982), 3, 16. Wyatt-Brown explains his view of the relationship between honor and Evangelicalism in "God and Honor in the Old South," *Southern Review* 25 (April 1989): 283–96.

37. David Brion Davis, *The Problem of Slavery in Western Culture* (Ithaca, N.Y.: Cornell University Press, 1966), esp. 222; Forrest G. Wood, *The Arrogance of Faith: Christianity and Race in America from the Colonial Era to the Twentieth Century* (New York: Alfred A. Knopf, 1990), xviii, 11; Jon Butler, *Awash in a Sea of Faith: Christianizing the American People* (Cambridge, Mass.: Harvard University Press, 1990), 129–51; Ford, *Origins of Southern Radicalism*, 19–37, quotation at 24; Lester B. Scherer, *Slavery and the Churches in Early America, 1619–1819* (Grand Rapids, Mich.: Eerdmans, 1975), 141–44; John R. McKivigan, *The War Against Proslavery Religion: Abolitionism and the Northern Churches, 1830–1865* (Ithaca, N.Y.: Cornell University Press, 1984), 7, 15; H. Shelton Smith, *In His Image, But . . .: Racism in Southern Religion, 1780–1910* (Durham, N.C.: Duke University Press, 1972), 129–207; Anne C. Loveland, *Southern Evangelicals and the Social Order, 1800–1860* (Baton

Rouge: Louisiana State University Press, 1980), 186–218; Tise, *Proslavery,* 292–307, 323–46; Drew Gilpin Faust, "Evangelicalism and the Meaning of the Proslavery Argument: The Reverend Thornton Stringfellow of Virginia," *Virginia Magazine of History and Biography* 85 (January 1977): 3–17; Jack P. Maddex Jr., "Proslavery Millennialism: Social Eschatology in Antebellum Southern Calvinism," *American Quarterly* 31 (Spring 1979): 46–62.

38. James D. Essig, *The Bonds of Wickedness: American Evangelicals Against Slavery, 1770–1808* (Philadelphia: Temple University Press, 1982), 115 (first quotation); Bailey, *Shadow on the Church,* 23 (second quotation); Mathews, *Religion in the Old South,* 136–84 (all subsequent quotations at 152, 173). On southern clergy and slavery, also see James Oscar Farmer Jr., *The Metaphysical Confederacy: James Henley Thornwell and the Synthesis of Southern Values* (Macon, Ga.: Mercer University Press, 1986), 195–233; and Mitchell Snay, "American Thought and Southern Distinctiveness: The Southern Clergy and the Sanctification of Slavery," *Civil War History* 35 (December 1989): 311–28.

39. Rollin G. Osterweis, *Romanticism and Nationalism in the Old South* (New Haven, Conn.: Yale University Press, 1949), 14–15; Oakes, *Ruling Race,* 119–20.

40. Arthur Egendorf et al., *Legacies of Vietnam: Comparative Adjustment of Veterans and Their Peers: A Study Prepared for the Veterans' Administration,* 97th Cong., 1 Sess., House Committee on Veterans' Affairs, House Committee Print No. 14 (Washington, D.C.: Government Printing Office, 1981), 729–30.

41. Sellers, "Travail of Slavery," 53. Percentage based on 395,216 slaveholders; see Oakes, *Ruling Race,* 260n6. Ira Berlin, *Slaves Without Masters: The Free Negro in the Antebellum South* (New York: Pantheon, 1974), esp. 138–57 at 149–50; Orlando Patterson, *Slavery and Social Death: A Comparative Study* (Cambridge, Mass.: Harvard University Press, 1982), 262–96, quotation at 217.

42. Sellers, "Travail of Slavery," 56–62; Patterson, *Slavery and Social Death,* 35–51, quotation at 45; Davis, *Problem of Slavery in Western Culture,* 31, 62.

43. Genovese, *Political Economy of Slavery,* 31–34 at 34; William J. Cooper Jr., *The South and the Politics of Slavery, 1828–1856* (Baton Rouge: Louisiana State University Press, 1978), 69–74, 238–44.

44. David Donald, "The Proslavery Argument Reconsidered," *Journal of Southern History* 37 (February 1971): 3–18; Drew Gilpin Faust, *A Sacred Circle: The Dilemma of the Intellectual in the Old South, 1840–1860* (Baltimore: Johns Hopkins University Press, 1977), esp. 112–31; Tise, *Proslavery,* esp. 75–96; Peter Kolchin, *Unfree Labor: American Slavery and Russian Serfdom* (Cambridge, Mass.: Harvard University Press, 1987), 371.

45. Takaki, *Pro-Slavery Crusade.* See also Barton J. Bernstein, "Southern Politics and Attempts to Reopen the African Slave Trade," *Journal of Negro History* 51 (January 1966): 16–35.

46. Gerald F. Linderman, *Embattled Courage: The Experience of Combat in the American Civil War* (New York: Free Press, 1987); Reid Mitchell, *Civil War Soldiers* (New York: Viking, 1988), 180–83; James I. Robertson Jr., *Soldiers Blue and Gray* (Columbia: University of South Carolina Press, 1988); James M. McPherson, *The Battle Cry of Freedom: The Civil War Era* (New York: Oxford University Press, 1988), 853–62; Beringer et al., *Why the South Lost the Civil War,* esp. 266–67; Stampp, "Southern Road to Appomattox."

47. Roark, *Masters Without Slaves,* 85–108; Leon F. Litwack, *Been in the Storm So Long: The Aftermath of Slavery* (New York: Alfred A. Knopf, 1979), 187–89; Dan T. Carter, *When the War Was Over: The Failure of Self-Reconstruction in the South, 1865–1867* (Baton Rouge: Louisiana State Uni-

versity Press, 1985), 82–95; Foster, *Ghosts of the Confederacy*, 22–24.

48. Drew Gilpin Faust, *The Creation of Confederate Nationalism: Ideology and Identity in the Civil War South* (Baton Rouge: Louisiana State University Press, 1988), 75–81.

49. Steven A. Channing does stress fear, and to that extent, he treats secession as irrational. He also discusses the complexities of southern attitudes toward slavery. See Channing, *Crisis of Fear: Secession in South Carolina* (New York: W. W. Norton, 1970).

50. Woodward, "The Irony of Southern History," in Woodward, *Burden of Southern History*, 167–91.

− 3 −

COMING TO TERMS WITH DEFEAT

POST-VIETNAM AMERICA AND THE POST−CIVIL WAR SOUTH

In the three decades since this essay first appeared, in 1990, the memorialization of the Vietnam War has continued, and many more monuments to the soldiers of the Vietnam War have gone up. Yet the nation still struggles to come to terms with the war, and many of its veterans still endure post-traumatic stress disorder. Kathleen Belew's 2018 book, Bring the War Home, *which chronicles the impact of the Vietnam War on veterans who later became part of white power paramilitary groups, has made even clearer that the war continues to haunt the nation. Perhaps this early attempt to explore parallels between the aftermath of the Vietnam War and of the Civil War remains helpful.*[*]

I N A RECENT EDITORIAL CARTOON, a perplexed couple emerges from a movie theater. Over their heads the marquee reads *"Platoon:* Now Showing." Beneath it, the man comments, "I liked it better when Rambo won the war." This cartoon exemplifies what might be called the United States' third Vietnam War. The first was the actual war in Indochina to preserve South Vietnam, a military intervention that lasted twenty-five years, cost some 58,000 American lives, and ended in frustration and failure. The second was the war at home over the morality and wisdom of that intervention, a battle that divided and disrupted the nation. The third is the battle to define what the wars in and over Vietnam meant. The fighting in this third Vietnam War appears to be escalating as new offensives are launched, not only in the growing number of histories, memoirs, and novels but also in popular movies, prime-time television shows, and even a comic book series.

In this inevitable third Vietnam War, Americans begin to come to terms with defeat in Vietnam. Once before, one part of the nation—the South—faced a similar adjustment. A comparison of the white South's experience with defeat and America's emerging response to its loss of the war in Vietnam may be helpful. Such a comparison need not ignore the substantial differences between the Civil and Vietnam Wars. The former was a domestic conflict, fought only on American soil. The latter was an American intervention in a complex foreign conflict, part civil war, part military invasion, an intervention abroad that led to confrontation at home and divided and scarred the nation. Yet, though the wars differed, an examination of their aftermaths reveals several points on which a cautious comparison may yield insights for Americans fighting the third Vietnam War. Americans now wrestle with three problems that the white South also faced: how to treat defeated veterans, how to reconcile former foes, and how to interpret defeat.

IN THE LAST YEARS of the Vietnam War and into the 1970s, American popular culture frequently presented Vietnam veterans as crazies or criminals, dysfunctionals who never quite succeeded in putting the war behind them. The vets rightly resented such portrayals, and to counter them they pointed proudly to the successful among their ranks. Recent polls have shown the successes to be far from uncommon and have suggested that fewer veterans failed to adjust to life after Vietnam than media stereotypes indicate. But if the stereotypes exaggerated, evidence still suggests that many Vietnam veterans have had difficulty in coping with their wartime experiences. The most troubled among them suffer from a debilitating condition, labeled post-traumatic stress disorder, whose victims relive the war in dreams and flashbacks. The war also haunts many for whom such clinical labels are inappropriate—even some of the "successes" counted in the polls.

Studies reveal that numerous factors contribute to postwar stress—the personal background of the soldier, the intensity of combat he experienced, the type of community to which he returned, and the personal support he received from friends and family. Yet such variables would be involved in the return of veterans from all wars. Among the factors offered to explain the peculiar difficulties of Vietnam veterans, two predominate: the unique character of the

Vietnam War and the welcome home or, more accurately, the lack of a welcome home the veterans received when they returned.

Those who attribute postwar troubles to the unique character of the war dwell on its brutality, its lack of established lines, and its confusion over who was friend and who was foe. They also point to the soldiers' youth and pattern of service. Almost seven years younger on average than his World War II predecessor, the Vietnam soldier found himself suddenly delivered, alone, into the war zone, where he served a one-year tour, and then, just as abruptly and still alone, he returned to the United States. While not necessarily disputing assumptions about uniqueness, other observers argue that the veterans' problem lay in the outcome of the war. Theologian W. Taylor Stevenson, for example, contends that the veteran suffers from a sense of defilement—a belief that he was dishonored and symbolically dirtied by breaking the taboos that protect Americans' sense of innocence and powerfulness. Still others argue that by 1968 Americans neither supported the war nor expected to win it. Consequently, at the time, veterans serving after 1967, and in retrospect all veterans, regarded their service as purposeless—"It don't mean nothing," in the refrain of the Vietnam soldiers in the recent movie *Hamburger Hill*. Surveys do show that veterans most likely to undergo postwar stress served after 1967, when the war had become increasingly unpopular and, for many, its purpose increasingly unclear.

Despite the partial validity of these arguments, whether combat in Vietnam was unique remains very much an open question. Certainly, the one-year rotation, a policy adopted in no other conflict save Korea, created many difficulties, but other aspects of the Vietnam War may not have differed as radically from those in previous conflicts as some accounts assume. The destruction of villages and murder of civilians may not have been as frequent or cold-blooded as movies like *Platoon* and memoirs like *A Rumor of War* make them seem, and clearly similar atrocities occurred in earlier wars. In World War II and Korea, according to one historian, civilian casualties probably equaled or exceeded those in Vietnam, and as James Reston Jr.'s *Sherman's March and Vietnam* serves to remind, even when Americans fought other Americans, they did not always spare civilians or towns.

Nor were other aspects of the Vietnam War totally different from those of the Civil War. The Confederate soldiers, no older than their Vietnam War counterparts, also faced horrifying brutality and suffering in an age of mass casualties but also of rudimentary medicine that could do little to heal them or ease their pain. Their war, a fight to overthrow their own government and to preserve slavery, could have led to a sense of defilement as readily as did the Vietnam War. Significant antiwar agitation occurred in the South toward the end of the war, and the Confederate soldiers, like the Vietnam vets, endured the conflicting emotions of a frustrated and defeated army. Yet little evidence of post-traumatic stress disorder appears in the postwar letters, diaries, and reminiscences of Confederate veterans. Though scarred by defeat, they seem to have suffered far less difficulty adjusting after the war than the Vietnam veterans have. The nature of combat in the two wars may help explain that difference, but of greater importance may be the way veterans of the two wars perceived their return from battle.**

The treatment of returning Vietnam soldiers has itself become an issue central to the third Vietnam War. Popular lore tells of returning soldiers who were harassed by antiwar civilians, but these accounts should not be accepted until systematic investigation confirms them. Clearly, however, veterans believe themselves to have been the victims of civilian hostility. Many talk of trying to hide their service; others who did not or could not hide it because of injury recount sad tales of harassment by angry or scornful fellow citizens. "Did you kill any babies?" they say people asked them. They tell of a passerby looking at their empty sleeve and hissing, "Serves you right" or of antiwar protestors spitting on them. The image of being spit on by civilians, whether fact or myth, aptly symbolizes what the veterans feel—a sense of defilement, a sense that society condemned their actions and rejected them as unclean.

Confederate soldiers, too, worried about whether defeat dishonored them, but few recounted tales of scorn. They talked instead of how white southerners warmly embraced them. A one-armed veteran likely met not a hostile comment but a bevy of adoring females. Towns throughout the South staged picnics and celebrations to welcome their soldiers. More important, in the ten to fifteen years after the Confederate surrender, southerners built Confederate cemeteries, erected funereal monuments, and held yearly memorial celebrations in honor of the dead and veterans. These celebrations and memorials, though avoiding the issues and passions of the war, publicly, ritualistically testified to the honor of the Confederate soldier; they signaled to the soldier that his society did not consider him defiled by war or defeat.

Exactly this sort of ritual of acceptance and honor was denied Vietnam veterans when first they came home, or even after the war ended. The one-year tour and the soldiers' return as individuals and not in units made organizing a triumphant parade unlikely, if not impossible. More important, some Americans were appalled by the war and others were frustrated by defeat; both groups shunned the Vietnam War's soldiers and avoided discussion of the conflict. For a time, Americans almost succumbed to a sort of collective amnesia. This initial failure to accept the returning Vietnam warriors, so very much in contrast to the South's reception of its armies after Appomattox, contributed significantly to the vets' adjustment problems.

War, as Vietnam veteran William Broyles Jr. and others point out, sets up conflicting emotions within soldiers. It both horrifies and fascinates. It demands that soldiers kill and destroy, actions that they have been taught to consider wrong in other situations, and at the same time generates tremendous excitement, since it is, in Broyles's analogy, the greatest of all games. Taught the standards and values of the game in basic training, what Robert Jay Lifton calls a rite of passage into another world, few Vietnam soldiers questioned the morality of killing the enemy or resorting to extreme violence. The ethics of war justified it, and the need to survive demanded it. But what was logical and moral in "Indian country," to use the significant slang of the soldiers, the veterans feared might not be seen as such "back in the world."

To ease their fears, soldiers may well need another rite of passage—a ritual welcome home, be it a grand parade, memorial day, or monument unveiling—to facilitate their return to "the world." Such a public, symbolic act helps the soldiers resubmit themselves to normal social values. And it allows society to welcome them back, allows it both to acknowledge its role and its acceptance of their temporary violation of moral dictates and to admit the nobility of the soldiers' sacrifice and the legitimacy of what has so fascinated them. Veterans of any war need such acceptance, but those who fought in a controversial, defeated cause, which brings with it feelings of failure and purposelessness, need it even more.

The returning Confederates received such ritualistic welcome; the returning Vietnam vets at first did not—a difference that helps explain why so many more Vietnam than Confederate veterans had a difficult time putting the war behind them. In the absence of a ritualistic acceptance, the psychological tensions and moral anxieties some veterans felt remained unresolved and unratified by society. As a result, some veterans felt defiled, in theologian Stevenson's term, or spat upon, in the image of popular accounts. But their feeling of uncleanness resulted less from the specific evils of Vietnam, less from special brutality or violation of American innocence and powerfulness, than from the absence of the usual postwar ritual of restoration and cleansing.

The welcome came later, and the veterans' enthusiastic, emotional response showed their need for ritual acceptance. In the late 1970s, two movies, *Coming Home* and *The Deer Hunter,* despite differing views of the war, won popular and critical acclaim, marking new, intense interest in Vietnam veterans and their war. Early treatments still stressed the vet's problems, and in some ways harkened back to the older antiwar spirit, but soon his image began to be rehabilitated. An early favorable presentation appeared on television as a new American frontier hero, a not-quite-so-innocent American Adam on that not-quite-so-innocent American frontier, Hawaii. There, Thomas Magnum battled for truth and justice between swims, volleyball, love affairs, and in his early seasons, flashbacks to Vietnam. *Magnum, P.I.* never really confronted the issues of the war but rather celebrated a noble, model veteran who took pride in having fought in Vietnam and cherished—indeed, with sidekicks T.C. and Rick, still enjoyed—the camaraderie of battle. The brief flashbacks not only advanced the plot but also offered viewers a sense of the experience of combat in Vietnam and of its aftereffects.

A few years later veteran Oliver Stone's *Platoon* put a vivid, bloody vision of this experience on the big screen. On one level, Stone's movie re-created the brutality and morality of "Indian country," of the war in Vietnam, in order to ask the civilians "back in the world" to understand what the vets had endured and done. The tremendous acclaim for *Platoon* seemed at last to signal society's acceptance of that behavior and to spur an emotional catharsis.

As this interest in Vietnam grew, Americans finally offered the veterans the ritualistic reassurance so long denied them. By 1986, 143 monuments to the Vietnam veterans had been planned or constructed in forty-five states at a cost of $20 million in privately raised funds. In 1982, the nation dedicated the most important of these monuments, the Vietnam Memorial, located on the Mall, not far from the Lincoln Memorial, in the nation's capital. It resulted from private fund-raising efforts led by veterans who sought to separate the government's war from the warrior, who sought reconciliation and acceptance, and who therefore strove to keep the project free from politics or ideology. In avoiding wartime issues and passions, their efforts resembled early Confederate memorial activities, and so, too, did the memorial's design. Conceived by a Yale University student, Maya Ying Lin, the monument was not, in her words, "meant to be cheerful or happy, but to bring out in people the realization of loss and a cathartic healing process." A grand review, the welcome home parade denied the veterans, marked its dedication, and soon thereafter this monument of mourning and purification was drawing 4 million visitors a year, making it the biggest attraction in Washington save for the National Air and Space Museum.

V-shaped, constructed of black marble panels sunk slightly into the ground so that visitors faced the some 58,000 names of the men and women who died in Vietnam, names etched in the seemingly endless order in which they died, the monument evokes, almost commands, mourning. "Nothing I had heard or written had prepared me for the moment," columnist James J. Kilpatrick wrote of his visit to the memorial. "I could not speak. I wept. . . . This memorial has a pile driver's impact. No politics. No recriminations. Nothing of vainglory or glory either." Or, as one of the judges who selected the design put it in imagery also used to describe Confederate Memorial Day, it "looks back to death and forward to life." The tourists who flocked to it searched for names they knew, made rubbings of names of friends and relatives, left flags, flowers, medals, or some personal token of love and respect. More than any single thing, the memorial on the Mall and its ceremony of dedication offered the ritualistic acceptance so long denied the Vietnam veterans.

Americans, then, have begun to recover from their collective amnesia. Hostility toward veterans has cooled, and the nation has at last formally offered welcome and cleansing. By stressing mourning, this memorial activity resembles the white South's treatment of its veterans. The South's adjustment to defeat, however, rested not only in its memorialization of its soldiers but also in its interpretation of the war and its reconciliation with the North. The three developments proved interrelated, because as reunion proceeded, the North joined in the homage to the veterans, and a shared, heroic interpretation of the war developed, thereby helping ensure that the veterans' sacrifice had purpose and meaning. The continued celebration of the Vietnam veterans may well also depend on whether and how the nation achieves reconciliation and reinterprets the war.

THE RECONCILIATION OF THE foes in the war over Vietnam, the "hawks" and "doves," in the lingo of the 1960s, has not kept pace with acceptance of the veterans. Some combatants have tried to bridge their differences, but as Myra MacPherson detailed in *Long Time Passing*, hostilities between soldiers of the war and protestors against it continue. James Fallows has perceptively argued that preexisting class differences between the mostly poor and disadvantaged who volunteered or were drafted and the comparatively rich and well-connected who avoided the draft help explain these persisting resentments. But estrangement results not just from class conflict, as a comparison with what happened after the Civil War suggests. The reconciliation of North and South occurred slowly, and only as the passions of the war dissipated and veterans on both sides deemphasized the issues of the war—slavery and secession—and focused instead on their common wartime experience, the camaraderie and excitement of battle.

Vietnam veterans, though, share such memories with the Vietnamese, as revealed in William Broyles's *Brothers in Arms,* a Marine veteran's account of his return to Vietnam. In passages that resemble reflections by Civil War veterans, Broyles describes visits to former battlefields and with former foes and concludes that confrontation in battle created bonds with his one-time enemy. For the foes in the war over Vietnam, the warriors and antiwarriors, there exists no such shared experience on which to build reconciliation. Indeed, as Fallows and others have pointed out, the two groups have starkly different memories of the war: one of the army and combat, the other of college and protest. These differences make a second feature of the post–Civil War reconciliation of Blue and Gray, a willingness by each side to celebrate the other's heroism and motives, even more important in the reconciliation of the two sides in the war over Vietnam. That willingness, though, may ultimately depend on how Americans interpret the war in Vietnam, just as it did on how the North and South came to view the Civil War.

The white South, after a brief period of examination and debate, developed an interpretation of defeat that facilitated acceptance of the veterans and reconciliation with the North but hindered any learning of lessons or gaining of wisdom. Southerners rejected any notion that defeat constituted a judgment upon their cause; instead, they concluded that they had fought the war over valid constitutional principles and therefore had acted morally and legally. God had allowed their defeat not because He judged their cause evil but because He planned to use them for some greater purpose. Certainly, defeat had not resulted from any failing of the South or, more specifically, any shortcomings of Confederate soldiers. This interpretation helped Confederate veterans cope with defeat by telling them that even though they lost, they had acted nobly and heroically, and by reassuring them that their sacrifice had been part of a divine plan. It also meant that by the time of national reconciliation during the Spanish-American War, most southerners accepted national myths of divine mission and powerfulness, just as most northerners did.

The North had always assumed that God directed its cause and that it had acted heroically and nobly in saving the Union and freeing the slaves. Robert Penn Warren labeled this moral self-satisfaction the North's "Treasury of Virtue," a treasury that provided moral capital to underwrite the corruption and materialism of the subsequent Gilded Age. By the early twentieth century, northerners not only believed that they had acted rightly but also had come to share the southerners' assessment of Confederate soldiers. With both sides celebrating their role and seeing themselves as part of God's plan for the nation, the Civil War had been rendered a battle in which everyone had been right and everyone had fought heroically—a war, in other words, that on some level everyone had won. Hence, neither side perceived the conflict's tragic dimensions but instead interpreted the war as a vindication leading to reaffirmation of God's mission for the United States in the world.

No such simple, creative consensus about Vietnam has come to dominate public thinking as the third Vietnam War for the historical hearts and minds of the American public escalates. The divisions of the war years persist; proponents and opponents of the war alike continue to consider their side to have been right and to refight the war pretty much along old lines. Thus, Stone's *Platoon*, though "new" in its vivid and sympathetic re-creation of the experience of combat in Vietnam (which may explain its popularity), still takes a traditional antiwar approach by dividing American attitudes toward the war between good and evil and by portraying the United States role as one of almost unrelieved brutality, violence, frustration, and failure. Two recent histories of the war,

Loren Baritz's *Backfire* and Gabriel Kolko's *Anatomy of a War*, each in its own way echoes antiwar arguments of the 1960s, the former in its condemnation of America's bureaucratic, technological society and the latter in its romanticizing of the Viet Cong and North Vietnamese.

Many doves, of course, do not perceive any need to rethink the war or their role in it because they believe they rightly opposed American involvement and won the battle at home over Vietnam. Some even seem to suffer from their own "Treasury of Virtue." They know they were right about the war all along and that therefore they have built up a treasury of moral capital for a new gilded age of BMWs and Rolexes. Events in Indochina since 1973 and new evidence about the North Vietnamese war effort, however, indicate that some doves do need to reconsider their simplistic conception of a peace-loving peasantry attacked by a brutal imperialistic America, or to revise their belief that only American intransigence prolonged the war. The antiwarriors might even question whether the shrillness of some protestors dangerously escalated the war at home or consider whether an absence of will among the antiwarriors actually helped prolong the war. James Fallows and Myra MacPherson have argued that if the antiwar movement had been willing to pay a heavier price, if its partisans had gone noisily to prison rather than quietly avoiding the draft and marching noisily on the Pentagon, the war might have ended sooner.

Although their Treasury of Virtue has made it easy for the doves to avoid hard questions about their role in the Vietnam wars, defeat logically should have forced the hawks to rethink their position. But they have proved even less ready to do so than have most doves. For a time, hawks ignored the war or argued that its uniqueness precluded drawing any lessons from it. Beginning in the late 1970s, though, and with greater visibility in the 1980s, a few scholars, politicians, and polemicists took the offensive in the third Vietnam War. In 1978, Guenter Lewy published *America in Vietnam*, one of the first, and still one of the best, of such interpretations. It scathingly attacked the way the United States fought the war between 1965 and 1968 but still defended the legality and morality of the war and contended that the United States could have won. Public figures proved less critical and cautious than Lewy in championing this view of the war. Journalist Norman Podhoretz flailed the antiwar movement and proclaimed America's role in Vietnam an "act of imprudent idealism whose moral soundness" has been vindicated. In 1980, Ronald Reagan complained that Americans dishonor "the memory of 50,000 young Americans who died" in Vietnam "when we give way to feelings of guilt as if we were doing something shameful." He urged that they "recognize that ours was, in truth, a noble cause." Similarly, H. Ross Perot and other conservative critics of the Vietnam Memorial condemned Maya Lin's design for dishonoring the cause and its defenders and demanded a more heroic statue to the soldiers. These critics succeeded in securing an addition to the wall, a group of three representative soldiers placed to one side and to the front of the V-shaped memorial.

FOR THOSE WHO CONTINUE to believe the Vietnam War could have and should have been won, explaining defeat becomes crucial. No real consensus, though, has emerged on why the United States lost; the confusion that characterized the war still haunts its historiography. But most postwar critics of American policy have stressed two interrelated themes. The first, with antecedents in the debates of the 1960s, blames defeat on the policy of phased escalation; awesome force did not succeed because it was applied piecemeal rather than in one decisive blow. Lyndon Johnson and his civilian advisers, according to this argument, hesitated to approve bombing targets and to commit sufficient troops, thereby tying the military's hands and allowing the other side to match American force.

The second theme attributes defeat to a failure of public will to win. Leslie H. Gelb, in one of the best analyses of the decision to escalate the war, perhaps unintentionally gives aid and comfort to the proponents of this view when he stresses that the leaders of the Kennedy and Johnson administrations never really expected victory or dedicated enough resources to achieve it. Military analysts Harry G. Summers Jr. and Bruce Palmer Jr. catalog many American errors but still blame defeat in large measure on a loss of will among the politicians and the public. Summers claims that President Johnson never fully developed the national consensus essential to the war effort. Palmer, too, criticizes the civilian leaders for failing to sustain public support and identifies two crucial points at which the war was lost: in the wake of the Tet Offensive and during Watergate. Many critics join Palmer in arguing that during the Tet Offensive, a massive enemy attack in early 1968, the Americans and their South Vietnam allies won a decisive victory that irresponsible reporters and panicky politicians transformed into a defeat. Others, too, agree that Watergate kept President

Nixon from fulfilling his promise of additional aid and air support for South Vietnam after the American withdrawal, thereby leaving South Vietnam unable to repel the North's final offensive. In his *No More Vietnams*, Nixon himself flatly asserts that in "a spasm of . . . irresponsibility," Congress in 1973 threw away everything that had been "achieved in twelve years of fighting."

Together, both explanations—the failure of phased escalation and of will— support an even more simplistic interpretation of defeat. Politicians declare that American soldiers should never again be sent to fight a war that their nation is not willing to win. The movie *Rambo* presents a cartoon-like but nonetheless prototypical American hero, with glistening and glorious biceps, skilled with both the bow and modern weapons, who could have won the war by himself— if only he had not been betrayed by the wimps of the bureaucracy. Though they differ in many ways, *Rambo*, the politicians' pleas, and even Palmer's and Nixon's books share a common theme: the failure of will at home, to some extent the creation of craven journalists, disloyal protestors, and timid politicians, robbed the soldiers of victory. Such explanations resemble the "stab-in-the-back" thesis used in Germany in the 1920s and 1930s to explain defeat in World War I. The American version, however, emphasizes popular failure rather than a conspiracy by a few dastardly individuals.

Moreover, American proponents of a stab-in-the-back thesis, unlike their German counterparts who used theirs to nurse bitterness over the loss of World War I, employ it to explain away American defeat. In that regard, the emerging defense of America's role in Vietnam resembles the South's interpretation of defeat in the Civil War. The South, too, insisted upon the morality, nobility, and heroism of its cause and so celebrated its efforts in the war that southerners came to perceive their defeat almost as military victory. The same thing appears to be happening to Americans' views of Vietnam. Building from key points developed in the failure-of-will argument, political scientist Timothy J. Lomperis, who served in Vietnam, maintains that in some ways the United States *did* win in Vietnam. He even entitled his book *The War Everyone Lost—and Won*, a title that one can easily imagine for an early twentieth-century address before a Blue–Gray reunion. The complex argument in the text acknowledges that the United States lost the war to preserve South Vietnam but also contends that U.S. destruction of the Viet Cong during the 1968 Tet Offensive and its subsequent effort over the next five years left South Vietnam sufficiently strong to defend itself. The United States had, in effect, defeated the attempt through a people's war to overthrow the government of South Vietnam and thereby had denied legitimacy to the Communist government established after the North Vietnamese conquest of South Vietnam in 1975. Everyone won, everyone lost. Former President Nixon went even further in turning defeat into victory. "When we signed the Paris peace agreements in 1973, we had won the war. We then proceeded to lose the peace." In 1985, President Reagan expressed virtually the same sentiment as he blamed the fall of South Vietnam on Congress's refusal to supply aid to South Vietnam. "The truth of the matter is," he said, "we did have victory. . . . We continue to talk about losing that war. We didn't lose that war. We won virtually every engagement."

Interpreting American involvement in Vietnam as a justified, moral, and noble crusade, one all but won militarily only to be lost because of timidity and a failure of will at home, constitutes a major, new offensive in the third Vietnam War—a frontal assault on the doves who condemn the American war effort as both hopeless and wrong. Many leaders of the charge come from the ranks of the right, and it clearly supports conservative political and foreign policy objectives. Yet this interpretation has an appeal beyond its utility to conservatives. Proclaiming the nobility of the war, blaming defeat on a failure of will, and assuming the nearness of victory supports efforts to rehabilitate the reputation of the veterans. Moreover, as the South's experience suggests, defeated Americans may well find such an explanation not just appealing but believable.

Deciding exactly what the American public believes about any issue is difficult, especially so in this case because polls often seem contradictory. One taken in 1985 showed that almost three-quarters of the American people considered the United States involvement in Vietnam to have been wrong, though this total may include many who believed in the morality and wisdom of the war but opposed the way it was fought. This same poll, however, suggests that the hawks may be succeeding in convincing Americans of the war's nobility. The proposition that Vietnam was a noble crusade received its highest levels of support among eighteen- to twenty-two-year-olds, the group with no personal memory of the war. Americans also seem quite receptive to the failure-of-will explanation for defeat. In 1980, 47 percent strongly agreed and another 26 percent somewhat agreed with the statement "The trouble in Vietnam was that our troops were asked to fight a war which our political leader in Washington would not let them win." That the majority of Americans accepted the validity of this statement, and that Vietnam veterans—and again the young with no memory of the war—concurred most readily of all, suggests the existence of attitudes on which the proponent of a positive view of the war may build.

Despite its growing popularity, though, this interpretation makes coming to terms with defeat difficult. It portrays irresolute leaders and domestic opponents of the war as villains who cost the nation victory. Already, surveys show tremendous resentment toward those who refused to serve and reveal less support for those who protested than for those who fought. But just as veterans want and need public acceptance of their actions during the war in Vietnam, protestors want and need public approval for their role in the war at home over Vietnam. To withhold it, or worse, to blame defeat on the antiwarriors, can only hinder reconciliation of the former foes. Reconciliation with regard to the war in Vietnam must rest on mutual respect and acceptance of each side's position in the conflict—as the South's post–Civil War reunion with the North suggests. Similarly, the South's experience after the Civil War indicates that an interpretation of defeat that simply reaffirms the righteousness of the cause and the heroism of the armies without wrestling with the implications of failure leads only to a trivialization of the memory of the war and to a failure to derive any special insight from it.

The tendency toward trivialization also emerges in a second recent offensive in the third Vietnam War, one that does not frontally assault older, antiwar positions but rather outflanks them by focusing on the Vietnam combat experience. *Magnum, P.I., Platoon,* and similar portrayals of the war in popular culture attempt to explain what the war was like to those who never fought there—a healthy, necessary corrective to the early tendency to ignore the war and its warriors. But explanation very easily becomes glorification. The movie *Hamburger Hill,* for example, answers its own refrain—"It don't mean nothing"—by celebrating the camaraderie, courage, and sacrifice of the warriors, which the film implies gave meaning and purpose to the war. Therein lies the danger of the new emphasis on the experience of combat: it makes the soldiers' heroism sufficient justification for the cause.

The South and the North did much the same thing following the Civil War, which made sectional reconciliation possible because it ignored the divisive issues and celebrated common experiences, but it ultimately trivialized the meaning of the war. In the case of Vietnam, the emphasis on the camaraderie and excitement of combat does not foster reconciliation but rather further divides warriors from antiwarriors. In *Hamburger Hill*, the antiwarriors almost become the enemy, and the movie comes close to saying they had no right even to comment on the war. The emphasis on the Vietnam combat experience may thus further polarize the nation. It also ignores and thereby trivializes the war's issues and its meaning—or worse, renders Vietnam only another setting for popular culture adventure stories, perhaps the ultimate trivialization.

Neither of the two offensives—neither the reinterpretation of the war nor the glorification of combat—appears likely to yield a victory in the third Vietnam War, to lead Americans successfully to come to terms with defeat. Nor, for that matter, do the continued attacks of the doves, who, secure in their virtue, still slug it out along old fronts. Few on either side seem to have found a way out of the difficulties inherent in the third Vietnam War. Just as the actual war came to be considered a no-win situation, so too may the attempt to come to terms with the meaning of Vietnam. An interpretation of the war that depicts the veterans' service as a purely noble, heroic undertaking renders the protestors' actions disloyal, thereby making reconciliation difficult. But the reverse is also true: making the antiwarriors into the force of light encourages casting the warriors as the force of darkness. And declaring both sides right or focusing only on the experience of combat trivializes the hard moral choices of the 1960s and may well prevent the nation from gaining insights from defeat.

The way out of the quagmire of the third Vietnam War, the strategy that will allow the United States to "win," necessitates that both opponents and proponents of the war be willing to take new positions. They must seek and accept new information. In studying contemporary history, those who lived through it too easily assume they know what happened and too readily reject evidence that challenges old beliefs. They must also develop a new appreciation for complexity and an openness to the views of the other side. In short, they must fight the third Vietnam War with a subtlety, with a consciousness of political and moral ambiguity, rarely displayed in the first two Vietnam wars and uncharacteristic of politics and popular culture. A "new Vietnam scholarship," as journalist Fox Butterfield put it, has already challenged "some of the most cherished beliefs of both the right and the left" and presented "a war that was more complex, more morally ambiguous, than either the doves or the hawks had maintained." But it has certainly not won the field from either the hawks or the doves. Nor has it begun to uncover all the facts or even ask all the pertinent questions. Much remains to be learned about the war itself, particularly about whether combat in Vietnam was unique, and more needs to be understood about the veterans' postwar adjustment.

Even as scholars begin to develop these and other points, Americans need some framework for understanding the war's meaning. Unless further evidence suggests another, Americans can probably do no better than to view the Vietnam War as Robert Penn Warren suggested they interpret the Civil War—as a tragedy. As with the Civil War, American participation in the Vietnam War cannot be blamed on any one group or person but on the policies and assumptions accepted by most Americans at the time. And no one group came out of the wars in and over Vietnam with a Treasury of Virtue; the fight besmirched both warrior and antiwarrior alike. Neither should be held up as model heroes, but both can claim heroism in the midst of tragedy, a shared experience that might serve as a basis for reconciliation.

Historians and the public alike can find inspiration for the task of reinterpreting the war as tragedy in the Vietnam Memorial on the Mall. The wall evokes mourning but also demands reflection. For, as the nation looks at those haunting black marble panels, looking through the names of those who died at its behest, it sees ultimately its own reflection. The memory of the Vietnam War should serve the same function and should force the nation not to bask in its reflection but to consider and reconsider it—to analyze, not glorify, the war.

NOTES

* Kathleen Belew, *Bring the War Home: The White Power Movement and Paramilitary America* (Cambridge, Mass.: Harvard University Press, 2018).

** Since this essay was first published, much scholarship has stressed the Civil War's intense psychological toll on its veterans. These works have been heavily influenced by the prevalence of post-traumatic stress disorder among veterans of the Vietnam and later wars, and they often cite that experience in explaining what happened to Civil War veterans. One of the first to make such connections was Eric T. Dean Jr., *Shook Over Hell: Post-Traumatic Stress, Vietnam, and the Civil War* (Cambridge, Mass.: Harvard University Press, 1997). More recent studies include James Martin, *Sing Not War: The Lives of Union & Confederate Veterans in Gilded Age America* (Chapel Hill: University of North Carolina Press, 2011); David Silkenat, *Moments of Despair: Suicide, Divorce & Debt* *in Civil War North Carolina* (Chapel Hill: University of North Carolina Press, 2011); and Diane Miller Summerville, *Aberration of Mind: Suicide and Suffering in the Civil War–Era South* (Chapel Hill: University of North Carolina Press, 2018). All three of these works have shown the difficulty of establishing the Civil War's impact on its veterans, but they still make a strong case that many Civil War veterans experienced mental health issues, which in some cases led to suicide. These historians have certainly demonstrated more evidence for PTSD among Confederate veterans than is indicated here, although the case for Confederate veterans having at least less, although maybe not far less, difficulty adjusting after the war may still be defensible.

— 4 —

WHAT'S NOT IN A NAME

THE NAMING OF THE AMERICAN CIVIL WAR

ISTORIANS OF THE U.S. Civil War once hotly debated whether it was the first modern war. They might well instead have considered it America's first postmodern one. Since 1989, the American military has consciously chosen nicknames for military operations, the author of an Army War College thesis explains, "with an eye toward shaping domestic and international perceptions about the activities they describe." Those nicknames then often served as the name of the war, as in Desert Shield and Desert Storm. Naming has not always been easy or successful; for example, a dispute developed over the name for the war on terror. Even so, along with the military, many other Americans have come to believe that the name is important in defining the purpose of a war and shaping support for it. Or, as one national security think tank put it in appropriately postmodern terms, wars "are socially constructed, as are their names."[1]

Both during and after the Civil War, northerners and southerners displayed an appreciation for the importance of naming the conflict. As the war started, Abraham Lincoln, Congress, and most northerners at first referred to a civil war or an insurrection but quickly came to call it the Rebellion, a name they hoped would reinforce the goal of preserving the Union even as it stigmatized secession and the South. Frederick Douglass and others proposed alternatives that made slavery central to the war, such as the Abolition War or the Slaveholders' Rebellion, but few northerners adopted them. In the first decades after Appomattox, northerners continued to refer to the Rebellion. White southerners objected to that name and used others, including Civil War and the War Between the States. By the end of the century, Civil War had become the most common public name, and between 1905 and 1911, Congress made it virtually the official name of the war. The United Daughters of the Confederacy then campaigned, but failed, to replace Civil War with War Between the States. Despite the persistent use of that and other alternative names for the war, particularly among white southerners and African Americans, Civil War was the most widely used name, as demonstrated in linguistic surveys conducted in the middle and late twentieth century.

In the end, then, the generic Civil War became the name of the war, one that allowed both sides to hold to their interpretation of the war and thereby helped obscure its meaning. The postwar debate over the name reveals a white South less united and intransigent than many assume and suggests that Americans deemphasized slavery's importance in the memory of the war. It also illustrates how the North willingly made concessions to the white South in hopes of fostering reunion and national reconciliation, even as it reveals the limit of those concessions.

ON THE EVE OF THE WAR, many Americans talked of a coming "civil war." In late December 1860, in letters exchanged between President James Buchanan and representatives of South Carolina, both sides lamented what they feared would be a civil war. The following January, in one of his last Senate speeches, Jefferson Davis, too, spoke of the country being on "the verge of civil war." In his first inaugural address, Abraham Lincoln told—or warned—the South, "In *your* hands, my dissatisfied fellow countrymen, and not in *mine*, is the momentous issue of civil war." Like these leaders, a fearful public in 1860 commonly referred to an impending civil war, though some northerners talked of "rebellion." A sample of newspapers shows that the use of "civil war" vastly exceeded that of "rebellion."[2]

When the Confederates fired on Fort Sumter, Lincoln's proclamation calling for the states to provide militia and summoning Congress to meet on July 4 made no mention of a civil war and included only a vague reference to "combinations" in the various states. Four days later, when proclaiming a blockade of the South, Lincoln described the situation as an "insurrection," and over the next three months, he most often referred to an insurrection. The need to establish the power to wage war against the Confederacy probably led him to use the word "insurrection." Since the 1790s, the federal government had called out troops, usually the militia, to put down domestic disturbances. When presidents did so, they acted on the basis of a 1795 law, passed in the wake of the Whiskey Rebellion. In that law and several that built on it, Congress delegated power to the president to deal with civil unrest, defined as "insurrection," following the clause in Article I, Section 8, of the U.S. Constitution, which authorizes calling out the militia. Even in his proclamation that suspended the writ of habeas corpus in Florida, Lincoln still referred to an insurrection rather than switching to "rebellion," the word used in Article I, Section 9, of the Constitution, which authorizes the suspension of the right of habeas corpus. He also used "insurrection" in two letters to Commanding General Winfield Scott that authorized him to suspend habeas corpus.[3]

Another factor may also have influenced Lincoln's early use of "insurrection." Emmerich de Vattel, whose *The Law of Nations* was at the time generally recognized as an authoritative source on international law, drew a crucial distinction between an insurrection and a civil war. In an insurrection, the party or region in revolt was not considered a belligerent. In a civil war, it was. Lincoln's initial use of "insurrection" instead of "civil war" may have been influenced by his hope of preventing other countries from recognizing the Confederacy or granting it rights as a belligerent. But his subsequent use of "rebellion," which under international law still denied the Confederates the rights of belligerents, made the same point but in a way that had a greater impact on the public, which probably had more to do with his choice than did the Confederacy's standing under international law. When Vattel drew a distinction between insurrection and rebellion, it rested in part on the size of the resistance, but primarily on the question of legitimacy. "Rebellion" was commonly applied to "open and unjust resistance," he wrote; indeed, a rebellion was "void of all appearance of justice." Perhaps the fact that "rebellion" cast just such a judgment on the South's actions made it appealing and useful to Lincoln; after the war, it certainly helped make the word anathema to the former Confederates.[4]

In any case, after a few months Lincoln's primary choice of a name changed from insurrection to rebellion. On July 4, he sent Congress a message, one on which he had been working through June. In it, Lincoln first referred to an "insurrectionary government" and the "giant insurrection" that Virginia had allowed "to make its nest within her borders." Later in the text, Lincoln introduced "rebellion." He mentioned it first in the context of the revocation of the right of habeas corpus, which could have reflected its use in the Constitution. He had not done so, however, in his earlier proclamations and letters on habeas corpus. Still later in his message, Lincoln made his purpose clear: "It might seem, at first thought, to be of little difference whether the present movement at the South be called 'secession' or 'rebellion.' The movers, however, well understand the difference. At the beginning, they knew they could never raise their treason to any respectable magnitude, by any name which implies *violation* of law." They offered, Lincoln went on, "rebellion thus sugar-coated." Lincoln thereby emphasized the illegality, the unconstitutionality of secession and chose "rebellion" as the word that encapsulated his and the North's conception of the conflict even as it put the blame squarely on the people of the South.[5]

In the debates that summer, members of Congress referred, variously, to a civil war, an insurrection, or a rebellion. In giving a title to perhaps the most important of the several laws that it passed, ratifying what Lincoln had already done and acknowledging his power to act going forward, Congress included the title of the 1795 law, which it formally amended, with its reference to "insurrection." The 1861 law's title, though, began "An Act to provide for the Suppression of Rebellion against and Resistance to the Laws of the United States." A phrase in its first paragraph echoed the title: "whenever, by reason of unlawful obstructions, combinations, or assemblages of persons, or rebellion against the authority of the Government of the United States." When soon-to-be peace Democrat Clement L. Vallandigham questioned adding the word "rebellion," Republican John A. Bingham, the bill's manager, explained that it was "incorporated in the bill, as an amendment, because that is the word used in the Constitution." He then added, "We put the word in the bill in order to make the object and purpose plain." "Insurrection" also appeared in the Constitution and in the clause most relevant to the bill's purpose. Making "the object and purpose plain" seemed more a matter of defining the North's conception of the war and rallying opposition to the South than of following the language of the Constitution. Both "insurrection" and "rebellion" appeared in the bill, though, and the use of "insurrection" persisted. Once the session ended, Lincoln again used it when he issued a proclamation banning intercourse with the "Rebel States," the latter reflecting his new interpretation of the South's actions. Indeed, throughout the war, Lincoln and other northerners continued to use "civil war" and "insurrection."[6]

Rebellion, however, became the most commonly used name. Lincoln most often said "rebellion" and did so more often each year, reaching 75 percent or more of the time in 1864 and 1865. Yet Lincoln may well have realized that calling the conflict a rebellion, with its incorporation of the Union's interpretation of the war and harsh judgment on the South, would make reunion more difficult. In any case, he used "civil war" in two speeches in which he sought to define the meaning of the conflict, the Gettysburg Address and his second inaugural. In the latter, in which he talked explicitly of healing the wounds of the war, he carefully avoided the term that southerners soon came to criticize. He referred not to rebellion, which put all the blame on the South, but to civil war, a more generic term that better allowed him to acknowledge and evoke shared failure and guilt. In doing so, he anticipated a postwar renaming of the Rebellion to Civil War, with one crucial difference. When northerners and white southerners later agreed on Civil War, they did so in part because it allowed each side to hold to its own interpretation of the war and preserve its own sense of innocence. The second inaugural maintained that the judgment of God fell on both North and South.[7]

Like Lincoln, during the war Congress and the military most often used "rebellion." Even though several of Congress's first acts in the July session mentioned insurrection in their titles, the *Congressional Globe* indexed them under "Rebellion" and continued to use that as the entry for war matters. When Congress named its documents, during the war's first Congress, Civil War most often appeared in the title, but for the remainder of the war, it all but disappeared and Rebellion replaced it. Within the documents, by 1863 "rebellion" appeared far more often than "civil war." The same proved true in military correspondence; in the *Official Records,* "rebellion" appeared five times as often as "civil war" and three times as often as "insurrection." The public, too, adopted "rebellion" After 1861, book titles shifted dramatically toward incorporating it. In newspapers, where "civil war" appeared more frequently in 1860 and even 1861, by 1862 "rebellion" came to be used more than 75 percent of the time.[8]

Given such popular usage, as well as use by Lincoln and Congress, Rebellion can be considered the all but official and certainly the most common public name for the war, though never the only one. Even President Andrew Johnson's proclamations declaring the war at an end termed it an insurrection and referred to civil war. In his General Orders No. 100, Francis Lieber included definitions of "insurrection," "rebellion," and "civil war." He defined insurrection in traditional terms and distinguished it from a rebellion primarily by its size. When he turned to civil war, as historian David Armitage argues, he first offered another traditional description: "Two or more portions of a country or state, each contending for the mastery of the whole and each claiming to be the legitimate government." Then, Armitage writes, he "made . . . up out of whole cloth," a second explanation; civil war, Lieber added, is "also applied to a war of rebellion when the rebellious provinces or portions of the State are contiguous to those containing the seat of government." Lieber then went on to define rebellion as "a war between the legitimate Government of a country and portions or provinces of the same who seek to throw off their allegiance to it and set up a Government of their own." Lieber's second description of civil war incorporated the Union's use of Rebellion into its definition. Both names thereby came to imply that the Confederates' cause lacked legality and legitimacy. Moreover, by incorporating "rebellion" into the definition of civil war and not vice versa, Lieber seemed to suggest that Rebellion was the more appropriate name. It better served the Union's cause. It fit the northern narrative of the war as one to preserve the Union against an unconstitutional and unjust attempt by white southerners to undermine a democratic system and destroy the Union. It implicitly denied that the Confederate States of America legally existed.[9]

EVEN AS REBELLION PROMOTED the narrative of a war for Union, it ignored the role of slavery. For some in the North, the war began as a war against slavery, and for many more it became one by 1863. Historians who recently have promoted the idea of the war as a Second American Revolution have pointed out that some northerners, primarily abolitionists, used "revolution" to describe the war, seeing it as part of an international revolution against slavery. Other names that acknowledged the role of slavery also emerged—the war for union and liberty (or for liberty and union), the slaveholders' war, the war for (or of) emancipation, and the war to free the slaves. None took hold in the public mind. The two most common names that tied the war to slavery were abolition war and slaveholders' rebellion. These entered public use, however, in very different ways.[10]

Almost from the beginning of the conflict, Confederates employed the term "abolition war" to attack the North's cause—and no doubt to mobilize their own supporters, who feared emancipation. In June 1861, the *New Orleans Daily Picayune* claimed that "though ostensibly and professedly" fighting "for the 'Union, the constitution, and the flag' of the United States," the North actually waged "an anti-slavery and abolition war." White southerners may have borrowed the phrase from northern Democrats. A September 1861 letter in the *Macon Daily Telegraph* reported that in Illinois, Indiana, and Iowa, many opposed the war and "openly denounce it" as "an unholy, unchristian, unjust Abolition War." Northern peace Democrats frequently employed the term to criticize the war effort or to warn that making it an abolition war would undermine public support. After the Emancipation Proclamation, some still linked calling the war an abolition war with opposition to the war. One "Loyal Democrat" referred to the cry of peace Democrats "that this is an 'Abolition War,' a 'Republican war,' a 'N—— war'" as "only an excuse behind which those who raise it, hide their opposition to the war for any purpose."[11]

But even Republicans, particularly in the midst of the 1864 campaign, sometimes denied that it was an abolition war. At a political rally in Hartford, Connecticut, Henry Wilson pointed to the "designs of the Democratic party— or copperhead party— . . . to divert the people from the true issue involved in this struggle. The charge made that the war is an abolition war is false. It is a war for the maintenance of the Union." Robert C. Ingersoll and Thurlow Weed made much the same case. The origin of "abolition war" among Confederates and Copperheads no doubt discredited it, as did lingering opposition to abolitionism, with its call for racial equality and other forms of radicalism. Moreover, the term seemed to leave the goal of preserving the Union out of the story.[12]

Some in the North, however, including Frederick Douglass, embraced the name abolition war. Like Lincoln, the abolitionist both realized the importance of naming the war and employed various names for it. In December 1861, he attempted to claim his opponents' name for his own cause. "It cannot be denied," Douglass told the American Anti-Slavery Society, "that this war is at present denounced by its opponents as an abolition war; and it is equally clear that it would not be denounced as an abolition war, if abolitionism was not odious." To applause, he continued, "I hold that it is an abolition war, because slavery has proved itself stronger than the Constitution" and "the Union." Douglass added that he considered it an "abolition war instead of . . . a Union war, because I see that the lesser is included in the greater"—that the destruction of slavery was necessary to victory and to the preservation of the Union and the Constitution. "Let us emblazon" abolition war "on our banners, and declare before the world that this is an abolition war, that it will prosper precisely in proportion as it takes upon itself this character." The adoption of the name, Douglass hoped, would help make the war one that would transform the Union into one in which "there shall be no North, no South, no East, no West, no black, no white, but solidarity of the nation, making every slave free, and every free man a voter." For a time after that speech, Douglass did not campaign on behalf of "abolition war," but he returned to promoting the name in 1864 when he felt abolition was more popular than it once had been.[13]

In the title of an 1862 address, Douglass used another name for the war, the Slaveholders' Rebellion. The second of the two most common names that acknowledged the role of slavery, it had the advantage of recognizing the role of slavery but keeping the idea of rebellion and the threat to the Union as well as placing the blame on the South. Moreover, it arose in a very different context than "abolition war." In the session of Congress that began on July 4, 1861, in which Lincoln and Congress helped make Rebellion the primary name for the war, Senator Samuel C. Pomeroy of Kansas entered a resolution "to suppress the slaveholders' rebellion." His bill referred to the role both slavery and the slave power had played in bringing on the rebellion, but its primary objective was to make emancipation the purpose of the war. Pomeroy's resolution was tabled and never got out of committee. The New York Times, however, praised the Kansan and his bill: "There are no white-glove touches in this bill, but it names the Southern revolt the 'Slaveholders' Rebellion.' Never was language more appropriate, and through all time shall this strife be signaled as the 'Slaveholders' Rebellion.'" During the war, the Times, the Chicago Tribune, and a few other newspapers occasionally referred to the Slaveholders' Rebellion. Along with Douglass, other northerners incorporated it into their speeches. Its use persisted after the war. J. Watts de Peyster, a wealthy New Yorker, former general in the Union army, prolific author on military history, and frequent ceremonial speaker, often used the phrase.[14]

Though it was the most popular and persistent of the names for the war that emphasized the role of slavery, Slaveholders' Rebellion never caught on. Douglass used it or "slaveholding rebellion," another name that emerged, but he also used Civil War, or more often, the Rebellion. The African American historian George W. Williams, in his 1886 book on the role of Black troops in the war, mentioned the Slaveholders' Rebellion but more often called it the Civil War and put the War of the Rebellion in the book's title. Many African Americans would follow Douglass and Williams in being comfortable with Rebellion or Civil War, but some would use a name that made the cause of emancipation more central to the war. Northern whites never embraced Slaveholders' Rebellion or any of the other names that incorporated the goal of ending slavery. Several historians have recently contended that white northerners remembered the war as a battle to preserve the Union *and* to end slavery. However, the choice northerners made in naming the war, along with the later debates over that name, suggest that for most white northerners preserving the Union proved more important than ending slavery.[15]

In the first years after the war ended, Rebellion continued to be used in the titles of congressional documents. As early as 1866, however, an act entered in Congress included the slightly amended "War of the Rebellion." When the War Department published the official military records of the conflict, according to historian Yael A. Sternhell, its title included "War of the Rebellion," a choice that reflected popular usage among northerners and that was made without debate. After 1874, when an infusion of spending revitalized the Official Records project, the *Congressional Record* changed its index entry for war matters from "Rebellion" to "Rebellion, War of." Despite such official use of War of the Rebellion, the shorter Rebellion remained the most common name the government and northerners applied to the war. In titles of congressional publications, book titles, and newspaper articles, Rebellion heavily outnumbered War of the Rebellion. In the mid-1870s, when Melvil Dewey first developed his catalog system for libraries, he recommended "Rebellion, Southern" as the subject heading for the war. Civil War, of course, continued to be used, and other names emerged as well. During the war and for almost two decades after it, though, some form of Rebellion proved substantially more common, in both official publications and popular usage.[16]

CONFEDERATES, LIKE THEIR COUNTERPARTS in the North, understood the importance of names, and they rejected the idea that secession constituted only "sugar-coated rebellion." "Their crusade was no mere rebellion," historian George C. Rable wrote of the Confederates, "yet whether *civil war* or *revolution* fit the case remained a point of contention." The idea of a Confederate revolution, Rable showed, did take hold. After the war, however, most Confederates quickly abandoned it, even as the search for an appropriate name became more important to them. Edward A. Pollard, in his influential 1866 history of the war, wrote, "Names are apparently slight things; but they create the first impressions; they solicit the sympathies of the vulgar, and they create a cloud of prejudice which the greatest exertions of intelligence find it impossible wholly to dispel." Thirty-five years later, a North Carolina veteran proclaimed a name "the most important thing in the world"—it is "to mankind the thing itself. . . . How imperative, then, it is upon us to see that neither ignorance nor prejudice nor malice mar the most heroic effort of our race by fastening upon it a bad name!" In 1930, a Daughter of the Confederacy similarly observed that a "name given to a struggle, and accepted as correct by both sides of that struggle, defines its nature and often determines the opinion of the world concerning it." Over the intervening years, white southerners debated a host of names. They readily agreed that the North had it wrong; there was no rebellion. But even though historians have stressed that white southerners embraced a unified view of the war, they did not easily agree on a name.[17]

Pollard dismissed the idea "that the war of 1861, brought on by northern insurgents against the authority of the Constitution," was a southern rebellion. His subtitle offered a different name, the War of the Confederates. His book's title, *The Lost Cause*, came to be used frequently, but most who talked or wrote of the Lost Cause, like Pollard himself, used it to refer to the Confederacy rather than to the war itself, although the distinction could become fuzzy, as it did with the northern use of "rebellion." Two years after Pollard's history appeared, in 1868, two prominent former Confederates, Raphael Semmes and Alexander H. Stephens, put War Between the States in the titles of their books. In the second volume of his *A Constitutional View of the Late War Between the States*, the former vice president of the Confederacy offered an even broader attack on northern names for the war than Pollard had. The war "was no Insurrection or Rebellion, or even Civil War in any proper sense of these terms," Stephens argued. All three assumed the war divided members of the same society, but "the people of the United States never did form or constitute *one Political Society*, or Body-Politic." "The war, therefore, was a war between the States regularly organized into two separate Federal Republics." Rather than emphasize the two republics, Stephens kept the focus on states' rights. The "object of the 'Confederates' was to maintain the separate Sovereignty of each State and the right of Self-government, which that necessarily carries with it." Neither Pollard nor Stephens, nor other white southerners who objected so vehemently to the terms "insurrection" or "rebellion," mentioned another possible factor in opposing them. In the years before the war, both "rebellion" and "insurrection" had often been used in conjunction with slave revolts, an association that surely appalled white southerners.[18]

Some southerners who, like Stephens, contended that the South had legally asserted a right of secession, preferred the War of Secession. Still others offered variations on Pollard's suggestion, the War of the Confederates. Right after the war, no doubt influenced by the wartime evocation of the revolutionary heritage, some former Confederates called it the Confederate War for Independence. Others used the shorter Confederate War. Authors put both in book titles, and one postwar journal was titled *Confederate War Journal*. Sumner A. Cunningham, the editor of another, more influential, postwar magazine, the *Confederate Veteran*, also advocated its use. Confederate War implicitly assumed the legitimacy of the South's actions and perhaps emphasized wartime experiences rather than the war's origins. In any case, Confederate War became a common name in the South.[19]

The Late Unpleasantness and the War of Northern Aggression, each of which folklore and even some historians have treated as the South's names for the war, were not commonly used. The Late Unpleasantness evoked either southern quaintness or an unwillingness to face the reality of defeat, but few white southerners actually used it, nor was it solely a southern formulation. A few northerners also used it to refer to the war, and some northerners as well as southerners on occasion referred to the Spanish-American War as the late unpleasantness. Almost no one in the late nineteenth century used War of Northern Aggression. Former Confederates did talk of the war in phrases that evoked its sentiment. Stephens briefly mentioned a "war of aggression," and later others spoke of the "War of Coercion." According to Google Ngram, which generates a graph based on a keyword search of American texts scanned by Google, "War of Northern Aggression" did appear a few times in the pages of books published in the early 1880s. It did not appear, however, in any title of a sample of books on the war published before 1915 or in a sample of southern newspapers from the years 1861 to 1920. In the *Southern Historical Society Papers,* the publication of the Southern Historical Society that scholars agree spoke for the most recalcitrant of white southerners, the phrase "war of coercion" appeared along with a couple of others that expressed similar sentiments, but never "War of Northern Aggression."[20]

Some white southerners did insist on calling it the War Between the States, including Jefferson Davis, who once apologized when he slipped and used Civil War. Nevertheless, the most common public name for the war among white southerners in the late nineteenth century was Civil War, which appeared slightly more often in the titles of books published in the South. In southern newspapers, references to the Civil War dramatically outnumbered those to the War Between the States." Two other public forums showed similar patterns. The *Southern Historical Society Papers* published accounts of the war by many people, and because the articles in it all discussed the same war, it did not need to be named. The most common reference was simply to "the war." From the first issue of the *SHSP* in 1876 until 1910, Civil War appeared more frequently than War Between the States. The United Confederate Veterans (UCV), formed in 1889, took a very strong stand against "offensive epithets" such as "rebellion" or "rebels." "Certainly, a decent respect for the many millions of Southern people, who are a patriotic and powerful part of our reunited country, will cause these epithets to be abandoned," its history committee demanded. "Their elimination . . . will demonstrate a proper expurgation of sectional feeling." Although it protested the use of Rebellion, the UCV did not at first advocate any specific alternative. Its constitution referred to the War Between the States, but in its proceedings speakers employed a plethora of names. Civil War was often heard, even from its commander.[21]

Only at the end of the century did Confederate societies come to endorse a single name for the conflict. In 1898, the UCV voted to call it the Civil War Between the States, and two years later it dropped "the civil." During the year in between, the UDC, which many historians consider the real power in shaping southern memory, endorsed War Between the States. Not too long thereafter, Cunningham and the *Confederate Veteran* dropped Confederate War and adopted War Between the States. What might be called the official arbiters of Confederate memory had moved toward advocating War Between the States as the conflict's primary public name. The name fits with the interpretation

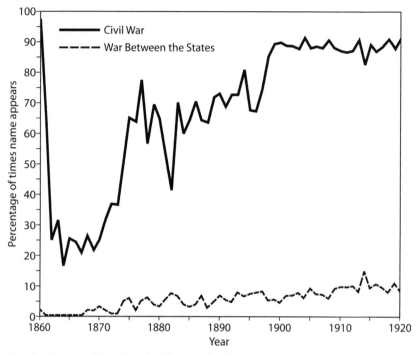

Note: See the appendix at the end of this essay for the methodology used to create this and the other graphs.

Graph 1. Usage of the terms "Civil War" and "War Between the States"
in southern newspapers, 1860–1920.

that secession was legal and constitutional and that therefore the Confederacy was an independent nation. War Between the States also eliminated the stigma that came with Rebellion—which elite white southerners wanted to avoid even more in the late 1880s and the 1890s, when the word "rebellion" had come to be associated with labor and anarchist violence.[22]

The emphasis on War Between the States by leaders of the Lost Cause occurred at about the same time as a culmination in the shift in national usage from Rebellion or War of the Rebellion to Civil War. A graph of newspaper usage of the keywords "Rebellion"/"War of the Rebellion" compared with "Civil War" shows that "Rebellion" peaked in 1864 and that a long, slow decline in its usage followed, probably reflecting a gradual easing of the war's tensions. The decline began in 1865, with the end of the war, and continued through the years of Reconstruction. The first of two major shifts in usage occurred between 1874 and 1878, no doubt because of the end of Reconstruction. In newspapers, Civil War then came to be used more frequently than Rebellion. Its dominance became even more pronounced after a second shift, between 1898 and 1903. At the time of the Spanish-American War, many northerners thought the South had demonstrated its loyalty to the nation. Even after that war, of course, some northerners still used Rebellion, and former Confederates still objected. Nevertheless, during the 1880s, Civil War became the most frequently used public name for the war.[23]

The shift to use of Civil War occurred more slowly in formal or official contexts. In book titles, which carry greater gravitas and assume greater permanence than newspaper columns, Civil War appeared more often after the end of Reconstruction, but no clear pattern of usage emerged in the 1880s or early 1890s. In the 1890s, however, shifts toward the use of Civil War did occur

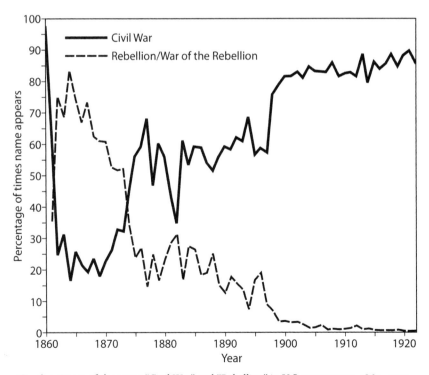

Graph 2. Usage of the terms "Civil War" and "Rebellion" in U.S. newspapers, 1860–1920.

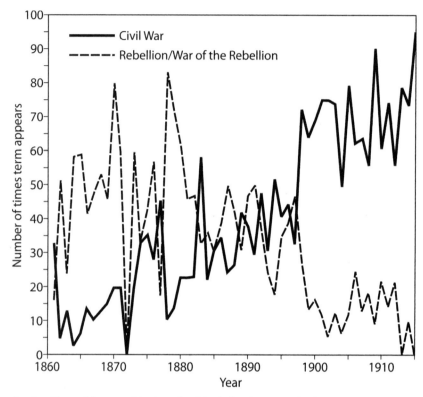

Graph 3. Usage of the terms "Civil War" and "Rebellion" in a sample of book titles, 1861–1915.

in other public documents. Melvil Dewey, who had included only "Rebellion, Southern" in his classification system published in 1876, added a heading for "Civil War" in the 1894 version. The following year, in its *List of Subject Headings for Use in Dictionary Catalogs*, the American Library Association had entries for "Civil War" and "Rebellion," in both cases referring the reader to "U.S. History, Civil War."[24]

In book titles, a significant change occurred after the outbreak of the Spanish-American War in 1898, when use of Civil War became dramatically more common than the use of Rebellion. The federal government soon followed suit, and the use of Civil War in the titles of congressional publications increased after 1900. Although the *Government Style Manual's* 1894, 1898, and 1900 editions offered no guidelines on the name for the war, its rules on capitalization called for putting "war of the rebellion" in lower case, with no mention of "civil war."

The 1903 edition for the first time specifically addressed the names of wars and stipulated the use of "civil war." Public preferences apparently led to changes in official policy.[25]

Congress soon ratified the style manual's stricture. It voted three times to substitute "Civil War" for "Rebellion"; together these votes constituted as close to an official change in the name of the war as occurred. A private survey of leading Americans conducted at roughly the same time showed that most Americans concurred with Congress. Both the congressional debates and the survey suggest that the choice of Civil War reflected a desire to promote reunion and reconciliation but also revealed that neither the North nor the South had significantly changed its interpretation of the war. So, too, did the failure of the UDC's attempt to make War Between the States the official name.

On three occasions, in 1905, 1907, and 1911, Congress took a stand on what to call the war. In March of 1905, with the Senate rushing to pass appropriation bills during the session's final days, Louis E. McComas of Maryland entered an amendment giving preference in the Railway Mail Service to those who had served honorably in "the war of the rebellion." Augustus O. Bacon of Georgia quickly proposed that he "strike out the words 'war of the rebellion' and insert 'civil war.'" McComas readily agreed, although he defended his original choice by saying "war of the rebellion" was used "in the civil-service regulations." Bacon reiterated his request, McComas again agreed to the change, at which point Edward W. Carmack of Tennessee recommended that "war of secession'" be inserted instead of "civil war." "No," Bacon replied. "The term 'civil war' is all right. That is now recognized as the courteous nomenclature." Perhaps because it was the end of the session, the interchange received little attention. Bacon and Carmack, though, would soon be involved in a more substantial debate over the name.[26]

In January of 1907, the Senate began a discussion of a pension bill for soldiers in the "war of the rebellion." Both Bacon and Carmack objected to its use in the title, and Carmack moved that "civil war" be substituted. The bill's sponsor, Porter J. McCumber, a Republican from North Dakota, observed that "war of the rebellion" was the usual term, but he had no objection to the substitution. It appeared the Senate would make the change quickly and easily, as it had in 1905. Then Hernando D. Money of Mississippi jumped to his feet, "clamoring to be heard." More conservative than either Carmack or Bacon, Money insisted that the proper name for the war should be the "war between the States" because "it was a war between sovereign States." Carmack quickly backtracked, saying he did not offer "civil war" as "embodying what I considered a correct definition or description of that war" but simply to conform "to what I believe has been the best practice and the usual descriptive words as employed in legislation and in official documents." He admitted, though, that he actually agreed with Money that "it was not a civil war any more than it was a war of rebellion." He continued to favor "war of secession." Money then reiterated that it should be the "war between the States." McCumber responded that he did not object to "civil war," that it might even be the "better" term, but that he could not accept Money's suggestion.[27]

"The meek-appearing but bellicose" Henry M. Teller, a Colorado Democrat, then entered the fray. Earlier, before Carmack moved to change the wording, Teller had used "civil war" several times; in reply to Money, though, he said it was not a war between the states but a rebellion, and that is the "proper term." "It may be an offensive term" but it "was a rebellion against the Government of the United States." It started out as a rebellion by the states, he added, but became one by the people. Money stood his ground, although he said he did not mind being called a rebel, and then told a story of a conversation he had once had with former senator Henry Blair of New Hampshire, in which they agreed that during the war all good men should have fought on one side or the other. Teller, picking up on Money's acceptance of being a rebel, returned to the idea of using "rebellion," pointed out it was in the Fourteenth Amendment, and then echoed Money's celebration of postwar reconciliation. Teller's recommendation of "rebellion" brought Bacon to his feet, and in a long speech he denounced the use of "rebellion." He stressed that the South had acted within the law and fought to settle the question of states' rights and the original nature of the Union. It was, he said more than once, too great a war to be a rebellion. But he also added that the outcome of the war had made "two great peoples . . . one indivisible people."[28]

After Bacon finished, Nathan B. Scott, a Republican of West Virginia, repeated a story he had told "with effectiveness on the stump." One of his constituents, killed while serving in the Spanish-American War, was brought home to the same cabin and buried in the same cemetery as his father, a fallen Confederate soldier. "Wrapped about [the son's] coffin was the flag of a united country—the Stars and Stripes." Votes on other amendments to the pension bill interceded, and then James O. Patterson of South Carolina made one final speech in which he praised the sectional reconciliation on display and then suggested the name "the war of secession." The Senate ignored Patterson's suggestion and unanimously passed the amendment to use "civil war." When Scott had finished his story, Carmack went over and shook his hand, as did other southerners, later. "The best of feeling seemed to prevail after the sectional debate," a reporter for the *Washington Post* wrote. One of his colleagues added that it looked as "if the Senate would have a good, old-fashioned cry."[29]

A similar but briefer discussion occurred in 1911, this time in the House and not regarding the title of an act but a reference to the "war for the suppression of the rebellion" buried in a section of a bill to codify the laws. Charles L. Bartlett from Georgia, the son of a Confederate veteran, moved to substitute "during the Civil War from 1861 to 1865." When someone worried that the dates might complicate determining service, he changed it to just "Civil War." Joseph W. Keifer, former Speaker of the House and a Republican from Ohio, asked, "What is to be accomplished by that?" James R. Mann, an Illinois Republican, explained, "Good feeling, that is all; but that is worth something." Bartlett then added, "We have got far enough away from that era in our history not to use the word 'rebellion.'" "It is used in the Constitution," in the Fourteenth Amendment, Keifer replied, apparently forgetting about the clause on suspending the right of habeas corpus. Bartlett then complained that "rebellion" was put there "right after the war." Keifer persisted in his contention that the new wording accomplished nothing and insisted that in fact the war was a rebellion. Bartlett disagreed, although other than saying it "was no more a rebellion than the Revolutionary War was," he did not offer a constitutional defense. Instead, he said, to repeated applause, that sectional reconciliation had proceeded to the point that the words "used in the heat of that bloody conflict" and the days that followed could be abandoned. He added that he felt sure that those on the other side now "respect the views and the sentiments of those against whom they fought." Keifer bristled and accused Bartlett of lecturing him. Bartlett assured him he had too much respect for him to do that. Keifer then claimed that, more than the language of the bill, Bartlett's comments revived the feelings of the war. He quickly added that he did "not particularly object to substituting the words "Civil War" for "the rebellion." He did resent being lectured about sectional reconciliation. He then recalled his own "kindly" feelings for the other side at the end of the war and during later veterans' reunions. He concluded by saying that during the Spanish-American War he had sons of Confederate veterans in his unit and treated them all fairly. Bartlett apologized again, Keifer said he bore no ill feelings, and the House agreed to the amendment unanimously.[30]

Newspapers covered the 1911 discussion over the name of the war, but the press devoted more extensive coverage to the 1907 debate. Even then, some papers ignored Congress's actions on the name. The major story that week concerned events in Brownsville, Texas, where Black soldiers had allegedly attacked a bar and one white man was murdered. President Theodore Roosevelt had issued dishonorable discharges to the whole unit, generating considerable public controversy. Contemporary race relations, apparently, commanded more attention than Civil War memory. Many papers, however, did mention the 1907 debate. The Associated Press included a two-sentence account in a story on the pension bill in which the name of the war had become an issue. A few papers highlighted the development in a subheading or even in a headline. "'Rebellion' Cut Out of the Bill," proclaimed the Raleigh, North Carolina, *News and Observer*. "No 'Rebels' Bore Arms in Legions of the South," read the *Atlanta Constitution*. In the *Washington Post*, the subheadings were more explicit: "Not 'War of the Rebellion': Bill Provides That Late Unpleasantness Shall Be Known as 'The Civil War.'" Over a somewhat tongue-in-cheek account that concluded that there had been no "War of the Rebellion," only a "Civil War," the *New York Times* ran the headline "No Rebellion in '61, Declares the Senate." Most accounts did not address the question of the provenance of the change; the *Post*, for instance, wrote that it was only for "this particular measure." However, the *Constitution*, like the *Post* and the *Times* headlines, implied that it was for all official documents.[31]

The *Constitution* may have been correct. Following these three congressional debates, the federal government appeared even more committed to using Civil War as its official name for the conflict. At the time, however, not everyone agreed that such a decision had been made. In 1910, the superintendent of documents claimed, "So far as I am aware, the Government has never formally approved any particular name for the war between the North and the South from 1861 to 1865." The Office of the Adjutant General, which oversaw the military's use of a name, declared in June 1907 that the "War Depart. has no knowledge of any official designation of a title for the war of 1861–65." But the adjutant general added that "the question of the use of the terms 'war of the rebellion' and 'the civil war' was discussed in the Senate [in January,] when the latter term was substituted for the former in a pension bill then under consideration." Five years later, and after the third debate in Congress, the adjutant general's office decided that "in consideration of the growing sentiment to omit reference to the Civil War as the rebellion, it may be desirable to refer to that war as the Civil War in future orders, changes, etc., except in cases where the exact language of an act, law or statement is required and such language contains any other designation for that war."[32]

Along with the army's new policy, indexing in the *Congressional Record* and in the titles of government publications pointed to a change in policy following the congressional debates. After 1874, the *Congressional Record* had indexed references to the war as "Rebellion, War of." Beginning in 1896, "Civil War" appeared in the index, but with the instruction "see Rebellion, War of." Then, in the first volume published after the 1907 debate, the *Record* reversed its policy; "Rebellion, War of" included the directive to "see Civil War." Other than in the volumes completing the publication of the military and naval records of the Rebellion, the use of Rebellion as a name of the war appeared in only one more title in the congressional series.[33]

The shift to Civil War in official documents points to the importance of the 1905 to 1911 debates, during which members of Congress three times took a unanimous stand in favor of its use. What members of Congress did not say in these debates may be as important as what they did. No one mentioned slavery's role in the war, or the achievement of emancipation. The turn-of-the-century rise of a radical white racism no doubt played a role. In such a climate, few whites emphasized the emancipationist legacy of the war or listened to African Americans who did. Also significant in the congressional debates was that the change always came at the behest of southerners. The northerners agreed, most because they thought the term "Civil War" was at least accurate yet still offered a way to encourage good feelings between the sections—in other words, to make white southerners happy. Wanting to do so indicates a desire for not just reunion but also at least a degree of reconciliation. Southerners preferred other names—War Between the States or the War of Secession—but realized that there were limits to how far their former foes would go. Their northern counterparts, some of them quite testy and emphatic about it, made it clear they had no intention of calling it War Between the States. Indeed, some still considered the Confederate cause a rebellion. No one seemed to have changed his mind; they just agreed to find a name acceptable to both sides.

The two extensive debates, in 1907 and 1911, included a speech by a northerner that mentioned the Spanish-American War and southern support for or sacrifices in it. A discussion of what to call the Civil War did not naturally lead to such comments; they surely were offered as evidence of southern loyalty to the nation and of the success of reunion. Their inclusion in the debates supports the conclusion that the Spanish-American War, in which the white South demonstrated its loyalty, helped shift American usage away from Rebellion and its implication of disloyalty.[34]

An informal survey taken at about the same time as the congressional debates provides additional insight into what Americans thought about the name of the war. Shortly after the 1907 debate, Senator Benjamin R. Tillman of South Carolina spoke in Seattle, Washington, and reported that Congress had adopted the name War Between the States. Edmund S. Meany, the registrar at the University of Washington and a professor of history with an interest in geographic names, heard him. Meany initially believed Tillman's comment to be true, soon learned it was not, and then decided to find out what people actually did call the war. He prepared a pamphlet that reprinted the Senate debate of 1907 and included a very brief introduction that asked everyone who received a copy "to send me his choice of a name for the war and, if convenient, to state his reasons." Meany sent the pamphlet to three thousand people across the nation and from various walks of life. He received 176 replies, twenty-six of which simply acknowledged receipt of the pamphlet. The other 150 offered a variety of names.[35]

Only six respondents mentioned slavery, and only two of them proposed names that focused on its role in the war: the Slavery War and the War for Slavery. The Missouri businessman who offered the latter acknowledged that it would not be acceptable but had "the advantage of truthfulness," since the war was fought to perpetuate "negro slavery." Meany included these two suggestions in a long list of possible names but did not otherwise mention them. Eight respondents ignored slavery but still held to the earlier northern names, the Rebellion or the War of the Rebellion. One of them, George W. Pollitt, was commander in chief of the Sons of Veterans. He cited Lincoln's use of the name and maintained that the war was "an armed rebellion in which the authority of the Government was denied in certain sections of this country." "It was a rebellion, pure and simple and nothing else." A surprising eighteen respondents, all but one from the North, proposed the War of [or for] Secession. They included historians Charles Francis Adams and Edward Channing. Channing thought War for Secession "precisely" described a war "fought to determine whether a state had the right to secede or had not that right." Thirteen respondents, including eight southerners, favored War Between the States.[36]

Although Meany's survey revealed continued diversity in the choice of names, an overwhelming number of his respondents reported Civil War as the common and proper name. Even southerners agreed. Thirty of them thought Civil War the appropriate name, more than three times the number who favored War Between the States. Overall, 93 of 150 respondents said the name was and should be Civil War, which reinforces the conclusion that it had become the primary name for the war. The reasons they offered for that choice echoed the emphasis on good feelings among the sections heard in the congressional debates. Meany favored Civil War and cited three factors. First, "it is entirely free of any possible offense to the adherents of either side of the conflict." Second, it was more accurate because the "war was greater in scope, size, duration, and purpose than could be inferred from such titles as 'Rebellion' or 'insurrection.'" Third, it is "most frequently used by the Government and therefore it is the duty of the people and of writers of history to adopt in general use this official name of 'Civil War.'"[37]

Meany's respondents gave various reasons for choosing this name. More than one mentioned its brevity. Like Meany, though, several stressed that it avoided giving offense to either side. They explained that it was "acceptable to North and South," that it did not imply a "reproach to either party of Americans," or that it "relieves the South from embarrassment." Or they mentioned being "charitable" or showing "courtesy." One who preferred War of Secession said that if she had to pick another name it would be Civil War. "Not that 'War of the Rebellion' would be a misnomer," she added, "but I think with you that there is no need to keep rubbing in the bitterness of defeat by a harsh title."[38]

Two of the longer replies Meany received, perhaps not surprisingly, came from professional historians. One of the nation's most prominent historians, J. Franklin Jameson, expressed views similar to those offered on the floor of the Senate in 1907. After making clear that he spoke only for himself and not for the American Historical Association, he boldly stated that he believed "the term 'War of the Rebellion' is historically correct. But there is an odious sound about the word 'rebel' and it is objectionable to many persons." He preferred Civil War, which "is perfectly applicable to every war the contestants in which have previously been living under the same government." Another historian, George Wells Knight, a Michigan native who taught at Ohio State University, listed seven reasons why Civil War was the most appropriate name, including its accuracy, its widespread acceptance, and its adoption by Congress. He also preferred it because of, not despite, its obscurity. "It describes a *fact* without importing into the descriptive name any one or another *theory* of governmental or constitutional organization" and "still leaves each person free to hold any theory he chooses as to the cause of the war."[39]

The actions of Congress and the responses to Meany's pamphlet indicated that the nation as a whole had embraced the name Civil War and made clear that the name constituted a concession to southern sensibilities. For white northerners, it nevertheless still acknowledged that the South had wrongly and illegally tried to destroy the nation, but Civil War did so without saying it as explicitly and critically as Rebellion had. White southerners thought Rebellion could not be interpreted any other way but Civil War could be compatible with their belief that secession had been legal and their actions honorable. White northerners had certainly moved away from the anti-southern animus of the war and Reconstruction. Some southerners, however, did not think the northerners had gone far enough.

In 1911, the United Daughters of the Confederacy launched a campaign to convince Congress to designate War Between the States as the official name of the war. UDC leaders objected to the term "civil war." South Carolinian Isabella D. Martin complained it made no concession to southern attitudes and claimed that she even preferred Rebellion, which "means what it says." She considered "civil war" "an insidious device of the enemy to make us acknowledge we were a 'so-called government,'" because a civil war is a fight between different sections of a nation. But, she insisted, "the legitimate righteous, well organized government of the Confederate States in support of which thousands of precious lives were given" was a nation. The petition a UDC committee prepared advocating War Between the States made the same point. For "four years we maintained an entirely separate government from that of the United States, being an entity known the world over as the Confederate States." The petition did mention "State sovereignty" as an "inherent doctrine" that was "our main justification for resisting Federal aggression," but it was only one of several rights the Confederacy sought to preserve. Indeed, the petition made it clear that the "States" in War Between the States did not "imply that it was a war between individual States." Instead, the word referred to the "contending parties," the "'United States' and the 'Confederate States.'" The UDC's insistence on the term "War Between the States" supported a states' rights interpretation of the origins of the war but put less emphasis on it than Alexander Stephens had. Not only did the UDC insist that the South had the right to secede, but by evoking the phrase "Confederate States," it declared that the Confederate nation, a noble one, had in fact existed.[40]

The UDC adopted its campaign at its annual meeting in 1911; the following year the chair of the War Between the States Committee reported that her congressman had advised waiting before approaching Congress. In 1913, at the behest of the committee, Charles G. Edwards of Georgia entered a bill to change the name of the war, and the following December, Ollie M. James of Kentucky introduced the UDC's petition and had it printed in full in the *Congressional Record*. Congress did not take up the matter that session. In 1916, the committee continued its efforts, including sending a copy of the petition to former president William Howard Taft and asking his support. Taft wrote back, curtly but politely, that the name should be Civil War.[41]

Nothing ever came of the bill to change the name. During the 1907 Senate debate, northern senators had made it clear they opposed the name War Between the States, and several of the people who responded to Meany's survey were even more emphatic in their opposition. Some called the name "idiotic," or "offensively inaccurate." One, more cool-headed, declared it "objectionable" because it assumes "the Southern point of view." That comment went to the heart of northern objections, which were fully developed by J. Franklin Jameson. He thought the idea of using War Between the States "preposterous." "Peace, kind feeling, and magnanimity are all excellent traits. But here when a conflict is admitted to have settled for all time a great constitutional question and given it the answer which the Federal Government constantly maintained that it should have—why should those living under that government stultify its course and deny positions steadily maintained by the executive, legislative, and judiciary, by adopting a name which can be justified only by adopting and approving the constitutional doctrines of the secessionists?" Given widespread, strong opposition in the North, the UDC's campaign to convince Congress to change the name from Civil War went nowhere.[42]

Although they failed to change the official name, the Daughters persisted in their fight to make War between the States the dominant public name. Some people, even in the South, questioned its logic. In the 1950s, E. Merton Coulter, as much a professional southerner as he was a professional historian, considered it "cumbersome" at best and thought most people would never grasp the idea that "States" referred to the Confederate States and the United States rather than just individual states. The UDC's own reports sometimes expressed frustration that veterans and even the Daughters continued to use Civil War. The Daughters' campaign clearly had an impact, however. Many in the South did employ the UDC's preferred name, and even a few U.S. presidents incorporated it into their speeches on occasion. A Google Ngram view shows a constant rise in its appearance in books between 1920 and 1940. It leveled off in the 1940s and then declined. War Between the States also showed up in various government documents, and in 1995, along with Civil War, appeared at the top of a sheet of commemorative stamps.[43]

EVEN THOUGH War Between the States and other names persisted in vernacular usage and had their champions, by the early twentieth century, a national consensus had developed that made Civil War virtually the official and certainly the public name for the war. Over the course of the century, the use of Civil War continued and increased—as demonstrated in the Linguistic Atlas of the United States and Canada, a survey of American usage conducted from the late 1930s into the 1970s, and in a public opinion poll conducted in 1994. Seeking to understand regional variations in word choice and pronunciation, the scholars who compiled the atlas selected representative communities in several regions and chose subjects within each community from a breadth of socioeconomic levels. Field-workers then went into the communities and asked a series of usage questions, one of which inquired what the subjects called the war of 1861–65. Two of the survey leaders concluded that Civil War was "overwhelmingly the most prevalent in all states, North and South, and among all age groups."[44]

Broken down by region, the survey revealed interesting patterns within that consensus. In New England, where the first of the studies was conducted in the late 1930s, Civil War proved to be the most common choice among the 412 people interviewed. Seventy-six percent used it; only 17.8 percent cited Rebellion or War of the Rebellion, with the use of Rebellion being three times more common. Only in the New England survey were respondents allowed to offer more than one name, and Rebellion frequently appeared as a second choice, further testifying to its persistence. In their third or fourth choices, respondents offered names that involved slavery. Two mentioned "abolition war," the term coined by opponents of emancipation, and five offered "n——war"; both suggested not a commitment to emancipation but a continuing racist response to it. Use of Civil War did not vary dramatically by age, but more educated people were more likely to use it. Respondents with little education offered a wider variety of names. In the Upper Midwest survey, almost 88 percent of the 256 people interviewed in the late 1940s used Civil War, only a little under 4 percent Rebellion or War of the Rebellion. The 502 subjects in the Mid-Atlantic states, interviewed during the 1930s, used Civil War less often, only 68 percent of the time. Around 17 percent of the people interviewed offered varying forms of Rebellion. One person called it a War of Slavery. In the border states, where interviews were conducted around the same time but in a region presumably with more southern influence, Civil War usage was even higher, at 75 percent. By midcentury, the North had clearly embraced Civil War, though the use of Rebellion had not totally disappeared.[45]

Usage in the South demonstrated a greater variety, as had been the case in the nineteenth century. Respondents in the South Atlantic states, interviewed over the course of three decades, had not overwhelmingly embraced the name Civil War; of the 1,067 respondents there, 36.3 percent used it. That was nearly twice as many as the next choice, Confederate War, named by 19.1 percent. It had persisted in the vernacular, although its usage may also have owed something to the newspapers. In 1943, Alabama journalist John Temple Graves maintained that "newspaper people, afraid of the Daughters but not able to find room for so long an expression as 'War between the States,' have hit on calling it 'The Confederate War.'" War Between the States was chosen by 14.7 percent of respondents; 10.3 percent called it "the war." Usage of War Between the States was about the same among men and women, but those with middle- and upper-class jobs and those the interviewers judged "cultured" were more likely to use it. The time period when the interviews were conducted also influenced their choices. Use of Civil War declined significantly in the years from 1941 to 1964, although it went back up a bit after that. Even so, resentment persisted in the vernacular tradition, as did the idea that the Confederates fought to preserve slavery. In 1946, one Georgian asked to name the war replied, with surprising realism and supreme racism, "The yankees whipped [us] and freed our n——s."[46]

The final survey, which covered the Gulf South states, was conducted in the early 1970s; it found that few people still used "the war" or "Confederate war," though almost 20 percent called it the War Between the States. A majority of the respondents, 55.3 percent, spoke of the Civil War. A demographic breakdown of those who gave one of the four most common answers (in other words, disregarding the outliers and the "don't knows") showed that men and women who offered a name said Civil War and War Between the States at roughly the same rate. But the use of War Between the States was related to class. Indeed, the scholars who conducted the study identified the use of War Between the States as one of four markers of middle-class status.[47]

The more frequent naming of the War Between the States in the Gulf South states may reflect the timing of the survey, the early 1970s. During the civil rights era, there was a revival of interest in the war among white southerners who championed states' rights in the cause of white supremacy. White southern fears of federal intervention in the South's system of racial repression began to rise in the late 1930s, when only a southern filibuster prevented passage of a federal antilynching bill. The appearance of the phrase "war between the states" in the Google Books collection peaked about the same time, in the early 1940s. Public use of War Between the States in the South Atlantic states rose in the 1950s and 1960s, at the height of white opposition to racial change. Its persistence in the Gulf South states in the early 1970s probably also reflected continued resentment of the federal government, as did the introduction of the name War of Northern Aggression. In a 1956 attack on northern advocates of racial integration, George Bell Timmerman, governor of South Carolina, used that name. At about the same time, according to Google, the phrase began to appear in books, although it appeared more frequently after 1980. By then, it was used by some neo-Confederates and other white southerners who were angry about the outcome of the civil rights movement, resentful of federal power, and frustrated by modern society. The name War of Northern Aggression also appeared in travel writing about the South, most often when northern writers promoted tours of a romanticized South and therefore sought to evoke the persistence of quaint customs among southerners who lived in an environment that had escaped the changes rife in modern society. Their reports, often made almost offhand, that southerners still referred to the War of Northern Aggression served their purposes well. Nevertheless, the name's use never became widespread. In the early 1970s, only eight residents of the Gulf South region (less than 1 percent of those interviewed) used it.[48]

Along with the white southern vernacular tradition persisted a very different tradition, in the African American community. The early American linguistic surveys interviewed only forty or so African Americans, and a summary article reported that when offering a name for the war they followed their white regional counterparts, even in the South. The later Gulf States survey included 181 African Americans, a minority of whom did indeed reply either "Confederate War" or "War between the States." More than 70 percent, though, said "Civil War," and it was probably the most common public usage among African Americans across the country. Two major African American newspapers in the twentieth century, the *Pittsburgh Courier* and the *Chicago Defender,* used the name almost exclusively, though both occasionally wrote of the War of the Rebellion, and the *Defender* on extremely rare occasions referred to the Slaveholders' Rebellion. Another source, the Works Progress Administration's collection of slave narratives from the 1930s, revealed a slightly more complex vernacular tradition. Some of the former slaves interviewed did cite names used by the whites around them, such as "de War Betwixt de States," "the Confederate War," or "de Secession War." Others, like most of their fellow Americans, referred to the Civil War. Still others offered names that focused on slavery's role in the war: "slavery war," "Freedom War," "the War for Freedom," or as one South Carolinian said, "de Holy War for da liberation of the poor African slave people." The continued use of such names testified to the persistence within the African American community of a memory of the war in which slavery was the central cause and emancipation its most important outcome.[49]

In 1994, a Southern Focus Poll, a representative sample of southerners and northerners conducted by the University of North Carolina's Odum Institute for Research in Social Science, showed that the African American vernacular tradition persisted. The survey discovered such names for the war as "prejudice war," "fight for freedom," "the war for the freedom of the colored people," and, undoubtedly a more recent formulation, "extension of the liberation struggle." Among whites, however, the use of the older terms had declined significantly. When asked what they called the "war between the North and the South in the 1860s," only four of 938 southerners replied "War of Northern Aggression." "Confederate War," once popular in the South, was named by only fifteen, "the war," by only eleven. Even "War Between the States" was cited by only 6.5 percent of southerners, most often by people who also answered, "Yes, I am a southerner." The majority—61.7 percent (65.5 percent of whites)—said "Civil War." Use of Civil War went up among people who lived in a metropolitan area as well as with the amount of education and wealth they had, a reversal of the social patterns found in the earlier surveys, when War Between the States was more common among the middle and upper classes. This suggests that persistent Confederate identity may be stronger among southerners outside the elite. Males gave "War between the States" as the answer to the question more often than females. Among northerners, 71.4 percent used Civil War. Only one respondent mentioned "the Rebellion." Together, the numbers suggest a consensus on Civil War as the name for the war, although in both sections almost a fifth offered a different name. Most surprising, 18.5 percent of southerners and 13.9 percent of northerners claimed not to know what the war was called, hardly testimony to the strength of Civil War memory in American society at the end of the twentieth century.[50]

Like the earlier Linguistic Atlas of the United States, the 1994 Southern Focus Poll demonstrated the persistence at the end of the twentieth century of the consensus that had emerged by its first decade. Despite the existence of vital vernacular usages, particularly among some white southerners and African Americans, the nation had adopted Civil War as its public, and for all intents and purposes official, name for the war that saved the Union and freed the slaves. Soon after the fighting began, Lincoln, Congress, and most northerners had adopted the name Rebellion in order to portray the war as one to subdue the unlawful, undemocratic, disloyal, and plainly treasonable actions of white southerners.

After the war ended, a slow, lengthy process began of changing the name to Civil War. White southerners had objected vehemently to Rebellion, and the move toward the use of Civil War clearly came in part as a white northern concession to white southern sensibilities. The timing of the shift, though, suggests that events, not Lost Cause arguments or stories, played the central role in the North's willingness to accommodate southern sensibilities. The use of the name Civil War jumped at the end of Reconstruction as the North turned away from the issues of the war and its aftermath and became dominant after the Spanish-American War, when they believed southerners had demonstrated their renewed loyalty to the nation.

White northerners adopted Civil War in large part because they sought re-union, one of their goals in the war. At least some of them were also committed to reconciliation; hence their expressions of concern for southern feelings. The 1907 debate in Congress and the survey conducted by Edward Meany, however, made it clear that northerners who used Civil War had not abandoned their view of the nature of the war. "Civil war" accurately described their view of the nature of the war, an illegal revolt within an existing nation. When the United Daughters of the Confederacy called for a change to War Between the States, which most northerners rightly thought was intended to incorporate a Lost Cause interpretation of the war, northerners refused.[51]

Interpreting what the white southerners' names for the war reveal about their memory of the war is more difficult. Their early use of Civil War and the variety of other names they offered suggests they may not have been as obsessed with or as unified in their memory of the Civil War as has been thought. By the early twentieth century, some insisted on War Between the States because their Confederate identity remained important to them. They held fast to an interpretation of the war that stressed that the South had acted rightly and had succeeded in establishing a nation, an interpretation that served the cause of states' rights and southern pride. Yet War Between the States never dominated southern usage. At the very least, the fact that Civil War became and remained the name most often used by white southerners reveals them to be open to re-union and reconciliation. It had to be achieved, however, without their having to repudiate their or their ancestors' honorable and just motives, which is why white southerners vehemently objected to calling the war a rebellion. Nevertheless, maintaining a Confederate identity may have proved less important to them than many have assumed. If War Between the States served as a Lost Cause shibboleth, a majority of white southerners failed the test. Its revival and the introduction of the more adversarial term "War of Northern Aggression" in the 1960s and 1970s indicates that for some the 1960s proved more important than the 1860s in shaping southern memory—but they remained a small group.

Despite the persistence of vernacular traditions, North and South did come together, and the nation adopted a generic name for the greatest threat to its unity, a name that placed much less opprobrium on the South than Rebellion. Americans not only abandoned it but also had long ignored usages such as Slaveholders' Rebellion or the War of Secession, which focused on slavery and the other issues of the war. Instead, they embraced a name that consciously fostered unity and reconciliation—at the great cost of obscuring the war's causes and consequences. The generic name allowed both white northerners and southerners to see their respective causes as right and just. The term "Civil War" not only obscured the meaning of the war; it also nurtured a sense of mutual innocence.

APPENDIX: NOTE ON METHODOLOGY

Graphs 1 and 2 were created through the same search procedure, but graph 1, on usage only in the South, was created by limiting searches by name to only newspapers in the eleven former Confederate states and Oklahoma. Here too, for clarity, only the two names with substantial usage, Civil War and War Between the States, are graphed, but I searched for all the names listed in the description of graph 2. The use of Civil War may have reflected the fact that southern newspapers either reprinted northern newspaper articles or ran copy provided by national press associations. Papers had the right to change such copy and could have changed the name of the war if that was of importance to them.

Graph 2, on usage in newspapers, comes from data collected using Readex's online database America's Historical Newspapers. When I completed my searches, in 2008, the website included more than three hundred newspapers from all states. I searched for the following names of the war: Civil War, Rebellion, War of the Rebellion, Slaveholders' Rebellion, War Between the States, Confederate War, War for Secession, the Late Unpleasantness, and the Lost

Cause. I recorded the total number of hits for each name by year from 1860 to 1920. Since hits on War of the Rebellion also turned up in a search for Rebellion, only the total for Rebellion was included in subsequent computations.

With the help of Katie Eskridge, a random 5 percent sample of stories that included either Civil War or Rebellion were read to determine whether they actually referred to the American Civil War. For each year, the percentage of stories that did concern the American Civil War was then applied to the overall total, with the resulting number used in the computations. To measure comparative usage (rather than the number of stories about the war in any given year), the total number of mentions of each name were then converted to a percentage of usage for that year. That year's percentages were then graphed. For clarity, the graph provided here includes only references to Civil War and Rebellion or War of the Rebellion. The other terms rarely exceed 3 to 5 percent of the total.

For graph 3, I compiled a database on books published on the Civil War between 1861 and 1915 through an online search of the Library of Congress catalog, using the keyword terms "War of the Rebellion" and "Civil War"—which included most books on the war, no matter the title. (For example, both Edward Pollard's *The Lost Cause* and Alexander Stephens's *A Constitutional View of the Late War Between the States* were included.) I then compiled a database of titles by year published, author, name, and where the book was published. Here, too, the raw numbers were converted into percentages of names used in each year. I then created a cross tab and graphs. As with the newspaper graph, the graph here includes only the two dominant names for the war. William Pencak uses a different sample, of memoirs and general histories cataloged in the two-volume *Civil War Books: A Critical Bibliography* and finds an emergence of Civil War as the common name in 1910, slightly later than the graph here. See Pencak, "The American Civil War Did Not Take Place," *Rethinking History* 6, no. 2 (2002): 217–21.

NOTES

1. Gregory C. Sieminski, "The Art of Naming Operations," *Parameters* 25 (Autumn 1995): 81; "World War IV—Naming World Wars," GlobalSecurity.org, http://www.globalsecurity.org/military /ops/world_war_4-name.htm. Historians have not ignored the name of the American Civil War; they have offered names they find more accurate, such as the Second American Revolution, or

more recently, the Wars of the Rebellions, linking it with the Indian Wars. See James M. McPherson, *Abraham Lincoln and the Second American Revolution* (New York: Oxford University Press, 1991), 3–42; Steven Hahn, "Slave Emancipation, Indian Peoples, and the Projects of a New American Nation-State," *Journal of the Civil War Era* 3 (September 2013): 309. Others have analyzed the various names given to the war. See E. Merton Coulter, "A Name for the American War of 1861–1865," *Georgia Historical Quarterly* 36 (June 1952): 109–31; William Pencak, "The American Civil War Did Not Take Place," *Rethinking History* 6, no. 2 (2002): 217–21; John M. Coski, "The War Between the Names: What Should the American War of 1861 to 1865 Be Called?," *North & South* 8 (January 2006): 62–70; Chandra Manning and Adam Rothman, "The Name of War," *New York Times*, August 17, 2013, http://opinionator.blogs.nytimes.com/2013/08/17/the-name-of-war. There is even a Wikipedia entry on the subject: "Names of the American Civil War."

2. James Buchanan to Robert W. Barnwell, James H. Adams, and James L. Orr, December 31, 1860, and Barnwell, Adams, and Orr to Buchanan, December 31, 1860, both in *The War of the Rebellion: A Compilation of the Official Records of the Union and Confederate Armies* [hereinafter cited as OR], 108 vols. (Washington, D.C.: Government Printing Office, 1880–1901), ser. 1, 1:115, 124; "Remarks of Jefferson Davis on the special message on affairs in South Carolina, Jan. 10, 1861," in *Jefferson Davis, Constitutionalist: His Letters, Papers and Speeches,* 10 vols., ed. Dunbar Rowland (Jackson: Mississippi Department of Archives, 1923), 5:11; "First Inaugural Address—Final Text," March 4, 1861, in *The Collected Works of Abraham Lincoln,* 8 vols., ed. Roy P. Basler (New Brunswick, N.J.: Rutgers University Press 1953), 4:271. On usage in newspapers, see graph 2 in the text. An explanation of its sources is in the appendix.

3. "Proclamation Calling Militia and Convening Congress," April 15, 1861, "Proclamation of a Blockade," April 19, 1861, "Proclamation Suspending Writ of Habeas Corpus in Florida," May 10, 1861, and Lincoln to Winfield Scott, April 27 and July 3, 1861, all in Basler, *Collected Works of Abraham Lincoln,* 4:331–33, 338–39, 347, 364–65, 419; "An Act to provide for calling forth the Militia to execute the laws of the Union, suppress insurrections, and repel invasions; and to repeal the Act now in force for those purposes," *U.S. Statutes at Large* 1 (1795), 424–25. For discussion of the presidential power in civil unrest, see Robert W. Coakley, *The Role of Federal Military Forces in Domestic Disorders, 1789–1878* (Washington, D.C.: Center of Military History, United States Army, 1988); Stephen I. Vladeck, "Emergency Power and the Militia Acts," *Yale Law Journal* 114 (October 2004): 149–94; Daniel Farber, *Lincoln's Constitution* (Chicago: University of Chicago Press, 2003).

4. Emmerich de Vattel, *The Law of Nations* (1758; Indianapolis: Liberty Fund, 2012), 644–45. The shift to "rebellion" came after England and France had recognized the Confederates' rights as belligerents, which reinforces the idea that Lincoln was primarily interested in shaping domestic opinion. Historians agree, though, that the Union operated from a dual conception of the war, treating the Confederates as both rebels and belligerents, making the Civil War both a rebellion and a war. That confusion over legal definitions may have been a factor in northerners' inconsistent use of "rebellion," "civil war," and "insurrection." See James G. Randall, *Constitutional Problems Under Lincoln* (1951; repr. Urbana: University of Illinois Press 1964), 48–73; Howard Jones, *Blue and Gray Diplomacy: A History of Union and Confederate Foreign Relations* (Chapel Hill: University of North Carolina Press, 2010), 51–55; Stephen C. Neff, *Justice in Blue and Gray: A Legal History of the Civil War* (Cambridge, Mass.: Harvard University Press 2010), 4–29. On foreign recognition, see Don H. Doyle, *The Cause of All Nations: An International History of the American Civil War* (New

York: Basic Books, 2015). Neff argues that neither the North nor the South considered it a civil war, and he sees the later use of Civil War as a "terminological compromise" (29), a conclusion similar to that reached here through different means.

5. Lincoln had previously used the term "rebel." See "Reply to Baltimore Committee," April 22, 1861; "Message to Congress in Special Session," July 4, 1861, both in Basler, *Collected Works of Abraham Lincoln,* 4:341, 427, 432–33. Adam Goodheart, *1861: The Civil War Awakening* (New York: Knopf, 2011), 356–62; Douglas L. Wilson, *Lincoln's Sword: The Presidency and the Power of Words* (New York: Knopf, 2006), 90–94.

6. For examples of use of "rebellion," "insurrection," and "civil war," see *Congressional Globe,* 37th Cong., 1st Sess., 42, 137, 289, 372, 394; Bingham quoted, July 16, 1861, 146. "An Act to provide for the Suppression of Rebellion against and Resistance to the Laws of the United States, and to amend the Act entitled 'An Act to provide for calling for the Militia to execute the Laws of the Union,'" *U.S. Statutes at Large* 37 (1861): 281–82; "Proclamation Forbidding Intercourse with Rebel States," August 16, 1861, in Basler, *Collected Works of Abraham Lincoln,* 4:487–88.

7. The frequency of Lincoln's usage was determined by keyword searches of the Abraham Lincoln Association's online version of the *Collected Works of Abraham Lincoln,* https://quod.lib.umich.edu/l/lincoln. David Herbert Donald says Lincoln most often used "rebellion," having found him using it more than four hundred times. See Donald, *Lincoln* (New York: Simon & Schuster, 1995), 302. "Address Delivered at the Dedication of the Cemetery at Gettysburg" and "Second Inaugural Address," both in Basler, *Collected Works of Abraham Lincoln,* 7:17–23, 8:332–33. I have no direct proof that Lincoln used "civil war" consciously in these two speeches, but Douglas Wilson rightly warns that "it is never safe to underestimate Lincoln." Wilson also shows how the second inaugural was structured "so as to emphasize that what is true of one [the North] is true of the other [the South]." Wilson, *Lincoln's Sword,* 86, 270.

8. *Congressional Globe,* 37th Cong., 1st Sess., viii. Frequency of use in titles and congressional documents based on keyword search of the ProQuest Congressional Publications database. The numbers from the OR are based on a very rough keyword search of the online version. At the time of the search, it was part of the Making of America Collection at Cornell University. It has now moved to the Hathi Trust Digital Library, http://catalog.hathitrust.org/Record/000625514. On newspaper usage, see graph 2 in the text; on book titles, graph 3.

9. Gerhard Peters and John T. Woolley, "Andrew Johnson: Proclamation 153—Declaring the Insurrection in Certain Southern States to Be at an End," April 2, 1866, *American Presidency Project,* http://www.presidency.ucsb.edu/ws/index.php?pid=71987; and Andrew Johnson, "Proclamation 157: Declaring that Peace Order, Tranquility and Civil Authority Now Exists in and Throughout the Whole of the United States of America," August 20, 1866, http://www.presidency.ucsb.edu/ws/index.php?pid=71992. See also "General Orders No. 100," April 21, 1863, OR, ser. 2, 5:681; and David Armitage, "Secession and Civil War," in *Secession as an International Phenomenon: From America's Civil War to Contemporary Separatist Movements,* ed. Don H. Doyle (Athens: University of Georgia Press, 2010), 45–46.

10. McPherson, *Lincoln and the Second American Revolution,* 3–6; Andrew Zimmerman, "From the Second American Revolution to the First International and Back Again: Marxism, the Popular Front, and the American Civil War," in *The World the Civil War Made,* ed. Gregory P. Downs and Kate Masur (Chapel Hill: University of North Carolina Press, 2015), 304–36. All of the names

mentioned can be found, in very small numbers, in the Readex America's Historical Newspapers database. Newspaper references to the Second American Revolution appeared primarily in the New Orleans *Daily Picayune,* which used it as the title for a column on war news. Google Ngram searches for "war to free the slaves," "slaveholders' war," and "war for emancipation" show that they appeared in a few books. "Second American Revolution" appears starting in the 1920s, when Charles Beard used it.

11. "Hypocritical Pretenses," *Daily Picayune* (New Orleans), June 7, 1861, 1; "The Working of Lincoln's Blockade," *Macon Daily Telegraph,* September 4, 1861, 1. See also "A Confederate Iron Clad at Charleston," *Richmond Examiner,* November 28, 1862, 2; "The Cotton Tax," *Macon Daily Telegraph,* May 1, 1866, 2; "A Loyal Democrat," *Chicago Daily Tribune,* March 18, 1863, 2.

12. Wilson in "A Glorious Meeting," *Hartford Courant,* April 4, 1864, 2; Ingersoll in "Grand Rally for the Union," *Chicago Daily Tribune,* October 7, 1864, 4; "From the Albany Atlas and Argus, Preventing the War: Mr. Weed's Testimony," *Pittsfield Sun* (Massachusetts), July 28, 1864, 1. See also "The Abolition War and Senator Seward," *New York Herald,* February 16, 1861, 6; "Russell's Letters to the London Times," *Baltimore Sun,* November 12, 1861, 1; "Got His Due," *Chicago Daily Tribune,* July 19, 1862, 2; "Treason! The Abolition War Against the Union," *The Crisis* (Columbus, Ohio), August 26, 1863, 246; "Abolitionist," *Wisconsin Daily Patriot* (Madison), March 27, 1863, 1.

13. "Emancipation, Racism and the Work Before Us," and "The Mission of the War," both in *Frederick Douglass Papers,* ser. 1: *Speeches Debates and Interviews,* 5 vols., ed. John W. Blassingame and John R. McKivigan (New Haven, Conn.: Yale University Press, 1979–92), 3:600–601, 609, 4:8–24; "Additional from the North," *Richmond Examiner,* February 6, 1864, 1; "Abolitionists," *New Hampshire Patriot and State Gazette* (Concord), April 6, 1864, 2; "Frederick Douglass," *Washington Bee,* July 17, 1886, 2.

14. "The Slaveholders' Rebellion," in *Frederick Douglas Papers,* 3:521–43; Senate Resolution 28, *Congressional Globe,* 37th Cong., 1st Sess., July 16, 1861, 134, 142. For a copy, see "Gen. Pomeroy's Bill to Suppress the Rebellion," *Chicago Daily Tribune,* July 23, 1861, 2. "Senator Pomeroy's Bill for Suppressing the Slaveholder's Rebellion," *New York Times,* July 21, 1861, 5; "England and the Pro-Slavery Rebellion," *Chicago Daily Tribune,* June 28, 1861, 2; "The Animus of the Great Rebellion," *Chicago Daily Tribune,* October 30, 1863, 2; "Wanted a Pro-Slavery Man," *Chicago Daily Tribune,* March 25, 1870, 2; "Hendricks and Reform," *Chicago Daily Tribune,* July 25, 1884, 4; "Lincoln Charged with Violating his Oath," *Chicago Daily Tribune,* May 15, 1889, 4. De Peyster's speeches and others in which "slaveholders' rebellion" appear are found in ProQuest's Civil War Era database. In the sample of books in the Library of Congress described in graph 3, four used it in their titles.

15. *Frederick Douglass Papers,* 5:47, 227; for "rebellion," see 4:154, 277, 5:48–49. Douglass also used "war for the union" (5:61, 177, 194, 198), and like white southerners, sometimes just said "the war" (4:297, 418, 5:44). George W. Williams, *A History of the Negro Troops in the War of the Rebellion, 1861–1865* (1888; repr. New York: Negro University Press, 1969), 65, 147. On the importance of slavery in northern memory, see Barbara A. Gannon, *The Won Cause: Black and White Comradeship in the Grand Army of the Republic* (Chapel Hill: University of North Carolina Press, 2011); Caroline E. Janney, *Remembering the Civil War: Reunion and the Limits of Reconciliation* (Chapel Hill: University of North Carolina Press, 2013); M. Keith Harris, *Across the Bloody Chasm: The Culture of Commemoration Among Civil War Veterans* (Baton Rouge: Louisiana State University Press, 2014).

16. S. 207, 39th Cong., 1st Sess., April 2, 1866, 1706. Yael A. Sternhell, "The Afterlives of a

Confederate Archive: Civil War Documents and the Making of Sectional Reconciliation," *Journal of American History* 102 (March 2016): 1037. Early legislation calling for an official history of the war continued to use Rebellion, but the resulting volumes and those of the naval history of the war always used War of the Rebellion in their titles. Observations on titles in other government documents are based on keyword searches of the ProQuest Congressional Publications database and the Readex U.S. Congressional Serial Set database. On newspaper usage, see graph 2 in the text; on book titles, graph 3. Melvil Dewey, *A Classification and Subject Index for Cataloguing and Arranging the Books and Pamphlets of a Library* (Amherst, Mass.: 1876), 36. Various sources, including Wikipedia and other websites, list the many names given to the Civil War. One of the most extensive lists in print appears in Jay S. Hoar, *The South's Last Boys in Gray: An Epic Prose Elegy* (Bowling Green, Ohio: Bowling Green State University Press, 1986), 524–25.

17. George C. Rable, "Rebels and Patriots in the Confederate 'Revolution,'" in *In the Cause of Liberty: How the Civil War Redefined American Ideals*, ed. William J. Cooper Jr. and John M. Mc-Cardell Jr. (Baton Rouge: Louisiana State University Press, 2009), 63–86; Edward A. Pollard, *The Lost Cause: A New Southern History of the War of the Confederates* (New York: E. B. Trent, 1866), 44; O. W. Blacknall, "The War for Southern Independence," *Confederate Veteran* 8 (November 1900): 485; *United Daughters of the Confederacy [UDC], Minutes of the Thirty-Seventh Annual Convention of the United Daughters of the Confederacy* (1930), 263.

18. Pollard, *Lost Cause*, 43–44. For examples of the use of "Lost Cause," see "Heap Black Guardism," *Flake's Bulletin*, February 14, 1866, 4; and "By Telegraph," *Georgia Weekly Telegraph* (Macon), May 30, 1871, 3. Raphael Semmes, *Memoirs of Service Afloat During the War Between the States* (1868; repr. Baton Rouge: Louisiana State University Press, 1996); Alexander H. Stephens, *A Constitutional View of the Late War Between the States; Its Causes, Character, Conduct and Results*, 2 vols. (Philadelphia: National Publishing Company, 1868–70), 2:425–27. The phrase, often rendered as a "civil war between the states," appeared in several newspapers at the beginning of or during the war. For example, see "A War Between the States," *Columbus Daily Enquirer* (Georgia), January 23, 1861, 2. For a further discussion of an earlier use of "war between the states," see Coski, "War Between the Names," 65.

19. S. D. McCormick, "War of Secession," *Confederate Veteran* 2 (November 1894): 330; Confederate War for Independence appeared in "Reminiscences of the Battle of Spotsylvania," *Daily Memphis Avalanche*, August 19, 1866, 1; "Glorious Women Whose Like We Shall Never See Again," *Macon Telegraph*, January 23, 1902, 4. Confederate War appeared in "Local News Items," *Columbus Daily Enquirer*, March 16, 1866, 3; "Death of ExGov. Allen," *Macon Telegraph*, May 18, 1866, 2; S. A. Cunningham, "The Name of Our War," *Confederate Veteran* 2 (April 1894): 112; R. J. Hancock, "Name—Confederate War," *Confederate Veteran* 11 (September 1903): 389. Confederate War or Confederate War for Independence was used in nine of the book titles in the sample used to create graph 3, and War of Secession was used nineteen times.

20. "Late unpleasantness" was used as a title in only one book in the sample described in graph 3; the phrase appeared in newspapers but never in more than 4 percent of the names in the search for any given year, and often less than 1 percent of the time in the sample compiled for graph 2. It was used three times in the *Southern Historical Papers*. For examples of use of "late unpleasantness" in the North, see "The Army During the War," *Daily Evening Bulletin* (San Francisco), June 4, 1880, 1; "Putting Down the Rebellion: An Incident of the Late Unpleasantness Recalled

by a Recent Meeting," *Kansas City Star* (Missouri), January 10, 1888, 2; "Marching on St. Louis: Veterans of the Late Unpleasantness Gathering for the Grand Army Encampment," *Daily Inter Ocean* (Chicago), September 26, 1887, 1; *New Haven Evening Register,* August 4, 1891, 1; "Some Odd Stories," *Idaho Daily Statesman* (Boise), July 28, 1893, 3; "People You Know," *Grand Forks Daily Herald* (North Dakota), August 11, 1906, 8. Even William A. Dunning used "our late unpleasantness" to refer to the Civil War; see Dunning to Edmund S. Meany, no date, Edward S. Meany Papers, box 103, folder 20, p. 61, Special Collections Division, University of Washington Library, Seattle. For examples of use with regard to the Spanish-American War, see "Spain," *Idaho Daily Statesman* (Boise), March 18, 1899, 2; "Spain's 'Morning Stamp,'" *Minneapolis Journal,* April 22, 1899, supp. 4; "Editorial Comment," *Philadelphia Inquirer,* March 10, 1909, 8; "He Sustains the Administration," *Dallas Morning News,* February 21, 1902, 6. Details on appearances of "war of northern aggression" determined using Google Ngram. Stephens, *Constitutional View of the Late War,* 2:44; "Editorial Paragraphs," "The Career of Leonidas Polk," and "Address of Honorable B. H. Hill before the Georgia Branch of the Southern Historical Society at Atlanta, February 18th, 1874," all in *Southern Historical Society Papers,* 3:302, 21:324, 14:484. On "War of Coercion," see J. William Jones, "Opposed to the Name Rebellion," *Confederate Veteran* 2 (July 1894): 199; UDC *Minutes,* 1905, 217.

21. Davis to A. Dudley Mann, November 7, 1881, in *The Papers of Jefferson Davis,* ed. Lynda L. Crist, 14 vols. (Baton Rouge: Louisiana State University Press, 1971–2014), 13:177–78, including note 1, 14:208. Among books published in the South and included in the sample of books (graph 3), Civil War outnumbered War Between the States 37 to 26. On southern newspaper usage, see graph 1 in the text. Usage in the *Southern Historical Society Papers* was compiled through a keyword search of the *Southern Historical Society Papers* CD-ROM from Eastern Digital Resources, Clearwater, South Carolina. United Confederate Veterans [UCV], *Minutes of the Eighth Annual Meeting and Reunion of the United Confederate Veterans* (New Orleans: Hopkins' Printing Office, 1899), 48–49; *Proceedings of the Convention for Organization and Adoption of the Constitution of the United Confederate Veterans, 1889* (New Orleans: Hopkins' Printing Office, 1891), 6; UCV *Minutes,* 1895, 12–14; 1898, 26.

22. UCV *Minutes,* 1898, 87; 1900, 78; UDC *Minutes,* 1899, 72–73; *Confederate Veteran* 13 (January 1905): 5. On the influence of the UDC, see, for example, W. Fitzhugh Brundage, "White Women and the Politics of Historical Memory in the New South, 1880–1920," in *Jumpin' Jim Crow: Southern Politics from Civil War to Civil Rights,* ed. Jane Dailey, Glenda Elizabeth Gilmore, and Bryant Simon (Princeton, N.J.: Princeton University Press, 2000), 115–39; Karen L. Cox, *Dixie's Daughters: The United Daughters of the Confederacy and the Preservation of Confederate Culture* (Gainesville: University Press of Florida, 2003). On rebellion and labor violence, see Gaines M. Foster, *Ghosts of the Confederacy: Defeat, the Lost Cause, and the Origins of the New South* (New York: Oxford University Press, 1987), 117–18, 143–44.

23. David C. Turpie questions southern support for the Spanish-American War; see Turpie, "A Voluntary War: The Spanish-American War, White Southern Manhood, and the Struggle to Recruit Volunteers in the South," *Journal of Southern History* 80 (November 2014): 859–92. But compare with Foster, *Ghosts of the Confederacy,* 145–49, 259n17; David W. Blight, *Race and Reunion: The Civil War in American Memory* (Cambridge, Mass.: Harvard University Press, 2001), 351–53; and Janney, *Remembering the Civil War,* 222–31.

24. See graph 3. Melvil Dewey, *Decimal Classification and Relative Index*, 5th ed. (Boston: Library Bureau, 1894), 41, 147; *List of Subject Headings for Use in Dictionary Catalogs* (Boston: Library Bureau, 1895).

25. For congressional publications, I have relied on ProQuest's Congressional Publications database and the Readex U.S. Congressional Serial Set database. *Manual of Style Governing Composition and Proof Reading in the Government Printing Office* (Washington, D.C.: Government Printing Office, 1894 [15–16]; 1898 [14–15]); *Manual of Style Governing Composition and Proof Reading in the Government Printing Office, Together with Decisions on the Board of Geographic Names* (Washington, D.C.: Government Printing Office, 1900), 15; *Manual of Style for Use in Composition and Proof Reading* (Washington, D.C.: Government Printing Office, 1903), 15.

26. *Congressional Record*, 58th Cong., 3rd Sess., March 1, 1905, 3733.

27. *Congressional Record*, 59th Cong., 2nd Sess., January 11, 1907, 929–30; "No Rebellion in '61, Declares the Senate," *New York Times*, January 12, 1907, 2.

28. "No Rebellion in '61"; *Congressional Record*, 59th Cong., 2nd Sess., January 11, 1907, 929–33. Bacon thought his speech important enough to publish in pamphlet form. See *The Civil War Was Not a Rebellion: Speech of Hon. A. O. Bacon, of Georgia* (Washington, D.C.: Government Printing Office, 1907).

29. "No Rebellion in '61"; "Pension Bill Passes," *Washington Post*, January 12, 1907, 4; "Capitol Gossip," clipping from *Washington Post,* January 12, 1907, in Precedent File 57-A-6002, #58 Civil War, Office of the Adjutant General, RG 94, National Archives, Washington, D.C.

30. *Congressional Record*, 61st Cong., 3rd Sess., February 1, 1911, 1787–88.

31. "'Rebellion' Cut Out of the Bill," *News and Observer* (Raleigh, N.C.), January 12, 1907, 1; "No 'Rebels' Bore Arms in Legions of the South," *Atlanta Constitution,* January 12, 1907, 1; "Pension Bill Passes," *Washington Post,* January 12, 1907, 4; "No Rebellion in '61." In another sign that concerns over current race relations took precedence over Civil War memory, Edward Carmack gave a speech on Brownsville about the same time he attacked the use of "rebellion." He received one letter of thanks for defending the honor of Confederates and a host of letters on the Brownsville speech. See Edward W. Carmack Papers, folders 23, 24, and 25a, Southern Historical Collection, University of North Carolina, Chapel Hill.

32. Superintendent of documents, quoted in Edward S. Meany, "Name of the American War of 1861–1865," Meany Papers, box 103, folder 18, p. 10. Reply by Gen. A[insworth] to A. H. Seymour, June 4, 1907; memo, F. C. Ainsworth, May 4, 1911; memo to Mr. Donnelly, December 4, 1912, all in File 57-A-6002, #58 Civil War, Office of the Adjutant General, Administrative Precedent File, RG 94, National Archives. I would not have found this rich file without Michael P. Musick, "Civil War Records: A War by Any Other Name," *Prologue* 27 (Summer 1995), http://www.archives.gov/publications/prologue/1995/summer/civil-war-records-2.html.

33. On titles of government documents, I again performed a keyword search in the Readex U.S. Congressional Serial Set database.

34. On the role of racism see, Blight, *Race and Reunion*.

35. Edmund S. Meany, *Name of the American War of 1861–1865* (Seattle, 1910); Meany, "Name of the American War." Meany's speech on the name of the war is quite good and reaches conclusions very similar to those here. On Meany, see, among other sources, the guide to his papers in

the Special Collections Library, University of Washington, Seattle, and *Dictionary of American Biography,* suppl. vol. 1:548–49. In fairness to Senator Tillman, it must be noted that he was absent during the 1907 Senate debate, but the next day, in a long speech on Brownsville, commended the Senate, in passing, for putting "its opinion in the law that the great war of 1861–1865 was not a war of rebellion, but a war between the States—a civil war." *Congressional Record,* 59th Cong., 2nd Sess., January 12, 1907, 1039.

36. Most of the response letters are in a numbered sequence without dates, and I have simply given the folder and page numbers as the best way to find them. See Meany Papers, box 103, folder 22, for L. M. Sedgwick (p. 191), Louis R. Ehric (p. 184), Herman Keifer (p. 152), J. N. Davidson (pp. 180–81), August Donath (p. 183), H. P. Scratchley (p. 190), and George W. Pollitt (pp. 176–77); folder 21, for Charles Francis Adams (p. 139) and Edward Channing (p. 144). Also Meany, "Name of the American War," 5.

37. Meany, "Name of the American War," 5–6.

38. Meany Papers, box 103, folder 20, for Gardner W. Allen (p. 43), Job Barnard (p. 48), Christopher B. Coleman (p. 56), Walter L. Fleming (p. 67), William Elliot Griffis (p. 76); Martin R. Andrews (p. 45), J. O. Batchelor (p. 49), and Paul L Haworth (p. 81); folder 21, for William Hayes Ward (p. 134) and Jeanne Elizabeth Winn (p. 136). For other letters that display concern for southern sentiments, see Meany Papers, box 103, folder 20, pp. 47, 53, 65–67, 70, 79, 83, 85–86; folder 21, pp. 112, 116, 121–122, 128, 131, 141, 146; and folder 22, pp. 174, 179–82.

39. J. Franklin Jameson to Meany, April 29, 1910, Meany Papers, box 103, folder 18; George Wells Knight, folder 20, pp. 90–92.

40. Martin, "What's in a Name: Correspondent Objects to Term 'Civil War,'" *The State* (Columbia, S.C.), July 5, 1911, 7; *Congressional Record,* 63rd Cong., 3rd Sess., December 12, 1914, 138.

41. UDC *Minutes,* 1911, 24–25; 1912, 315–16; 1913, 357–58; 1914, 296–99; 1915, 250–52; 1916, 307–8; *Congressional Record,* 62nd Cong., 3rd Sess., February 1, 1913, 2455; 63rd Cong., 3rd Sess., December 12, 1914, 138; L. E. Williams to Taft, March 14, 1916, microfilm, sec. 3, reel 164, and Taft to Williams, March 20, 1916, sec. 8, reel 538, both in William Howard Taft Papers, Library of Congress.

42. Meany Papers, box 103, folder 20, for Richard Henry Greene (p. 75), Theron W. Haight (p. 77); folder 18, for Jameson to Meany, April 29, 1910. For other letters that express opposition to War Between the States, see Meany Papers, box 103, folder 20, pp. 45, 59, 65, 68, 72, 79–81, 83, 88, 90–92, 94, 98; and folder 21, pp. 103–5, 107, 111, 113, 123, 128, 131–32, 138–40, 142, 145, 149, 152. One of the northerners who used War Between the States did say he did so to please southerners; see Reuben Gold Thwaites, Meany Papers, box 103, folder 22, pp. 170–71.

43. Coulter, "Name for the American War," 129; UDC *Minutes,* 1919, 315–16; 1922, 211–14; 1926, 206–8; 1930, 64–65; "New Deal Will Continue, Says Roosevelt," *Chicago Daily Tribune,* December 6, 1938, 1; "Capital Bids Its Farewell to Elizabeth," *Chicago Daily Tribune,* November 3, 1951, 1; "Military Rites for Last G.A.R. Veteran," *Chicago Daily Tribune,* August 3, 1956, 3. See also Google Ngram graph results for keyword "war between the states." For stamps on which "Civil War" appears in large letters and "War Between the States" in much smaller type, see, for example, "32c Civil War Pane of Twenty," Smithsonian National Postal Museum, https://postalmuseum .si.edu/object/npm_1996.2081.198.1-20.

44. Ravin I. McDavid Jr. and Virginia G. McDavid, "The Late Unpleasantness: Folk Names for the Civil War," *Southern Speech Journal* 34 (Spring 1968): 197.

45. The regional studies within the Linguistic Atlas project all reported their findings in different formats. The New England survey published a handbook along with six oversize volumes that placed the response by each subject on maps showing the geographic location of the respondent. Data on the Civil War appears in volume 3, map 551. No totals are provided. To find the age and educational level of each informant, a research assistant went through the maps to get the name of the war and the introductory volume. This information was entered into a database and the Statistical Package for the Social Sciences used to produce cross-tabulations. Hans Kurath et al., *The Linguist Atlas of New England,* 3 vols. in 6 parts (Providence, R.I., 1939–43). The Upper Midwest survey simply listed the names given in response to the question, followed by a list of the respondents by their numbers. Harold B. Allen, *The Linguistic Atlas of the Upper Midwest,* 3 vols. (Minneapolis, 1973–76), 1:381. What I have divided as the Mid-Atlantic, border, and South Atlantic states were all part of the *Linguistic Atlas of the Middle and South Atlantic States.* That project has a website and published a volume describing its work: William A. Kretzschmer Jr. et al., eds., *Handbook of the Linguistic Atlas of the Middle and South Atlantic States* (Chicago: University of Chicago Press, 1993). The project director, William Kretzschmer, very helpfully provided me an Excel file of respondents' answers to the question about the war, and demographic data on each of respondent. I subdivided the file into three regions—Mid-Atlantic (New Jersey, New York, and Pennsylvania), the border states (Delaware, the District of Columbia, Maryland, and West Virginia), and the South Atlantic (Florida, Georgia, North Carolina, South Carolina, and Virginia)—and compiled totals by those regions.

46. John Temple Graves, *The Fighting South* (New York: G. P. Putnam's Sons, 1943), 236. Numbers and quotation from Linguistic Atlas project.

47. The numbers for all responses were compiled from a list of names in Lee Pederson, ed., *Linguistic Atlas of the Gulf States,* 7 vols. (Athens: University of Georgia Press, 1986), 3:313–14. For key and listing of the four most common names, with demographic breakdowns, see 6:xviii, 215; for War Between the States as middle-class marker, see 6:xxiii.

48. On Timmerman, see Andy Hall, "'The War of Northern Aggression' as Modern, Segregationist Revisionism," *Dead Confederates, A Civil War Era Blog,* June 21, 2011, http://deadconfed erates.com/2011/06/21/the-war-of-northern-aggression-is-modern-segregationist-revisionism. For examples of references in tourism writing, see Horace Sutton, "Charleston: Tour Garden Spot Brimming with History," *Chicago Tribune,* May 21, 1978, F10; Larry Townsend, "Walk to Get the 'Feel' of Charleston," *Chicago Tribune,* March 17, 1991, K1; Mary T. Shmick, "True Grits: Down the Mississippi with Southern Style and Fading Myth," *Chicago Tribune,* April 21, 1991, E1. Pederson, *Linguistic Atlas of Gulf States,* 3:314.

49. McDavid and McDavid, "Late Unpleasantness," 202. Observations for the *Pittsburgh Courier* (1911–2002) and *Chicago Defender/Daily Defender* (1905–75) based on a keyword search of the ProQuest Historical Newspaper databases. For "War betwixt," see "Joe Morris," in *The American Slave: A Composite Autobiography,* 12 vols., ed. George P. Rawick (Westport, Conn.: Greenwood, 1977), suppl., ser. 1, 11:253. See Rawick, *The American Slave: A Composite Autobiography,* 7 vols. (Westport, Conn.: Greenwood, 1972), for "Emery Turner" (vol. 6, part 5:8); "Confederate War"

and "Eugenia Fair" (vol. 2, part 2:38); "George Briggs" (vol. 2, part 1:95); "Secession War" and "Phillip Evans" (vol. 2, part 2:37); "Civil War" and "John W. Fields" (vol. 6, part 5:79); "George Fortman" (vol. 6, part 5:92); "Betty Guwn" (vol. 6, part 5:99); "Ezra Adams" (vol. 2, part 1:5); on variations of freedom, see "John Love" (vol. 5, part 3:26); "Patsy Moses" (vol. 5, part 3:142); "Mary Kincheon Edwards" (vol. 4, part 2:15); "de holy" and "Harry D. Jenkins" (vol. 3, part 3:26). Kathleen Ann Clark, *Defining Moments: African American Commemoration and Political Culture in the South, 1861–1913* (Chapel Hill: University of North Carolina Press 2005), 15. White interviewers may have influenced the use of more traditional terms, although the question itself—"What do you remember about the war that brought you freedom?"—certainly encouraged names associated with emancipation or slavery. See Henry G. Alsberg to State Directors of the Federal Writers Project, July 30, 1937, copy in author's possession, originally downloaded from a Greenwood Press web page (http://aae.greenwood.com/from SundowntoSunup.htm) that was discontinued as of March 14, 2018.

50. "Frequencies" (question 44), "Crosstabs—Southern Sample" (question 44), and "Open Answers," all in Center for the Study of the American South, "Southern Focus Poll, Fall 1994" (Odum Institute for Research in Social Science, University of North Carolina at Chapel Hill, 2007), http://hdl.handle.net/1902.29/D-30614. On the shifting social basis of Lost Cause activism, see Thomas J. Brown, *Civil War Canon: Sites of Confederate Memory in South Carolina* (Chapel Hill: University of North Carolina Press, 2015), 216–26.

51. Changing usage of names for the Civil War speaks to the recent historiographical controversy over reunion and reconciliation, and particularly the interpretation in Blight, *Race and Reunion*. Undoubtedly, Blight's critics make a valid case that his work has underestimated the persistence of sectional hostilities and tensions among veterans—as did my own work. Yet the study here provides support for Blight's overall conclusion that reconciliation occurred and resulted in part from an agreement to focus not on the issues of the war, particularly slavery, but on the glories of the battlefield. It provides less support for his contention that the South succeeded in convincing the North to accept a Lost Cause memory of the war. By not adding a reference to slavery to the war's name, northerners appeared to emphasize the war as a battle for the preservation of the Union, long before the Lost Cause emerged. Northerners' opposition to War Between the States indicated that they had not accepted the South's interpretation of secession. For an excellent introduction to the literature on this issue, see Nina Silber, "Reunion and Reconciliation, Reviewed and Reconsidered," *Journal of American History* 103 (June 2016): 59–83.

— 5 —

THE FIERY CROSS AND
THE CONFEDERATE FLAG

DIXON, GRIFFITH, AND THE BIRTH
(AND REBIRTH) OF RACIST SYMBOLISM

WHEN *The Birth of a Nation* PREMIERED in 1915, the National Association for the Advancement of Colored People, Monroe Trotter, and others sought to ban the film. In his 2014 study of their campaign, historian Dick Lehr claimed that the resulting controversy, in the words of his book's subtitle, reignited America's Civil War. Lehr and his publisher drew on a widely held view that the film's director, D. W. Griffith, thoroughly imbued with the romance of the Lost Cause, sought to refight the war and champion the Confederate cause. Griffith's movie did help to nationalize the Lost Cause version of Confederate heroism and its outraged, and outrageous, version of Reconstruction—and rendered the Ku Klux Klan heroic in ending it. Too much, however, has been made of Griffith's refighting of the war and his celebration of the Lost Cause. *The Birth of a Nation*, as its title made clear, promoted a thoroughly reconciliationist vision of the Civil War and promoted a new American nationalism rooted in white Protestantism. It did so in part by helping to popularize the fiery cross as a symbol of Christian nationalism and it began a process of redefining an important Lost Cause symbol, the Confederate battle flag.[1]

Griffith took much of his movie from Thomas Dixon's novel *The Clansman*, also often portrayed as the epitome of the Lost Cause. Even as Dixon sought to defend the white South's view of Reconstruction, his novels offered a vision of American nationalism rooted in a violent white supremacy resting on a fear of racial intermixture. It was Dixon who introduced the vision of the Ku Klux Klan in white robes with crosses on them, as well as the image of the fiery cross that had been baptized in the blood of a white virgin. When Griffith filmed his version of Dixon's story, he departed from Dixon and also baptized a Confederate flag in the young girl's blood. The cross, but not the flag, then became incorporated into the rituals of the Ku Klux Klan of the 1920s, which perpetuated not the Lost Cause but a virulent form of white Protestant nationalism that would become even more influential a century later. Understanding the way in which these racist symbols came to be born—and in the case of the flag, more accurately, reborn—begins with an analysis of Dixon's attitudes and his introduction of the fiery cross and Klan regalia. It then explores how Griffith transferred both to the big screen and made the Christian symbols even more prominent. Finally, it recounts their incorporation into the rituals and public displays of the Ku Klux Klan after it formed in 1915.

BORN AT THE END OF the Civil War, Thomas Dixon grew up in Shelby, North Carolina, with vivid memories of Reconstruction. A beloved uncle rode with the Ku Klux Klan, and a young Dixon woke up one night to see Klansmen out his window. From Shelby, Dixon went off to Wake Forest University and then to graduate school at Johns Hopkins. Rather than become an academic, he tried acting, law, politics, and finally the ministry. In 1887, he left North Carolina to pastor churches in Boston and then New York. Though he embraced much of the new social gospel, Dixon became, as historian Joel R. Williamson termed him, a radical racist, whose writings described Black males as beasts and rapists, saw no place for Black people in America, and therefore thought the only solution to the race problem would be the expulsion of African Americans through colonization.[2]

Dixon did not, as some assume, celebrate the Old South and the Confederacy. He revered Confederate leaders but thought they should give way to new ones. Rather than cling to the Old South, he embraced a New South vision of mills and progress, and he renounced sectionalism. "I am no sectional fanatic," he wrote in a 1905 response to criticism of his novel *The Clansman*, "but a citizen of New York, with scores of warm friends in the great, rushing North. . . . This is my country—the whole of it, from sea to sea and from Alaska to the Keys of Florida. I love the people of the North, and I have promised that if God gives me strength they shall know mine own people of the South and love them too." He took very seriously his task of explaining the South to the North.[3]

In his early days in Boston, in 1887, Dixon went to hear Justin D. Fulton, a Baptist minister and anti-Catholic activist, speak at Tremont Temple. "I heard," Dixon recalled years later, "a silly old man . . . make a speech on the 'Southern Problem.'" Fulton had just returned from a six-week tour of the South and, apparently, condemned the region's continued disloyalty. "He sputtered, bellowed, stamped his feet and flung his arms far and wide," Dixon recounted. He then "quoted" from Fulton: "Before God, brethren, I warn you. The rebel flag still floats over every Southern town and village. The only way to save this nation from hell, today, is for Northern mothers to rear more children than Southern mothers." His words, Dixon recalled, "sent a shock down my spine and lifted me from the seat." Once on his feet, Dixon laughed out loud. When asked who he was, he replied, "A Southern white man who has lived in the South twenty-three years since the war and never saw a Confederate flag." After creating his disturbance, Dixon glared and walked out. Fulton's "challenge," Dixon observed, "determined my life's work." He decided then to write history and began to buy books to study the Civil War and Reconstruction. "I swore to destroy Sectionalism, reunite our nation and make the career of fools, like Fulton, impossible."[4]

Three years later, Dixon found himself in a very similar confrontation—this time in print rather than in person. In 1890, Elliott Shepard, a former abolitionist and editor of the *Mail and Express* in New York, attended the unveiling of the Robert E. Lee monument in Richmond. His paper then published an account of the ceremonies under a large headline, "Treason Glorified," with a smaller one adding "Tribute to the Memory of Benedict Arnold Lee." The occasion's main address, Shepard claimed, "breathed rebellion" in every line. Shepard also complained at great length about the Rebel flags seen "everywhere and cheered on all sides."[5]

As in Boston, Dixon did not let such statements go unchallenged. He responded to Shepard in a sermon delivered in his New York church and later published. He claimed Shepard's paper did not follow the Christianity or the God he knew and condemned Shepard for deliberately distorting the facts by implying that only Rebel flags were waved. Again, Dixon observed, "Why, I was born in the south and lived there twenty-three years and I never saw a Confederate flag." Dixon then offered a vision of reconciliation. "Men of the North and South we are brethren. Let us hear to-day the voices of the heroic dead.

They speak for peace and harmony. The brave and true never fight after the battle is closed. The time has come for us to take each by the hand and crush those influences that seek to perpetuate strife for a base, ignoble purpose. God help us that we may have, in deed and truth, our own glorious, united nation." The "base and ignoble" purpose Dixon saw might well have been Shepard's advocacy of the Force Bill to protect African American suffrage in the South.[6]

Dixon clearly associated flying the Confederate flag with a persistent southern sectionalism, and just as clearly believed that the white South had abandoned both the flag and the Confederacy and rejoined the Union. His historical research also grew out of his outrage when he saw a stage version of Uncle Tom's Cabin that he thought was a slander of his region. A year later, in 1902, he published the first novel in a trilogy, The Leopard's Spots; two others soon followed: The Clansman in 1905 and The Traitor in 1907. In between the latter two novels, Dixon produced a stage version of The Clansman.[7]

The Leopard's Spots and The Clansman, the two most popular and important of the three works, start at the end of the Civil War and tell the same story, about the horrors of Reconstruction fueled by northerners—including, in The Leopard's Spots, a character based on Uncle Tom's Cabin's Simon Legree. The central theme of both novels is the benighted brutality of the Black male, the corruption and horror of Black Republican rule during Reconstruction, and the triumph of white supremacy through the heroic and often violent efforts of the Ku Klux Klan. Into this theme, he weaves love stories and the emergence of a New South; a major character in the first novel is a Confederate general who becomes a factory owner.

In his novels, Dixon occasionally echoed themes prominent in the Lost Cause and included hints of a persistent sectional animosity. The Leopard's Spots, for example, points to the North's involvement in slavery and blames the war on abolitionists. It claims that the South did not fight for slavery; instead, white southerners opposed the trend of "nationalism, centralization, solidarity." In The Clansman, during Reconstruction, two southern women ask the novel's hero, Ben Cameron, to put on his Confederate uniform again. He does, but he also acquiesces when a Union military commander, citing as justification a ban on the display of the buttons, cuts them off and rips off the epaulets. In perhaps his most blatant evocation of the Confederacy, when Dixon staged The Clansman, the actor who played Cameron wore a Confederate uniform during Reconstruction.[8]

Dixon's novels as a whole, however, hardly fit into the Lost Cause celebration or the idea that the South still fought the Civil War. Dixon rarely wrote of the glories of the Old South. Nor did he defend slavery; he once claimed to hate it "more than I do hell." The South, he maintained, was better off without it. His novels, for the most part, start after the war ended and champion reunion and reconciliation. Early in *The Leopard's Spots,* Dixon describes the South after Appomattox. "There was nowhere a slumbering spark of war." Southerners "were glad to be done with" it, and happy "that the everlasting question of a divided Union was settled and settled forever. There was now to be one country and one flag, and deep down in their souls they were content with it." *The Clansman* does have some brief accounts of events during the war. In one, Elsie Stoneman, daughter of Austin Stoneman, a character based on Thaddeus Stevens, nurses Ben Cameron, a wounded Confederate, in a northern prison. Another is recounted by her brother, Phil Stoneman. In the only battle scene in the novel, he recounts how the same Ben Cameron stopped in the midst of a charge to give water to a wounded Yankee; the Union line cheered. Soon, Cameron resumed his charge.

> When the last man had staggered back or fallen, on came this boy, alone, carrying the colours he had snatched from a falling soldier, as if he were leading a million men to victory. A bullet had blown his hat from his head, and we could see the blood streaming down the side of his face. He charged straight into the jaws of one of our guns. And then, with a smile on his lips and a dare to Death in his big brown eyes, he rammed that flag into the cannon's mouth, reeled and fell! A Cheer broke out from our men.

Stoneman concluded, "It's a sin to kill men like that." The scene dramatized white northerners' celebration of southern heroism at the heart of the soldiers' postwar reconciliation.[9]

In describing Cameron's charge, Dixon refers only to the "colours," making no specific reference to a Confederate flag. When he writes about "the Clan," it carries a triangular flag with a dragon on it, as the Ku Klux Klan had during Reconstruction. Dixon's novels never mention a Confederate flag. In contrast, his novels do include more than once the claim that postwar southerners honored only one flag, the American flag. A Confederate general wants his son to put his sword beneath the "flag of our fathers," the Stars and Stripes. The South, in Dixon's accounts, embraced that flag, not the Confederate flag, reinforcing Dixon's emphasis on reunion.[10]

If the war brought reunion, Reconstruction provoked renewed division. In the play *The Clansman*, Nathan Bedford Forrest is described as the unconquered hero of the South. In *The Leopard's Spots*, another character observes that if Robert E. Lee had known what would follow in Reconstruction, he would have taken to the Appalachian Mountains and continued the fight. Dixon then explains that southerners "expected to lose their slaves and repudiate the dogma of Secession forever. But they never dreamed of Negro domination or Negro deification, of Negro equality and amalgamation, now being rammed down their throats with bayonets."[11]

In response, white southerners organized the Clan and fought "Negro domination." Dixon carefully avoids portraying the battle as a continuation of the Civil War; he specifically labels it a "new Revolution" or "a second war." In exposing the presumed evils of Reconstruction, Dixon sought to create a new nationalism based in white supremacy. If he could not convince northerners to embrace his radical racism, he at least wanted them to appreciate the danger he saw in the Black man and to support, if not colonization, at least the rigid repressive racial order the South had begun to establish. Dixon sought to create, in recent academic terms, a sense of whiteness that would become the basis of nationalism. On its most fundamental, even primeval level, Dixon based that common whiteness on a fear of what he called "amalgamation." Dixon felt confident that white northerners shared white southerners' deep fear of Black sexuality and racial intermarriage. Dixon described Reconstruction as a battle over whether the nation would be Anglo-Saxon or mulatto—a formulation he offered twice. The preservation of whiteness through the "protection" of white women from "pollution" by Black men became the centerpiece of Dixon's vision, but he also experimented with other ways to promote a common whiteness.[12]

As his references to Anglo-Saxons indicated, Dixon sometimes sought to tie whiteness to ethnicity, as many did in the late nineteenth century. In other places in *The Leopard's Spots*, Dixon refers to southern whites as Anglo-Saxons. The novel portrays the Clan as the Anglo-Saxon response to Black rule and calls its riders Anglo-Saxon knights. Yet Dixon also includes in the novel several references to his characters' Scotch-Irish roots and one passing reference to the Aryan race. In a speech before a Democratic state convention, one of Dixon's champions of white supremacy stresses Anglo-Saxon dominance but then includes within that group the Celts, Danes, Franks, Gauls, Normans, Romans, Spartans, and Vikings. Dixon proved rather cavalier in defining Anglo-Saxon and the ethnic roots of whiteness.[13]

In *The Clansman*, he virtually reversed his use of ethnic identities. Anglo-Saxons all but disappear; white southerners become Scotch-Irish. Dixon dedicated the book to his uncle, the "Scotch-Irish Leader of the South," describes the Clan as "the reincarnated souls of the Clansman of Old Scotland." This explains why he used the word "Clan" rather than "Klan," save in the book's subtitle, which reads Ku Klux Klan, perhaps so there would be no doubt as to his subject. Dixon also refers to Nathan Bedford Forrest, who organizes the Clan, as the "great Scotch-Irish leader." If by "Scotch" Dixon meant Highland Scots, as he appears to, or included the Celts, as he does at one point, then he chose an ethnic group that warred with the Anglo-Saxons.[14]

In *The Clansman*, Dixon shaded ethnic identity into a religious one. Southerners were not cavaliers, he observed, but Covenanters, a Scottish Presbyterian band that fought the English, and Huguenots, a militant group of French Protestants. Dixon, who had deep Christian beliefs, thereby tied the cause of white supremacy and its chief defenders, the Ku Klux Klan, to militant Protestantism. Dixon introduced symbolism that subtly but powerfully reinforced the idea of militant Protestantism. In *The Clansman*, Dixon described the uniform of the Clan as a "white robe . . . made in the form of an ulster overcoat with cape, the skirt extending to the top of the shoes." Each Clansman also "wore a white cap, from the edges of which fell a piece of cloth extending to the shoulders"—all made of "cheap unbleached domestic" cloth. On each man's breast appeared "a scarlet circle within which shone a white cross," introducing the Protestant symbol of the cross to the Clan costume. The novel's title page featured a drawing of a Clansman with mask, white robe, and a prominent cross on his chest. Later in the book, another illustration featured two Clansmen in similar uniforms, one holding a burning cross. In Dixon's play, the Clansmen likewise wore very similar costumes, and carried a fiery cross.[15]

Dixon, in both the novel and the play, made the fiery cross a central symbol of whiteness. Its introduction follows the rape of a white virgin and her subsequent suicide. Her father takes the sand that her blood has drenched and puts it in a silver cup, shows it to the gathered Clan, and proclaims, "Brethren, I hold in my hand the water of your river bearing the red stain of the life of a Southern woman, a priceless sacrifice on the altar of outraged civilization." Ben Cameron, her brother and the head of the Clan, looks at the prostrate Black man who has raped his sister, then "seized the cross, lighted the three upper ends, and held it blazing in his hand." He calls on the Clansmen to murder the rapist and dump his body on the lawn of the Black lieutenant governor. Cameron then explains the cross:

> "In olden times when the Chieftain of our people summoned the clan on an errand of life and death, the Fiery Cross, extinguished in sacrificial blood, was sent by swift courier from village to village. The call was never made in vain, nor will it be to-night in the new world. Here, on this spot made holy ground by the blood of those we hold dearer than life, I raise the ancient symbol of an unconquered race of men—"
>
> High above his head, in the darkness of the cave he lifted the blazing emblem—
>
> "The Fiery Cross of old Scotland's hills! I quench its flames in the sweetest blood that ever stained the sands of Time."
>
> He dipped its ends in the silver cup, extinguishing the fire, and handed the charred symbol to the courier, who quickly disappeared.

On the stage, the scene played out much the same way, although without any reference to Scotland but only to clansmen in the hills.[16]

In incorporating the cross, Dixon drew on an ancient ritual. The *Oxford English Dictionary* contains references to "fiery cross" from 1587, 1615, and 1747, and twenty-first-century Scottish heritage societies still claim it. Dixon, however, probably borrowed it from Sir Walter Scott's long poem "The Lady of the Lake," which tells of the use of a fiery cross to rally a Scottish clan and describes its baptism in goat's blood. (Neither folklore, Scott, nor Dixon bother to relight the fiery cross after its baptism—a puzzling aspect of the ritual, since it means a smoldering not a flaming cross is handed to the messenger.) No doubt because of Scott's popularity, by the time Dixon wrote, carrying the fiery cross had become a common metaphor and a frequently employed image. In the antebellum years, abolitionists summoned people to follow the fiery cross in opposition to slavery, and at the start of the war, both northerners and southerners used its imagery. In 1861, for example, a Connecticut paper wrote, "Thousands upon thousands are rushing from every valley and hillside of the North, as if summoned by the ancient fiery cross, to support the government." After the war, Union general and Lost Cause nemesis Benjamin Butler used it as metaphor to describe calls for Union troops, and Republicans brought the metaphor out at election time. Over the course of the nineteenth century, the fiery cross had become not a Scottish or southern symbol but an American one.[17]

The symbolism of the fiery cross marked a shift away from the Lost Cause, in which the Confederate flag, which Dixon never mentioned, would have been a central symbol. Although Dixon's novels offered a southern view of Reconstruction, *The Leopard's Spots*—and even more, *The Clansman*—avoided a celebration of either the Old South or the Confederacy. Both novels assumed and promoted an American nationalism, resting on both the South's and the North's determination to preserve white women from "pollution" by Black males and society from Black crime and political participation. Black and white was the significant division for Dixon. He offered only a limited vision of an alternative definition of whiteness but hinted at a religious basis for whiteness by referring to Clansmen as "Covenanters," placing the cross on the Clan costume, and making a fiery cross a Clan symbol. In his movie, Griffith incorporated Dixon's vision of a renewed nationalism rooted in shared white supremacy and featured the fiery cross and Christian symbolism even more prominently.

THE RADICAL RACISM IN Dixon's novels proved phenomenally popular; they sold an extraordinary number of copies, and not just in the South. When Dixon turned the second novel into a play, it faced more criticism for its racism than the book had and proved somewhat less popular. Nevertheless, *The Clansman's* combined success made it a promising story for a movie. Dixon himself first tried and failed to film a version of *The Clansman*; a second attempt by others failed as well. A decade would pass before an adaptation of Dixon's novels reached theaters.[18]

Reconstruction movies never became a genre, and only in 1908, according to film historian Eileen Bowser, did Civil War films become popular. At first, Civil War movies took a decidedly pro-northern view, she argues, but "producers soon discovered that the more romantic, noble, and heroic ideals to be found in the defeated South were attractive to both North and South. . . . From 1911 on, the films that seem to reflect a Southern point of view" outnumbered by 2 to 1 those that took a northern perspective. These films did not claim the South had "been correct politically, of course, but only that the film's heroes and heroines are the Confederates." They also commonly featured faithful slaves. If Bowser is right, northern audiences helped make a film like *Birth of a Nation* possible.[19]

Frank Woods, who at the time wrote scenarios for D. W. Griffith and had worked on one of the earlier attempts to film *The Clansman,* suggested that Griffith make a movie from Dixon's story. Griffith at once embraced the project. He and Harry and Roy Aitken, the brothers who owned his production company, met with Dixon and reached an agreement to secure the rights. The production team that would make and market the movie did not consist solely of white southerners. Woods, crucial in deciding to make the movie, in filming the movie, and in advertising it, came from Pennsylvania. The Aitken brothers, who raised much of the money for the movie and who one of them claimed should be given as much credit for it as Griffith and Dixon, had ties to southerners but grew up and lived in Wisconsin. Billy Bitzer, the cameraman, and his assistant, Karl Brown, both grew up in the North. The score, which some critics maintained proved crucial to the movie's success, resulted from a collaboration between Griffith and Joseph Carl Breil, another Pennsylvanian. The advertising campaign, which played an important role in the movie's reception, was led by Theodore Mitchell and J. R. McCarthy of the Shubert Theatre in New York. Mitchell had initially refused to take the job, but quickly agreed after seeing the movie. It may be that not all of these people thought making the movie a good idea. Bitzer "figured that a crazed Negro chasing a white girl-child" would be just another hack picture. "I was from Yankee country and to me the KKK was sillier than the Mack Sennett comedy chases." Brown, son of a Union veteran, dismissed Dixon's work as both racist and a typical celebration of the Confederacy. Both Bitzer and Brown, however, offered these observations many years later, long after public attitudes about the movie had changed.[20]

Of course, the two southerners, Dixon and Griffith, had no reservations whatsoever and had the greatest influence on the movie. Dixon played an important role in publicizing the movie, but he actually had surprisingly little direct influence on the plotting or shooting of the picture. His racist vision, drawn primarily from his play and the novel *The Clansman*, did provide the basis for the second half of the movie, on Reconstruction. Griffith added the first half on the Civil War and shaped the second on Reconstruction as well. Roy Aitken, who worked closely with Griffith on the film, found both Dixon and Griffith "deeply sympathetic to the problems of the South" and thought they wanted to show "the tortuous rebirth of their beloved homeland." Bitzer claimed that *Birth of a Nation* "was not just another picture for Griffith. He was fighting the old war all over again and, like a true Southerner, trying to win it or at least justify losing." Griffith's ties to the South clearly played a role, but the director produced a movie with a very different emphasis.[21]

Griffith was born in Kentucky in 1875, almost at the end of Reconstruction, and grew up there. In seeing the movie as Griffith refighting the war, Bitzer and a host of critics pointed not just to Griffith's Kentucky background but also to the influence of his father, "Roaring Jake," a Confederate veteran. The younger Griffith recalled hearing his father's war stories, although he would have only to age twelve, when his father died. Griffith also remembered his father's sword, which some scholars have made central to Griffith's Lost Cause vision and the movie itself. The specific story Griffith associated with the sword had nothing to do with a great battle or a heroic charge, only a bad haircut. One of the family's African American workers had taken the young Griffith into town to get his hair cut. When they returned, Roaring Jake did not care for his son's new, modern look. So he grabbed the old sword, threatened the Black man, and chased him around the yard—all to the delight of his son.[22]

Griffith's devotion to the Lost Cause can easily be exaggerated. For the subject of his first historical movie, he chose the American Revolution, and he made a host of Westerns, which were popular, before he made a Civil War movie. He began making them about the time they, too, became popular. Not all the Civil War films he made fit neatly into the Lost Cause celebration. His 1910 *House with Closed Shutters* told the story of a Confederate courier who deserts and flees to his home. His mother takes him in, tells everyone he has died in battle, and even after the war, hides him in their house. When the son deserts, his sister dons a Confederate cloak and delivers the message he was supposed to carry to the troops. Once she gets to the battlefield, she picks up a fallen Confederate battle flag and charges the Union lines, only to be shot.

In *Swords and Hearts,* which came out a year after *House with Closed Shutters,* a Confederate officer visiting an aristocratic woman ties up his horse outside her home. A poor white woman sees the Yankees approaching and takes the officer's cloak and horse. She leads the Yankees away from the house and thereby saves the officer. When he returns at the end of the war, the aristocratic woman he planned to marry has wed a northerner. The intertitle or title card, the printed text filmed and inserted in a silent movie, reads, "Defeated in war, rejected in love." The officer then marries the woman who had earlier impersonated and saved him. The Lost Cause rarely featured stories of Confederate cowards, cross-dressing females in battle, or southern women marrying Yankees.

Other of Griffith's early Civil War films did feature Lost Cause themes, perhaps most clearly *His Trust,* which included heroic Confederate armies at war. The film's sequel, *His Trust Fulfilled,* focused on the loyalty of a former slave, a theme with echoes in *Birth of a Nation.* In the earlier film, a loyal slave returns after the war and restores his fallen master's sword to its place in the home—a particularly interesting way to show African American loyalty, given the memory Griffith associated with his father's sword.[23]

Like *His Trust Fulfilled, Birth of a Nation* fit relatively easily but not completely into the Lost Cause narrative, in many ways more closely than Dixon's novels. Like Dixon, Griffith had little interest in glorifying the Old South. *Birth of a Nation* includes the requisite cotton fields with happy slaves at work. The "manor house," however, sits right on a town street, with its front elevation looking more like a middle-class dwelling than a plush plantation home. Unlike Dixon, who wrote little about the war itself, Griffith devotes almost half his movie to it. He begins it with the Africans brought to America, a hint that the war was about slavery, then quickly implies that the abolitionists' crusade for emancipation led to the war. After that, he explicitly states that the South fought for state sovereignty. He renders the South the victim of northern aggression and makes it very clear that the Confederate cause was just. These points hewed closely to Lost Cause tradition, as did his portrayal of the Confederate soldiers as brave, heroic, fearsome warriors.[24]

Even in the Civil War sections, however, Griffith incorporated strong reconciliationist themes, more so than Dixon's novels had. Like *The Clansman, Birth of a Nation* centers on two families, the southern aristocrats, the Camerons, and the northern abolitionists, the Stonemans. The sons of the two families become chums at boarding school, and before the war, the Stoneman boys have an idyllic visit at the Camerons' home. When the war comes, the sons of the families march off to war, the Camerons with the Confederacy and the Stonemans with the Union. During the war they come together. In an almost homoerotic image of brotherhood, a young Stoneman dies in the arms of a Cameron, uniting in death the families that symbolized each section.

Griffith also dramatized the story told in Dixon's *The Clansman* of Ben Cameron's charge toward the Union line. In the film as in the novel, Ben Cameron temporarily halts the charge to provide water to a wounded Union soldier. He then resumes his attack, and when he reaches the Union lines is halted, but not before he rams a Confederate flag into the mouth of a Union cannon. The Yankees cheer both his succor for their fellow soldier and his heroic charge. Stoneman, his friend who commands the Union defensive line, saves him from Union fire and takes him prisoner instead. Later, Elsie Stoneman, Phil's sister, ministers to Ben as a prisoner of war, and at the request of his mother, Abraham Lincoln pardons him from the charge of being a guerrilla.

In the movie's second half, Griffith provides additional images of reconciliation, in particular in a story line that appears in neither Dixon's play nor his novel. Toward the end of the movie, African American troops are chasing Cameron's father because he has shot a federal soldier. Befriended by white Union veterans, who have a young daughter with them, Cameron, his wife and daughter, and a former Cameron slave take refuge in the Union soldiers' log cabin. In that prototypical American symbol, they constitute a microcosm of a new America. They join together to hold off an attack by Black troops until they are rescued by the Clan. White supremacy restored, the movie ends with not one but two intersectional marriages: a Stoneman son marrying a Cameron daughter, and a Cameron son marrying the Stoneman daughter who had nursed him when he was a prisoner of war.[25]

In having the two families united in marriages, Griffith employed a trope central to sectional reconciliation, though he went further. In many novels and stories, reconciliation came through the marriage of a northern man and a southern woman; he has that, but also has a southern man marrying a northern woman. And the movie's very last title card quotes Daniel Webster, "LIBERTY AND UNION, one and inseparable, now and forever." The quote serves to emphasize the movie's main point: the nation had been saved and reunited by the Clan.[26]

The name of the movie, after all, was *The Birth of a Nation*—a title suggested by Dixon after watching the film. Griffith, like Dixon, sought in part to show the North what the South had experienced and thereby to evoke sympathy for the region and its racial practices. The movie follows the white South's views and those of contemporary white scholars, including Woodrow Wilson and William A. Dunning, by interpreting Reconstruction as a tragic mistake. It portrays African Americans as incapable of exercising or even understanding the franchise. When the movie is not treating African Americans as buffoons and toadies, it portrays them as brutal sexual predators after white women. The film does feature a few faithful Black servants, including one in the cabin. Griffith probably was not as radical a racist as Dixon but rather what Williamson termed a conservative racist, one who saw the possibility of a subservient role for Black people in America, but he was a white supremacist nonetheless. Like Dixon's novels, *Birth of a Nation*'s presentation of African Americans offered a justification for white supremacy.[27]

Also like Dixon, Griffith did not ground white supremacy in the Confederacy or the Lost Cause because like Dixon he had no desire to refight the Civil War, save when he filmed battle scenes. He gave far less attention than Dixon had to a racial identity based on ethnicity. He never mentions the Anglo-Saxons and makes only a passing reference to Scotland's hills. One intertitle does refer to an "Aryan birthright," an identity Dixon had barely mentioned and that Griffith never develops. As historian Matthew Frye Jacobson rightly observed, *Birth of a Nation* "rested upon the dualism of black and white." For Griffith, like Dixon, the purity of white women symbolized that dualism. The movie has frequent references to the goal of the Black Republicans being intermarriage, and its plot and the Clan's role in it revolves around not one but two threats to white womanhood.[28]

One threat involves the daughter of Austin Stoneman. Stoneman, modeled after the abolitionist and Republican radical Thaddeus Stevens, plots the African American domination of the South. Stoneman's Black protégé, Silas Lynch, wants to marry Stoneman's daughter, Elsie. Despite her earlier support for the Republicans' drive for Black equality, the daughter rejects the proposal and fights when Lynch tries to kiss her. He then holds her hostage and plans a forced marriage. Stoneman himself at first accepts the idea of Lynch marrying a white woman, but when he learns it is *his* daughter, he goes berserk. When it came to intermarriage, Griffith implies, northerners think about Black people much like southerners do. Even before that, Stoneman's son, a Union veteran, has joined the Camerons' fight against Black Republican rule.

The other threat to white womanhood leads to the initial gathering of the Clan and becomes the movie's centerpiece: the chase of Flora Cameron, a virginal symbol of carefree girlhood, by Gus, the former slave turned into a sinister danger by the Radical Republicans' empowerment of African Americans. Much has been written about this chase. Some scholars and critics, particularly those who want to make *Birth of a Nation* seem a little less racist, minimize the threat Gus presents. They point to Gus's comment to Flora, "I won't hurt yeh," and other aspects of the staging to assign Gus more benign motives than rape. Historian Russell Merritt, whose study of the film is often insightful, even described Gus's pursuit as "curiously restrained" and a "scene structured to include the possibility of a tragic misunderstanding." The NAACP and others who protested the movie's distribution did not agree. They forced some changes to the chase, but even after these deletions, it still involves a Black man intending to rape a white virgin. To avoid that fate, Flora jumps off a cliff.[29]

Griffith clearly sought to incorporate Dixon's image of the "Black beast" rapist into the film. Gus, as film critic Richard Schickel observed, runs doubled over and therefore appears more like an animal than a human. Karl Brown, who helped shoot the movie, reported that Griffith provided peroxide for Gus to drink so he would therefore literally foam at the mouth, which can be seen twice in the movie. At the time he filmed the scene, Brown thought Gus ran "with a low, stooped gait," almost like a hound with his nose to the ground. Later, when he watched it, Brown decided Gus resembled a shambling gorilla. In a list of scenes shot, someone titled the chase sequence "Claw of the beast," and in the negotiations with the mayor of San Francisco over cutting scenes from the movie, one of the people demanding changes referred to the chase sequence as "the rape situation."[30]

Birth of a Nation, in sum, followed Dixon in emphasizing Black sexual outrages, the horrors of Republican rule, and white southern suffering during Reconstruction—even as it celebrated the victory of the Ku Klux Klan. Like Dixon, Griffith also minimized the role of Confederate memory as a basis of white supremacy and stressed the healing of wartime divisions. The movie celebrates the birth of a new nation based on a shared white supremacy tied to opposition to intermarriage and an obsessive commitment to white female purity. Griffith, though, also associated white supremacy with two symbols, one that Dixon had ignored, the Confederate flag, and another that he had introduced, the fiery cross. Griffith baptized both in the blood of a white virgin, but then the flag does not appear again in the movie, whereas the fiery cross appears often as a Clan symbol. The new Ku Klux Klan that formed as the movie appeared and whose growth it encouraged followed the same pattern; it adopted the cross and eschewed the Confederate flag.

Griffith devoted half his movie to the Civil War, whether from a desire to tell his father's story, the realization that Civil War movies had become very popular, or the artistic challenge of filming battle scenes. Once he decided to make the war central, he could not avoid the Confederate flag as Dixon had. But which Confederate flag to use? Some historians argue that by 1915, if not before the war ended, the Confederate battle flag had become *the* Confederate flag. A case can be made that it was not yet as central a symbol either of the Lost Cause or of white supremacy as it would later become. During and after Reconstruction, it had occasionally been used on behalf of political causes; generally, though, southerners displayed the flag primarily on ceremonial or memorial occasions. Dixon, after all, claimed not to have seen one in twenty-three years. White southerners still recognized and flew different Confederate flags.

What would become the most accepted Confederate flag, a square flag that featured the Saint Andrew's cross on a red field, was actually the battle flag flown by many Confederate armies. The Confederacy's first official national flag had one red, one white, and one blue stripe, with a circle of stars in a blue field in its corner. It became known as the Stars and Bars. The Confederate government later adopted a second national flag that put the battle flag in the corner of a white field. When that flag proved problematic—it could easily be confused with a white flag of surrender—they kept the same design but added a red bar at the end of the white field. In early Civil War movies, the battle flag appeared most often, but others did as well. Griffith's earlier films had used the battle flag, although in *The House with Closed Shutters* Lee's camp flew both the battle flag and the Stars and Bars.[31]

Almost everyone who worked with Griffith on *Birth of a Nation* commented on his determination to ensure historical accuracy, and his research included several books with pictures that included flags. *Battles and Leaders of the Civil*

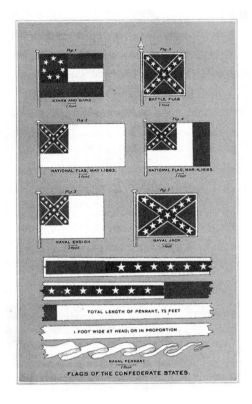

Flags of the Confederacy.
(From United Confederate Veterans,
The Flags of the Confederacy, 1907)

War had pictures of the Stars and Bars, but more of its photographs featured the battle flag. *The Soldier in Our Civil War* featured a picture of the Stars and Bars with the caption "The Flag of the Confederacy" and included many pictures of it flying (mostly over fixed installations), although other images showed the battle flag. The book also included a picture of the city of Petersburg with the second flag of the Confederacy flying above it. Still another source Griffith consulted, *Frank Leslie's Illustrated History of the Civil War,* had pictures that incorporated the Stars and Bars, the battle flag, and the second flag of the Confederacy. It included an illustration of the Battle of Petersburg that showed either the second or the third (it is impossible to make out whether the red bar appears) flying over Confederate lines.[32]

Like the picture books he consulted, Griffith used several different Confederate flags in his movie: a perhaps invented state flag, the Stars and Bars, the third official flag of the Confederacy, the Confederate battle flag, and a small, rectangular version of the battle flag. Toward the beginning of the movie, the state flag is introduced by a title card reading "The Spirit of the South," and the flag itself features the motto "Conquer we must—Victory or death—for our cause is just." It hangs in the Camerons' parlor but does not reappear in the movie. The battle flag plays a surprisingly limited role in the movie's Civil War scenes. A brief glimpse of it, carried by some cavalry troops, appears as they prepare to march off to war at the beginning of the movie. Later, in two scenes, a supply train cut off from the action at Petersburg carries a battle flag that hardly moves. In the movie's most dramatic battle scenes, during the confrontation at Petersburg, the shots of the Confederate forces include numerous vigorously waving third official flags, with their white fields and red bars.[33]

Third official flag of the Confederacy flown over the battlefield.
(Still image from *The Birth of a Nation*)

Griffith makes more of the Stars and Bars than either of the other two Confederate flags. He introduces it with the intertitle "The first flag of the Confederacy baptized in glory at Bull Run." A long shot of Ben and a young woman holding up the flag follows, and then a close-up of the flag. Men and women at a farewell ball for the troops toast and cheer the flag. When the summons to duty comes and the soldiers mount up and ride off to war, the Stars and Bars flies prominently at the head of their column. A later scene of the parents and family grieving the troops' departure includes not one but two Stars and Bars flags. Much later in the movie, it reappears, in the scene in which Ben Cameron charges the Union lines. When a color bearer falters, Cameron stops and picks up a fallen banner. Even though the Confederates in the battle lines had waved the third flag of the Confederacy, and even though the color bearer left those lines with the same banner, when he falters and falls, Ben picks up not the third flag but a tattered Stars and Bars, the first official flag of the Confederate government. It is this flag that he rams into the mouth of a Union cannon, marking the high point of Confederate valor in the movie but also signaling an end to its cause.[34]

Cameron spikes a Union cannon with the Stars and Bars.
(Still image from *The Birth of a Nation*)

Even before the scenes with the Stars and Bars, *Birth of a Nation* introduces a very different Confederate flag in a starkly different context. Shortly before he rides off to war, Ben Cameron teases his youngest sister, Flora, with a small Confederate battle flag. One scholar has called it a "miniature" flag and compared it to a handkerchief. It was clearly rectangular, unlike the original battle flag, and probably twenty-four or so inches long. It looks eerily like the battle flags that became popular in the 1950s and were so often waved by angry white segregationist mobs. At this point in *Birth of a Nation*, Ben hardly treats it with reverence; he dangles it over his sleeping sister's face and tickles her with it. The small flag certainly does not evoke the sense of awe that the Stars and Bars commands a few scenes later. When Flora wakes, she grabs it and later clutches it to her chest as Ben leaves for war.

Cameron dangles a small battle flag over Flora's head.
(Still image from *The Birth of a Nation*)

This flag reappears only much later, during Reconstruction, when Ben wants Flora, in the room where her mother and sister are sewing Clan robes, to promise not to betray the Clan. She leaves and returns with the small Confederate battle flag draped over her shoulder and pledges her loyalty and silence. Shortly thereafter, she appears with the flag wrapped and tied around her waist—again, treatment that hardly suggests a revered or sacred banner. She wears it as she leaves for the spring and throughout the chase by Gus. When Griffith first shot the chase scenes, Mae Marsh, who played Flora, forgot to tie the flag around her waist. Griffith insisted on reshooting the sequence. When Flora jumps off the cliff, Ben finds her, wipes her face with the flag, and clutches it to her as he hugs her. She then dies in his arms.[35]

After Gus's murder, when the Clan gathers, Ben takes Flora's battle flag and dips it twice into a basin. The following title card reads, "Brethren, this flag bears the red stain of the life of a Southern woman, a priceless sacrifice on the altar of an outraged civilization." This battle flag's baptism evokes comparisons with the movie's earlier references to the baptism of the Stars and Bars, the official flag of the Confederacy. It had been baptized in the glory of the soldiers, and presumably in their blood. It served as the flag of not just its armies but also its government; it was directly tied it to the Confederacy and its independence, and when spiked in the cannon's mouth, it symbolized the end of the Confederate nation. Now a battle flag that had never gone to war had been baptized in the blood of a white virgin, symbolically associating it with white womanhood and the attendant white supremacy. It had been reborn as a symbol of white supremacy. Its ties to the Confederacy and the fight to preserve slavery obviously persisted, but its association with a white supremacy, independent of Confederate nationalism, had been enhanced.[36]

Cameron baptizes the small battle flag in Flora's blood.
(Still image from *Birth of a Nation*)

But Griffith—and as it turned out, Americans—would only hold that symbol in reserve. After its baptism, the flag disappears from the movie. When the Clan rides in *Birth of a Nation,* it does not carry the Confederate flag but one with a dragon on it, a flag barely visible in the movie and one few today would recognize. The Clan, as in Dixon's account, prominently displays the fiery cross, and after the movie came out, it would become the central totem of a new Klan.

At the same Clan gathering in which Griffith has the battle flag baptized, he follows Dixon more closely in baptizing a cross. Right after the flag, Ben takes the cross in his hand and dips it in the same basin filled with Flora's blood. The title card explains, "Here I raise the ancient symbol of an unconquered race of men, the fiery cross of old Scotland's hills. I quench its flames in the sweetest blood that ever stained the sands of Time." After their baptisms, Ben hands not the Confederate flag but the cross to a rider and sends him to gather the Clans. A lighted cross will appear several more times. *Birth of a Nation* makes the cross far more of a symbol of white supremacy than the battle flag, and makes far more use of it than Dixon had.[37]

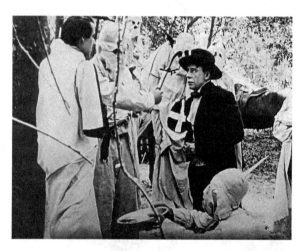

After baptizing the flag and a flaming cross, Cameron hands only the cross to the rider. (Still image from *The Birth of a Nation*)

In a scene right after the Clan proclaims Gus guilty and shortly before the cross's baptism, Clansmen gather with a small, burning wooden cross standing among them. A larger burning cross, planted in the ground, briefly appears in the midst of the Clan gathering where the baptism of the flag and smaller cross takes place. In *Birth of a Nation*, flaming crosses standing alone mark Clan gatherings. No such uses of the cross occurred in Dixon's novels, but it would become common in the twentieth-century Ku Klux Klan. Still another small cross appears stuck in the ground at a trail crossing where the rider sent to summon the Clans stops to meet fellow riders. And the cross serves not just to summon but also to lead the Clan. In the midst of Lynch's proposal and attack on Elsie Stoneman, Griffith intercuts scenes of mounted Clansmen carrying the fiery cross as they ride to retake the town and, as it turns out, to rescue Elsie.

All the Clansmen in the movie wear robes similar to those described by Dixon. Rather than the ulster overcoat, though, they appear in flowing white robes. They resemble the sheets after which they were modeled. Griffith explains the inspiration for the Clan's robes in a scene in which young white children, hiding under a sheet, scare several young Black children. Ben Cameron sees them and adopts the disguise for the Clan. Griffith followed Dixon more closely in putting on the chests of those white robes a large red circle, and within it a white cross. Officers, like Ben Cameron, wore robes with two circles, each with crosses. All rode horses that had white sheets across their backs, again with a circle and a cross in the middle, and even had white hoods with eyeholes. The flowing white robes with their crosses repeatedly filled the screen, and the movie rendered the Clansmen Christian knights.

In the cross, Griffith had chosen a symbol closely identified with Protestantism. He reinforced the repeated use of both the flaming crosses and the cross on the Clansmen's robes with visions of Jesus at the end of the movie. Some critics have explained Jesus's appearance as an appeal for peace in an antiwar movie. A Congregationalist magazine editorial of the time, critical of the film's racism, described the scene as "representing allegorically the birth of the nation in a group of all white people over which appears the figure of Christ in benediction." White-clad knights bearing crosses had saved—or as Griffith saw it, created—a nation, and Jesus's benediction strengthened the evocation of a white Protestant nationalism.[38]

While critics have made much of the influence of Griffith's father and his Lost Cause tales in shaping his son's historical vision, few have said much about his mother's influence. He was, Griffith wrote in his autobiography, "raised by women who were all very religious." As a child, when walking to school during a sleet storm, he thought he saw the face of Jesus in an ice-laden branch lit by the sun. As a youngster, his mother took him to camp meetings, and in the 1919 movie *A Romance of Happy Valley*, he filmed one. A visitor to the set, who watched the action, said Griffith could have been evangelist Dwight L. Moody. For a time as a young adult, Griffith sold subscriptions to the *Baptist Weekly*. A hard drinker and womanizer, Griffith may not have been religious himself, but he certainly was quite comfortable with religious imagery. Someone who saw Jesus in an icicle could readily offer an image of Jesus blessing the nation.[39]

Advertising for *Birth of a Nation* reinforced the emphasis on nationalism rather than sectionalism and often featured the fiery cross. In southern cities, robed Clansmen sometimes appeared for the premiere, and people dressed as southern belles and Confederate soldiers served as ushers. In New York and other northern cities, women ushers also dressed in antebellum costumes, but men donned either Confederate or Union uniforms. On at least a few occasions, Grand Army of the Republic chapters were invited to attend for free, and newspaper stories told how Griffith had sought the help of northern veterans in making the movie. A 1917 color postcard advertising the movie made the message explicit by featuring a Union and a Confederate veteran shaking hands over a chasm. They stood under American flag bunting that framed the card; pictures of Lee and Grant anchored the bunting.[40]

Newspaper ads did not offer such explicit emphasis on sectional reunion. The most common newspaper ad featured a huge black ball, exactly why is not clear, and enthusiastic praise for the movie. When *Birth of a Nation* opened in a city or town, papers often published still shots from different parts of the movie. They occasionally featured mounted Confederate soldiers, possibly flying a Confederate battle flag. More often, they included a battle scene with the third flag of the Confederacy, or Cameron's spiking of the cannon. In each case, with the poor reproduction, someone might have thought they were seeing the battle flag. Papers also reprinted images of robed Clansmen, with the cross clearly featured on their chests. The most widely used poster advertising *Birth of a Nation* featured a mounted Clansman, horse reared, cross clearly visible on his chest and on his horse's blanket, holding in his hand a fiery cross—much more the Christian knight than a sectional warrior. It became the Ku Klux Klan's iconic image.

Birth of a Nation's release immediately set off tremendous controversy. Led by the NAACP, African Americans and their liberal allies attacked the film's horrendous and pervasive racism. They protested its exhibition and demanded it be banned. A few cities did ban it for a time, and Kansas and Ohio for a longer period. The campaign forced changes in the movie, although the removal of a few scenes hardly diminished the movie's racism. The protests centered on the film's racism and its encouragement of violence against African Americans, but some critics also pointed to its treatment of the Civil War.

One of the foremost African American newspapers of the time published a letter from a Grand Army of the Republic leader that criticized *Birth of a Nation* for making the South look right and the North wrong. An Ohio paper quoted the report of a local Grand Army of the Republic post and offered a

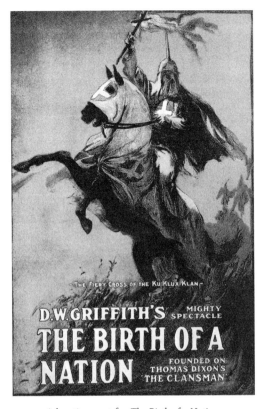

Advertisement for *The Birth of a Nation*.

similar critique: "The main point of the play seems to be to show that as to slavery and secession the South was altogether right, and that in the civil war and reconstruction the men who defended the Union were wholly wrong." A Kansas newspaper, discussing the movie and Dixon's novels, similarly claimed their "purpose is to degrade the Negro and the Union soldiers and boost the 'lost cause' of the rebels and portray to the American people that Jeff Davis and his gang were right."[41]

Many northern moviegoers left not outraged but with what they described as a new appreciation for the views and suffering of the South, which no doubt pleased Dixon, who sought just that, along with support for his and the Democratic Party's views on race. Historian Thomas Cripps, in his pioneering and insightful history of images of African Americans in early cinema, contended that *Birth of a Nation* and other movies helped southerners convert northerners to their Lost Cause and racial views. In a 1996 essay, however, Cripps repudiated that interpretation. Influenced by African American historian John Hope Franklin's work, he acknowledged that white northerners did not need to be converted. Facing the influx of African Americans during the First Great Migration, and fearing the new immigration, they shared the white South's white supremacy.[42]

The movie's national reception can hardly be interpreted any other way. *Birth of a Nation* had lengthy runs in cities across the country and continued to circulate for several years. The audiences that flocked to the movie did not just watch, they cried, they applauded, they cheered. One northern critic complained that when he saw the movie, "the crowd cheered the Stars and Bars and it was not moved by the Stars and Stripes. It applauded 'Dixie' and greeted 'Marching Through Georgia' with silence." The popular response to *Birth of a Nation* testified to an embrace of sectional reconciliation and the growth of a nationalism based on a shared sense of whiteness. The movie encouraged the Confederate battle flag's association with white supremacy, which the audiences cheered, rather than Confederate nationalism, and people interpreted the fiery cross as a new, powerful symbol of white Protestant nationalism. A new Ku Klux Klan took up the fiery cross and its message, further popularizing this white Protestant nationalism.[43]

WILLIAM J. SIMMONS FOUNDED the modern KKK in 1915, shortly before *Birth of a Nation* premiered in Atlanta, where he lived, and the new Klan developed a "symbiotic" relationship with the movie. Although Dixon condemned the Klan and Griffith avoided association with it, *Birth of a Nation* did contribute to the growth of this new Klan, which had no direct ties to that of Reconstruction. Yet Dixon's and Griffith's imagery became so thoroughly identified with the Klan that people often assume the use of flowing white robes and fiery crosses originated during Reconstruction. Even historians' books confuse the issue. The 1971 paperback edition of Allen W. Trelease's study of the Reconstruction Klan featured a flaming cross on its cover, and more recently, Jill Lepore's history of the United States illustrates its discussion of the 1860s Klan with the cover of a 1916 Klan pamphlet emblazoned with an image of a mounted Klan horseman holding a fiery cross.[44]

Yet Reconstruction-era Klansmen did not burn crosses; they also rarely dressed in white flowing robes with crosses on their chests as the Clansmen in *Birth of a Nation* did. One Reconstruction Klan leader in North Carolina decorated his robe with a cross; others did not. A few wore white robes or clothing. Most did not. In choosing their disguises, historian Elaine Franz Parsons shows, Reconstruction-era Klansmen drew most heavily on northern minstrel shows. They wore costumes of various cuts and many colors—red and black among them—with all sorts of decorations on them. The modern image of Klansmen in white robes and hoods, with crosses on the robe, gathered around a burning cross, originated in the twentieth century, not during Reconstruction.[45]

Simmons did claim that the Klan costumes served as a "memorial" to the original Klan and that during his youth African Americans had told him of its ghostly disguises, but such stories probably represented his attempt to exploit the memory of the earlier Klan. When *Birth of a Nation* premiered in Atlanta, Simmons published an ad for the new Klan that featured a drawing of a Klansman that closely resembled the movie's poster. The Klan of the 1920s adopted much of its symbolism from Dixon's book and Griffith's movie. Like them, the modern Klan made little appeal to the Confederate past and no use of the Confederate flag. It adopted as its banner a triangular flag with a dragon on it. Much more often the Klan flew the American flag, which was required to be present at Klan meetings. The modern Klan's costumes owed little to Reconstruction and instead drew from Dixon's and Griffith's vision and featured the flowing white robes with a cross in a red circle, albeit a smaller one than in the movie. The Klan also made the fiery cross a powerful symbol, perhaps the order's central one. It thereby did much to enhance a vision of national identity associated with white Protestantism.[46]

The first cross burning in Atlanta occurred before the Klan formed. In 1913, Leo Frank, the Jewish owner of an Atlanta pencil factory, was convicted of the murder of Mary Phagan, a young girl who worked in his factory. After Frank's many failed appeals, the governor of Georgia commuted his death sentence in 1915, but a mob then broke Frank out of prison and lynched him. Two months later, a group calling itself the Knights of Mary Phagan burned a large cross on Stone Mountain in Georgia. The November before *Birth of a Nation* opened in Atlanta, Simmons officially organized the new Klan with a cross burning atop Stone Mountain. Why both groups chose Stone Mountain, besides its physical size and local prominence, is not clear. It had no apparent ties to the original KKK. The previous year, talk of turning it into a Confederate memorial had begun, but nothing had been done to make that a reality.[47]

As the Klan grew, the fiery cross, an invented tradition of Dixon and Griffith, quickly became its central totem. On occasion it served the cause of vigilantism and intimidation. Klansmen burned crosses, for example, to intimidate an African American student at Columbia University and a Black family that moved into a white neighborhood. They placed crosses in front of Catholic churches and on a hill not far from where Catholic Al Smith made an address. Rather than just serving as a threat, though, the fiery cross proved far more important as a unifying symbol of patriotism and community, part of the ritual creation of a brotherhood. The 1920s Kloran, a sort of manual for Klan rituals, called for the cross to be central to the gathering of the Klavern. When asked, "What means the fiery cross?," members replied, "The emblem of that sincere, unselfish devotedness of all Klansmen to the sacred purpose and principles we have espoused." And, they added, "We serve and sacrifice for the right." In the long prayers that followed, they asked that "God save our Nation!" and "Keep ablaze in each Klansman's heart the sacred fire of a devoted patriotism to our country and its Government," by which they meant the national government, not a southern one.[48]

Klan meetings often occurred in fields or on hilltops, with members gathered around a huge, flaming cross. After the Klan's 1925 parade down Pennsylvania Avenue in Washington, D.C., it gathered by night around a tall fiery cross in a field across the Potomac. Ceremonies to induct new members almost always employed burning crosses. In Klan parades, a fiery cross often led the way. The fiery cross that Klansmen gathered around and that they followed served as symbol of their identity, one clearly tied to Protestantism. Some Klansmen also incorporated the symbol of a fiery cross into life's transitions, weddings and funerals. The Indiana Klan named its magazine *The Fiery Cross,* and the cover of a national one, *The Imperial Night-Hawk,* bore a picture of a Klansman almost identical to the iconic poster advertising *Birth of a Nation.* The Klan put the fiery cross on its stationery. One version had an image of a standing Klansman holding a fiery cross in front of a red background, with the title "Fiery Summons" at the top of the sheet. Another letterhead had on each side of the top a small drawing of a mounted Klansman carrying a flaming cross, an image again very much like the poster for *Birth of a Nation*. Klansmen also incorporated references to the symbol into songs; 78 RPM records featured musical homage to the fiery cross, such as "That Dear Old Fiery Cross," "The Bright Fiery Cross," and "The Cross in the Wildwood." The latter two songs, in an amazing syncretism of white supremacy and Protestantism, were set to the music of the popular Protestant hymns "The Old Rugged Cross" and "The Church in the Wildwood."[49]

In its rituals and public display, the Klan's use of the cross solidified the identification of a central symbol of the Protestant faith with white supremacy and an ethnic nationalism rooted in an identity as white Protestants. Neither the Klansmen, Griffith, nor Dixon had created that identity; many Americans had long seen themselves as part of a nation of white Protestants. But all three intensified that sense of identity, made it more militant, and gave it a new visible symbol. For many years the fiery cross, not the Confederate battle flag, served as perhaps the primary symbol of militant white supremacy.[50]

In the late 1930s, the battle flag, which Griffith had baptized in the blood of a white virgin, reemerged. By then, Thomas Dixon, a southern progressive turned reactionary, took to calling himself an "unreconstructed Rebel." In 1936, Eugene Talmadge of Georgia organized a mass meeting in opposition to Franklin D. Roosevelt and the New Deal, in part in hopes of promoting a presidential bid of his own. The man who had laughed at the idea that southerners still flew the Confederate flag spoke at a rally standing in front of a battle flag. Dixon appeared with segregationist Talmadge and the anti-Semitic firebrand Gerald L. K. Smith and delivered a speech in which he condemned a federal antilynching bill and Eleanor Roosevelt's outreach to African Americans. *Time* magazine described the rally as refighting the Civil War, and much later historian Jason Morgan Ward saw echoes of the Lost Cause in the movement Talmadge's rally helped to foster.[51]

But perhaps the Lost Cause was not so important to the flying of the Confederate flag after the late 1930s. Consciously or not, Griffith had helped make the battle flag less a symbol of the Confederacy and more a national symbol of white supremacy tied to a militant Protestantism. In the 1950s, the battle flag became the primary symbol of white supremacy and of the 1950s Klan, although the Klan still gathered around a burning cross. The battle flag also served as a banner for the anti-Semitism that became an increasing part of the

Klan's message, something foreign to the Lost Cause but easily incorporated into the 1920s Klan's white Protestant identity. In the early twenty-first century, the flag would also be readily adopted by white nationalist groups throughout the nation, not just in the former Confederacy.

Dixon and Griffith had helped to define and promote a symbol embraced by later white nationalists. They did not seek to revive the Confederacy or re-fight the Civil War; they sought to move beyond it. They embraced sectional reconciliation in the context of a nationalism based in white supremacy, and a white supremacy, in turn, identified with outraged white womanhood. They introduced, and identified with a martyred white virgin, a new symbol of white supremacy—the fiery cross. The 1920s Klan then used the cross in the cause of white Protestant nationalism, fueling a sense of ethnic identity. More than a century after *The Birth of a Nation* first drew mass audiences to the movies, that identity still exerts a powerful influence in the United States.

NOTES

1. Dick Lehr, *The Birth of a Nation: How a Legendary Filmmaker and a Crusading Editor Reig-nited America's Civil War* (New York: Public Affairs Press, 2014), 275. On *Birth of a Nation* in the context of South's promotion of the Lost Cause, see also Russell Merritt, "Dixon, Griffith, and the Southern Legend," *Cinema Journal* 12 (Autumn 1972): 26–45; Robert Lang, "The Birth of a Nation: History, Ideology, Narrative Form," in *The Birth of a Nation: D. W. Griffith, director*, ed. Lang (New Brunswick, N.J.: Rutgers University Press, 1994), 3–24; Melvyn Stokes, *D. W. Griffith's "The Birth of a Nation": A History of the "Most Controversial Motion Picture of All Time"* (New York: Oxford University Press, 2007); David Culbert, "Film History, Reconstruction, and Southern Legendary History in *The Birth of a Nation*," in *Hollywood and the American Historical Film*, ed. J. E. Smith (New York: Palgrave Macmillan, 2012), 11–25.

2. Joel Williamson, *The Crucible of Race: Black–White Relations in the American South Since Emancipation* (New York: Oxford University Press, 1984), 140–76 and passim. On Dixon's life and work, see also Raymond A. Cook, *Fire from the Flint: The Amazing Careers of Thomas Dixon* (Winston-Salem, N.C.: John F. Blair, 1968); Anthony Slide, *American Racist: The Life and Films of Thomas Dixon* (Lexington: University Press of Kentucky, 2004); W. Fitzhugh Brundage, "Thomas Dixon: 'American Proteus,'" in *Thomas Dixon Jr. and the Birth of Modern America*, ed. Michele K. Gillespie and Randal L. Hall (Baton Rouge: Louisiana State University Press, 2006), 23–45.

3. Thomas Dixon Jr., "'The Clansman,': Its Author, Thomas Dixon, Jr., Replies with Spirit and Good Humor to Some of His Critics," *New York Times*, February 25, 1905, 118. Interestingly, this was republished as "Comments Concerning 'The Clansman,'" *Confederate Veteran* 13 (May 1905): 227.

4. M. Karen Crowe, "Southern Horizons: The Autobiography of Thomas Dixon, A Critical Edition," (PhD diss., New York University, 1982), 270–71. Cook, *Fire from the Flint*, says Dixon was almost arrested, but his and other accounts do not mention the comment on Confederate flags (71).

5. "Treason Glorified," *Mail and Express* (New York), May 29, 1890, 1.

6. "Sectional Newspapers," *Daily Picayune* (New Orleans), June 6, 1890, 2.

7. On *Uncle Tom's Cabin*, see Crowe, "Southern Horizon," 360; and Cook, *Fire from the Flint*, 105–6. Thomas Dixon Jr., *The Leopard's Spots: A Romance of the White Man's Burden—1865–1900* (New York: Doubleday, Page, 1902); Dixon, *The Clansman: An Historical Romance of the Ku Klux Klan* (New York: Doubleday, Page, 1905); Dixon, *The Traitor: A Story of the Fall of the Invisible Empire* (New York: Doubleday, Page, 1907).

8. Dixon, *Leopard's Spots*, 26, 332; Dixon, *Clansman*, 256–57. For pictures of Cameron in the play, see the pamphlet *The Clansman by Thomas Dixon, Jr.* (New York: American News Company Publisher's Agents, n.d.), an advertisement for the play that included pictures from the New York opening. Available from Hathi Trust Digital Library, https://babel.hathitrust.org/cgi/pt?id=nc01 .ark:/13960/t5n87970b&view=1up&seq=7.

9. Cook, *Fire from the Flint*, 119; Dixon, *Leopard's Spots*, 34; Dixon, *Clansman*, 6–8.

10. Dixon, *Clansman*, 8, 332–33; *Leopard's Spots*, 13–14. For a picture of an original Klan flag, see the website of the American Civil War Museum, Richmond, Virginia, https://acwm.pastper fectonline.com. Dixon and Griffith both referred to the "Clan," and I have followed their spelling, save when the reference is to the actual Ku Klux Klan of the Reconstruction era or that founded in 1915 and active later.

11. Thomas Dixon Jr., "The Clansman: An American Drama," *Nineteenth Century Theatre and Film* 34, no. 2 (Winter 2007): 99–92; Dixon, *Leopard's Spots*, 136.

12. Dixon, *Leopard's Spots*, 83, 194, 333, 383. Other scholars have put Dixon's novels into the context of whiteness. See Scott Romine, "Thomas Dixon and the Literary Production of Whiteness," in Gillespie and Hall, *Thomas Dixon Jr. and the Birth of Modern America*, 124–50; R. Stephen Prince, *Stories of the South: Race and the Reconstruction of Southern Identity, 1865–1915* (Chapel Hill: University of North Carolina Press, 2014), 244–45.

13. Dixon, *Leopard's Spots*, 150, 441. On Anglo-Saxon, see also 24, 48, 122, 149, 154, 158, 200, 309, 329, 408, and 436–37; on Scotch-Irish, 122, 154, 175; on Aryan, 435.

14. Dixon, *Clansman*, 8, 295. On Scotch-Irish, see 101, 108, 187.

15. On Covenanters and Huguenots, see Dixon, *Clansman*, 129, 187, 315, 342, and unnumbered illustrations. Illustrator Arthur Ignatius Keller, born and based in New York City, drew the images in the book. For photographs from the play, see Dixon, "The Clansman: An American Drama."

16. Dixon, *Clansman*, 324–27; Dixon, "The Clansman: An American Drama," 107.

17. George B. Alton, ed., *Sir Walter Scott's Lady of the Lake* (New York: Allyn and Bacon, 1926), 68–70, 75–79. On Scott's influence on Dixon and Griffith, see James Chandler, "The Historical Novel Goes to Hollywood: Scott, Griffith, and Film Epic Today," in Lang, *Birth of a Nation*, 225–49. For examples of use of the fiery cross by antislavery forces, see "The Philadelphia Fair," *National Anti-Slavery Standard*, December 1, 1842, 3; "The Election," *National Anti-Slavery Standard*, October

31, 1844, 3; "Letter from Josiah Quincy," *National Anti-Slavery Standard,* June 7, 1856, 2. Also see "The Great Republican Meeting at Hamilton Yesterday," *Ohio State Journal* (Columbus), October 1, 1856, 2; "New England at the War," *Hartford Daily Courant,* September 17, 1861, 2; "Samuel Mc-Gowan," *The State* (Columbia, S.C.), August 12, 1897, 2. On Butler, see "Through Baltimore," *New York Herald,* August 4, 1869, 3; "Gen. Butler's Oration," *New York Times,* May 31, 1881. On use of the fiery cross by Republicans, see "The Big Time, the Republicans Had the City Last Night," *Register* (Wheeling, West Virginia), October 20, 1882, 4; "Are Ready to Bear Quay's Fiery Cross," *Philadelphia Inquirer,* July 12, 1897, 1.

18. Fred Silva, *Focus on The Birth of a Nation* (Englewood Cliffs, N.J.: Prentice-Hall, 1971), 3, 71–72; Cook, *Fire from the Flint,* 112, 131; Stokes, *D. W. Griffith's "The Birth of a Nation,"* 53–54.

19. Eileen Bowser, *The History of the American Cinema,* vol. 2: *1907–1915,* ed. Charles Harpole (New York: Charles Scribner's Sons, 1990), 177–79.

20. Stokes, *D. W. Griffith's "The Birth of a Nation,"* 81–109; "Growth and Development: Lecture by Frank Woods, The Academy of Motion Picture Arts and Sciences, at the University of Southern California, February 27, 1927," in *Introduction to the Photoplay,* ed. John C. Tibbetts (Shawnee Mission, Kans.: National Film Society, 1977), 48–50; Roy E. Aitken, as told to A. P. Nelson, *The Birth of a Nation Story* (Middleburg, Va.: Denlinger, 1965) 5, 25, 51–52; A. P. Nelson and Mel R. Jones, *A Silent Siren Song: The Aitken Brothers' Hollywood Odyssey, 1905–1926* (New York: Cooper Square Press, 2000), 25; G. W. Bitzer, *Billy Bitzer: His Story* (New York: Farrar, Straus and Giroux, 1973), 106; Karl Brown, *Adventures with D. W. Griffith,* ed. Kevin Brownlow (New York: Farrar, Straus and Giroux, 1973), 31–33.

21. Aitken, *Birth of a Nation Story,* 10; Bitzer, *Billy Bitzer,* 107.

22. On Griffith's life, see Robert M. Henderson, *D. W. Griffith: His Life and Work* (New York: Oxford University Press, 1972); Richard Schickel, *D. W. Griffith: An American Life* (New York: Simon and Schuster, 1984). For the sword story, see Robert E. Long, *David Wark Griffith: A Brief Sketch of His Career* (New York: D. W. Griffith Service, 1920), 25. Griffith himself recalled hearing Civil War stories as a youth. See D. W. Griffith, *The Man Who Invented Hollywood: The Autobiography of D. W. Griffith,* ed. James Haret (Louisville: Touchstone, 1972), 23; Henry Stephen Gordon, "The Story of David Wark Griffith, Part One," in *D. W. Griffith Interviews,* ed. Anthony Slide (Jackson: University Press of Mississippi, 2012), 31–32, 59; and Walter Huston, "Walter Huston Interviews D. W. Griffith," in Slide, *D. W. Griffith Interviews,* 187–88. On the emphasis on the sword, see Schickel, *D. W. Griffith,* 15–16; and for a very distinctive interpretation, see Michael Rogin, "'The Sword Became a Flashing Vision': D. W. Griffith's *The Birth of a Nation,*" in Lang, *Birth of a Nation,* 250–93.

23. *The House with Closed Shutters,* 1910; *Swords and Hearts, His Trust, His Trust Fulfilled,* and *The Battle,* 1911.

24. *The Birth of a Nation,* 1915. A complete copy is available on YouTube and also as a DVD, *The Birth of a Nation and the Civil War Films of D. W. Griffith,* Kino Video. See also John Cuniberti, *"The Birth of a Nation": A Formal Shot-by-Shot Analysis Together with Microfiche* (Meriden, Conn.: Research Publications, 1979). I will not give time references to the various scenes in the movie, but if quoting a title card, I will reference the appropriate page in Cuniberti. Seymour Stern and Linda Williams both point out that the house is not a feudal estate but of the Old South's middle class. Stern, "Griffith: The Birth of a Nation, Part I," *Film Culture* 36 (Spring-Summer 1965): 56;

Williams, *Playing the Race Card: Melodramas of Black and White from Uncle Tom to O.J. Simpson* (Princeton, N.J.: Princeton University Press, 2001), 117.

25. Cuniberti, *Birth,* 168. Both Schickel, *D. W. Griffith* (153–54), and Williams, *Playing the Race Card* (115), point out that Griffith often used scenes of people trapped in a cabin and in need of rescue.

26. On intersectional marriages, see Nina Silber, *The Romance of Reunion: Northerners and the South, 1865–1900* (Chapel Hill: University of North Carolina Press, 1993). Cuniberti, *Birth,* 168.

27. Williamson, *Crucible of Race.*

28. Cuniberti, *Birth,* 134, 142; Matthew Frye Jacobson, *Whiteness of a Different Color: European Immigrants and the Alchemy of Race* (Cambridge, Mass.: Harvard University Press, 1998), 118. Some scholars do stress the reference to an Aryan birthright and ethnic identity. See Stern, "Griffith," 160–61; and Everett Carter, "Cultural History Written with Lightning: The Significance of *The Birth of a Nation,*" *American Quarterly* 12 (Autumn 1960): 347–57. As with Jacobson and the argument here, several scholars have emphasized "whiteness" in the movie. See, for example, Daniel Bernardi, "The Voice of Whiteness: D. W. Griffith's Biograph Films (1908–1913)," in *The Birth of Whiteness: Race and the Emergence of U.S. Cinema,* ed. Bernardi (New Brunswick, N.J.: Rutgers University Press, 1996), 103–128; Richard Dyer, "Into the Light: The Whiteness of the South in *The Birth of a Nation,*" in *Dixie's Debates: Perspectives on Southern Culture,* ed. Richard H. King and Helen Taylor (New York: New York University Press, 1996), 165–176; Cedric J. Robinson, "In the Year 1915: D. W. Griffith and the Whitening of America," *Social Identities* 3 (June 1997), 161–92. Lang, "Birth of a Nation," also argues that protection of white womanhood is central to the movie (12 and passim).

29. Cuniberti, *Birth,* 123; Russell Merritt, "D. W. Griffith's *The Birth of a Nation:* Going After Little Sister," in *Close Viewings: An Anthology of New Film Criticism,* ed. Peter Lehman (Tallahassee: Florida State University Press, 1990), 227–28.

30. Dixon, *Leopard's Spots,* 125; Schickel, *D. W. Griffith,* 232; Brown, *Adventures,* 71, 94. Cuniberti, *Birth,* reproduces the list of scenes (174). An original is on microfilm edition, David W. Griffith Papers, Museum of Modern Art, New York (hereinafter cited as the Griffith Papers), reel 2; Eileen Bowers, "*Birth of a Nation* Script Notes," says that Lillian Gish thought "Claw of the beast" was one of the notes made by Jimmie Smith, a cutter, during production. Bowers, "Part of the proceedings of a meeting held before the Mayor at City Hall, Thursday morning, April 1, 1915, in reference to a motion picture film entitled 'The Birth of a Nation," Griffith Papers, reel 2. Along with Merritt, others have tried to make the chase less threatening. See Schickel, *D. W. Griffith,* 232; Paul O'Dell, "The Simplicity of True Greatness," in *Focus on D. W. Griffith,* ed. Harry M Geduld (Englewood Cliffs, N.J.: Prentice Hall, 1971), 92.

31. John M. Coski, *The Confederate Battle Flag: America's Most Embattled Emblem* (Cambridge, Mass.: Harvard University Press, 2005); Robert E. Bonner, *Colors and Blood: Flag Passions of the Confederate South* (Princeton, N.J.: Princeton University Press, 2002). The United Confederate Veterans, the United Daughters of the Confederacy, and the Sons of Confederate Veterans all used a different Confederate flag as their flag. The UCV still made a point of discussing the various flags. See, for example, United Confederate Veterans, *The Flags of the Confederate States of America* (New Orleans: William E. Mickle, 1907); and Walter A. Montgomery, "Flags of the Confederacy," *Confederate Veteran* 24 (June 1916): 196–98. I know of no systematic study of Confederate flags in

early movies. Most of the movies I have seen use the battle flag, but in addition to the exception mentioned above, *The Coward* (1915), which also featured the battle flag, and *Battle of Bull Run* (1913) prominently displayed the third flag of the Confederacy.

32. Stokes, *D. W. Griffith's "The Birth of a Nation,"* 176–77; Robert W. Johnson, *Battles and Leaders of the Civil War*, 4 vols. (New York: Century Company, 1887–1888); Paul F. Mottelay and T. Campbell-Copeland, *The Soldier in Our Civil War*, 2 vols. (New York: Stanley Bradley, 1890), 1:19 (on the flag), 2:274–75 (on Petersburg); Louis Shepheard Moat, ed., *Frank Leslie's Illustrated History of the Civil War* (1895; Fairfax, Va.: Fairfax Press, 1977), 488–89. Stokes and others mention Mathew Brady's photographs, but the collection of them published shortly before Griffith started the project did not have any pictures with flags. Bensel J. Lossing, *Mathew Brady's Illustrated History of the Civil War, 1861–65* (1912; Fairfax, Va.: Fairfax Press, 1978).

33. Cuniberti, *Birth*, 55.

34. Ibid., 53. Schickel considers this one of the great scenes of the movie. See Schickel, *D. W. Griffith*, 248.

35. Lillian Gish with Ann Pinchot, *Lillian Gish: The Movies, Mr. Griffith, and Me* (Englewood, N.Y.: Prentice-Hall, 1969), 139; Merritt, "D. W. Griffith: The Birth of a Nation," 225.

36. Cuniberti, *Birth*, 133. Scholars have paid surprisingly little attention to the baptism of the flag. Thomas Cripps wrongly says the cross is quenched by the flag. Cripps, *Slow Fade to Black: The Negro in American Film, 1900–1942* (New York: Oxford University Press, 1977), 50. Merritt, "D. W. Griffith," interprets it as "Flora and the South are resurrected" (227).

37. Cuniberti, *Birth*, 134.

38. Quote in *A Play with a Purpose* reprinted from *The Congregationalist and Christian World*, May 13, 1915, in Griffith Papers, reel 2. Others have pointed to the use of white Protestantism in the movie. See Stern, "Griffith," 159–60.

39. Parts of an autobiography, Griffith Papers, reel 2, 9 and 11; Long, *David Wark Griffith*, 107–9.

40. On ushers, see Arthur Lennig, "Myth and Fact: The Reception of 'The Birth of a Nation,'" *Film History* 16, no. 2 (2004): 123, 127. Stern, "Griffith," maintains that Confederate uniforms were used in the upper South, Klan dress in the lower South (78). On Union soldiers, see *Kansas City Journal*, November 21, 1915, Griffith Papers, reel 26; "Old Soldiers Are Invited to see 'The Birth of a Nation' at the Grand," Terre Haute, Indiana, January 6, 1916, Griffith Papers, reel 26; and "Soldiers of the Past and Present to See War Drama as Guests of the *Chronicle*," *Houston Chronicle*, February 1, 1916, Griffith Papers, reel 27. For 1917 postcard, see Ku Klux Klan Collection, box 1, file 12, Stuart A. Rose Manuscript, Archives, and Rare Book Library, Emory University, Atlanta. The Griffith Scrapbooks in the Griffith Papers are filled with clippings with stills from the movie. Posters are widely available online.

41. Lehr, *Birth of a Nation*; "Sweeney's Opinion of 'The Birth of a Nation' Sustained by Percy Hammond," *Chicago Defender*, June 14, 1915, 4; editorial, *Chicago Defender*, September 11, 1915, 8; "The Birth of a Nation," *Cleveland Gazette*, September 11, 1915, 2; "The Birth of a Nation," *Topeka Plaindealer*, January 28, 1916, 1.

42. Cripps, *Slow Fade to Black*, 3, 5, 8, 10, 30, 33, and passim; Thomas Cripps, "The Making of *The Birth of a Race*: The Emerging Politics of Identity in Silent Movies," in *The Birth of Whiteness: Race and the Emergence of U.S. Cinema*, ed. Daniel Bernardi (New Brunswick, N.J.: Rutgers

University Press, 1996), 40; John Hope Franklin, "'Birth of a Nation': Propaganda as History," *Massachusetts Review* 20 (Autumn 1979): 417–34.

43. For examples of positive northern response, see "The Birth of a Nation," unidentified clipping, Griffith Papers, reel 24; "A Tribute to 'The Birth of a Nation' by Rupert Hughes," in *Souvenir: The Birth of a Nation*, Griffith Papers, reel 2; Michael Gordon, "'The Birth of a Nation'—A Masterpiece of Photography," March 30, 1915, Griffith Papers, reel 24; "Made Old Soldiers Weep," *Baltimore Sun*, March 28, 1916, Griffith Papers, reel 26; and "'The Birth of a Nation,' *Battle Creek Moon-Journal* (Michigan), February 6, 1926, Griffith Papers, reel 2. "Crowd" quote in Percy Hammond, "'The Birth of a Nation': A Great Spectacle," in Chicago Section, Griffith Papers, reel 25.

44. Allen W. Trelease, *White Terror: The Ku Klux Klan Conspiracy and Southern Reconstruction* (New York: Harper Torchbooks, 1971); Jill Lepore, *These Truths: A History of the United States* (New York: W. W. Norton, 2018), 319.

45. Elaine Frantz Parsons, *Ku Klux: The Birth of the Klan During Reconstruction* (Chapel Hill: University of North Carolina Press, 2015), 78–101. For a Klansman with a cross, see Albion W. Tourgee, *The Invisible Empire: A New, Illustrated, and Enlarged Edition of A Fool's Errand, by One of the Fools* (New York: Fords, Howard, & Hulbert, 1879), facing page 225; a similar picture appears in Michael Newton, *The Invisible Empire: The Ku Klux Klan in Florida* (Gainesville: University Press of Florida, 2001), 2. On Klan costumes, see also Tourgee, *Invisible Empire*, 419–23; J. C. Lester and D. L. Wilson, *Ku Klux Klan: Its Origins, Growth, and Disbandment* (1905; New York: AMS Press, 1971), 58–59; Walter L. Fleming, *Civil War and Reconstruction in Alabama* (New York: New York University Press, 1905), 674–76; Wyn Craig Wade, *The Fiery Cross: The Ku Klux Klan in America* (New York: Touchstone, 1987), 33, 59–60; Bradley D. Proctor, "The K. K. Alphabet: Secret Communication and Coordination of the Reconstruction-era Klan in the Carolinas," *Journal of the Civil War Era* 8 (September 2018): 472–73.

46. Tom Rice, *White Robes and Silver Screens: Movies and the Making of the Ku Klux Klan* (Bloomington: Indiana University Press, 2015), 16, 20. On Simmons and the origins of the Klan, see, among a host of books, Wade, *Fiery Cross*; and Linda Gordon, *The Second Coming of the Klan: The Ku Klux Klan of the 1920s and the American Political Tradition* (New York: Liveright, 2017), 72; William Joseph Simmons, *The Klan Unmasked* (Atlanta: Wm. E. Thomson, 1923), 22–23, 87–88, 284–85. For copy of ad, see William G. Shepherd, "How I Put Over the Klan: Col. William Joseph Simons, Father of the Ku Klux Klan, Tells His Story," *Colliers*, July 14, 1928, 7. Many others make the point that the Klan's costumes and use of the cross came from *Birth of a Nation*. See, for instance, Rice, *White Robes*; and Felix Harcourt, *Ku Klux Kulture: America and the Klan in the 1920s* (Chicago: University of Chicago Press, 2017), 104–7. A keyword search for appearances of "Confederate flag" and "Ku Klux Klan" in the *New York Times* shows that both are mentioned for the first time in a single article in 1952.

47. On Knights of Mary Phagan and organization of the KKK, see Wade, *Fiery Cross*. Glenn Feldman says the initial cross burning came on land borrowed from a leading family in the original Klan, but that hardly seems an important tie. Feldman, *Politics, Society, and the Klan in Alabama, 1915–1949* (Tuscaloosa: University of Alabama Press, 1999), 13. Grace Elizabeth Hale, "Granite Stopped Time: Stone Mountain Memorial and the Representation of White Southern Identity," in *Monuments to the Lost Cause: Women, Art, and the Landscapes of Southern Memory*, ed. Cynthia Mills and Pamela H. Simpson (Knoxville: University of Tennessee Press, 2003), 219–33.

48. For examples of use of the fiery cross as intimidation, see "Negro at Columbia Defies His Critics," *New York Times*, April 3, 1924, 12; "Klan Cross Torn Down," *New York Times*, October 15, 1923, 1; "Negroes in Fear of Flaming Cross," *Times-Picayune* (New Orleans), August 18, 1926, 14; "Fiery Cross Greets Negro," *New York Times*, July 18, 1926, E1. See also "Smith Denounces Coolidge's Silence on the Ku Klux Klan," *New York Times*, October 19, 1924, 8; "Bombs and Crosses Set Off Near Ball," *New York Times*, October 12, 1924, 58; "The Kloran of the 1920s Klan, with Other Documents," in Wade, *Fiery Cross*, appendix B, 419.

49. See "Klan's Big Rally Ends with Outcry," *New York Times*, August 10, 1925, 26; "Thousands Witness Public Initiation of the Ku Klux," *Miami Herald*, May 17, 1922, 1; *Daily Herald* (Gulfport, Mississippi), June 16, 1922, 1; "Klan Initiates 652," *New York Times*, July 24, 1923, 23; "1,000 Out to See Klan Hold Funeral," *New York Times*, November 16, 1924, 19; "Fiery Cross Lights Hall for Wedding," *Times-Picayune* (New Orleans), October 17, 1926, 15; "KKK Attend Funeral," *Miami Herald*, September 4, 1922, 4; "Klan Rites Are Held Over Body at Depot," *Fort Worth Star Telegram*, January 26, 1922, 14. For a picture of Imperial Knight-Hawk, see Kelly J. Baker, *Gospel According to the Klan: The KKK's Appeal to Protestant America, 1915–1930* (Lawrence: University Press of Kansas, 2011), 23. On stationery and songs, see Ku Klux Klan Collection, Stuart A. Rose Manuscript, Archives, and Rare Book Library.

50. Among the many sources on a white Protestant identity, see Allen Lichtman, *White Protestant Nation: The Rise of the American Conservative Movement* (New York: Atlantic Monthly Press, 2008); Edward J. Blum, *Reforming the White Republic: Race, Religion, and American Nationalism, 1865–1898* (Baton Rouge: Louisiana State University Press, 2005). On the Klan and a white Protestant identity, see Baker, *Gospel According to the Klan*.

51. "National Affairs: 'Goober Democrats,'" *Time*, February 10, 1936, 17; Jason Morgan Ward, "'Negroes, the New Deal, and . . . Karl Marx': Southern Antistatism in Depression and War," in *Nation Within a Nation: The American South and the Federal Government*, ed. Glenn Feldman (Gainesville: University of Florida Press, 2014), 102–21; Glen Jeansonne, *Gerald L. K. Smith: Minister of Hate* (New Haven, Conn.: Yale University Press, 1988), 47.

– 6 –

THE MARBLE MAN, ROBERT E. LEE, AND THE CONTEXT OF HISTORICAL MEMORY

Whereas, now honor is accorded Robert E. Lee as one of the great military leaders of history, whose exalted character, noble life, and eminent services are recognized and esteemed, and whose manly attributes of precept and example were compelling factors in cementing the American people in bonds of patriotic devotion and action against common external enemies in the war with Spain and in the World War, thus consummating the hope of a reunited country that would again swell the chorus of the Union.[1]

T HE "WHEREAS" CLAUSE HERE, particularly its early section, easily could have begun a United Daughters of the Confederacy motion praising Lee, but it came at the beginning of a resolution entered in the United States Congress by a Michigan Republican. The resulting law, passed in 1924, called for the restoration of the Lee mansion in Arlington Cemetery. Congress's vote inevitably honored Lee himself and testified to his incorporation into the pantheon of American heroes. A little south of Arlington and a little short of a century later, the decision to take down a Lee monument, erected in Charlottesville, Virginia, the same year the Arlington resolution passed, led to massive protests and the murder of a young woman who was there to support the monument's removal. Some pundits proclaimed the Charlottesville confrontation was part of the continuing Civil War, but it can best be understood within the changing contexts of America's historical memory—how the white South's and the nation's memory of Lee, of what has been called the Marble Man, developed, and the role those memories have played in American society.

The white South made Lee central to the Lost Cause and created an image of Lee that persists and, on many points, complements the image that came to dominate the national memory—a Lee of national unity. That Marble Man was of spotless character; free from an association with slavery, secession, and the Confederate cause; and of unmatched military skill. Most important of all, he was a postwar force for reunion and reconciliation. An evaluation of how well Lee's life conformed to that memory offers insights into the latest debates over Lee statues. Lee's life and role in history prove far more ambiguous than either the Lee of the Lost Cause or the Lee of national unity would have it. Unlike the Marble Man, the real Lee hardly proves to be a hero or a model for a nation that in the early twenty-first century still struggles to make its civic ideals real for all Americans.

UNDERSTANDING LEE'S PLACE in the memory of the Civil War begins with an appreciation of the purposes his image served for both the white South and the North. At the end of the war, some in the North respected Lee the general; many more condemned him as a rebel and traitor. The government, after all, had charged him with treason, although in the end it dropped the case. One apt symbolic expression of northern opinion came in the treatment of Lee's home, Arlington. Early in the war, Quartermaster General Montgomery Meigs, who deeply despised Lee for his role in the war, took control of Lee's plantation. He turned it first into a village for freed people and then into a cemetery for Union soldiers, in both cases partly to demean Lee.[2]

For the white South, in contrast, Lee had become an unassailable hero. During the war, he commanded most Confederates' loyalty, and he and his Army of Northern Virginia, as historian Gary W. Gallagher has shown, were central to Confederate nationalism. Lee became an almost literal embodiment of the Confederate nation. After the war, white southerners' worship of Lee only increased. His death just five years after the war enhanced the adulation and allowed his partisans free rein to create their own vision of Lee. The Lee of the Lost Cause, as that image might be termed, boasted a spotless character, a commitment to duty and honor, and a deep religious faith. He became for many a saintly if not a Christlike figure.[3]

Most important, his partisans proclaimed him the war's great general, a military genius, defeated only by overwhelming numbers and resources, or, in their most extreme claim, only because of the failings of his lieutenant, General James Longstreet, at Gettysburg. Lee's image thereby served to vindicate the Confederacy. A nation and a region that produced such a glorious, virtually victorious figure must have fought well and honorably. A few Lee partisans tied him to the cause of the war, but most disassociated Lee from it, claiming he did not support slavery or secession. They also praised his role in promoting reunion and sectional reconciliation after the war. The Lee of memory, what Thomas Connelly aptly labeled the Marble Man, thereby served to justify the Confederacy even as it ignored the war's cause, slavery.[4]

The Marble Man first took physical form in a statue by Edward Valentine sculpted in the 1870s but not unveiled until 1883, at Washington College. The next year, New Orleans dedicated another statue to Lee, and in 1890 Richmond unveiled a third. These monuments symbolized the South's increasing sense of vindication. In the first, Lee lies down, said to be asleep. In the second, he stands up, atop a high column. In the third, he mounts his horse and sits grandly on a high pedestal.

When Richmond unveiled the mounted, triumphant Lee, white southerners cheered, but others did not. African Americans and some white northerners condemned the celebration of Lee in Richmond. The *New York Age*, an influential African American newspaper, acknowledged that Lee was a great general but then called him a "traitor" who "gave his magnificent abilities to the infamous task of disrupting the Union and to perpetuating the system of slavery. Where then is the wisdom or the propriety of wasting any sentiment on Robert E. Lee? Let the reconstructed Democracy of the South glorify him and his memory as they will, but let the patriots of the Nation indulge in none of it." Elliott Shepard, a white journalist, former abolitionist, and still a radical, admitted he was "an admirer of Gen. Lee and could applaud an honest, loving tribute to his memory by the men who followed his battle banner, but I think the time has come when the youth of the land should be taught that it is a grander thing to be an American than a Virginian." Shepard found it "blasphemous" that a speaker at the unveiling placed "Robert E. Lee on position with God himself."[5]

In 1903, Virginia began a campaign to put a Lee sculpture in the relatively new Statuary Hall in the United States Capitol; many northerners objected, especially veterans in the Grand Army of the Republic. The Virginia senator who had broached the idea dropped it. Three years later Virginia funded the

Recumbent of General R. E. Lee by Edward V. Valentine. Washington College, Lexington, Virginia, 1883. (Library of Congress, Prints and Photographs Division)

Monument of Lee standing, New Orleans, 1884. (Library of Congress, Prints and Photographs Division)

Lee sitting grandly on horseback, Richmond, Virginia, 1890. (Library of Congress, Prints and Photographs Division)

statue, and in 1909 quietly placed it in the Capitol. Some in the North persisted in their opposition. At its 1911 National Encampment, a few members of the Grand Army of the Republic still objected to Lee's presence and demanded removal of the statue. The encampment, however, voted overwhelmingly against a formal protest. Lee stayed in Statuary Hall, although at the time without any ceremonial reception and celebration. On several occasions in the early twentieth century, legislators entered proposals to put up Lee memorials elsewhere in Washington; Congress never even considered them.[6]

Northern attitudes, though, had begun to change. In 1901, Charles Francis Adams, descendant of *the* Adams, began a decadelong celebration of Lee in speeches and articles. Others in the North shared his views. By 1920, apparently confident of Lee's national reputation, General Electric placed in a New York newspaper an advertisement for a washing machine that featured a picture of General Lee. Perhaps the strongest testimony to Lee's new status as a national hero, and an indication of the reasons behind it, came in Congress, which in theory speaks for the nation.[7]

Congress in 1924 passed two measures with an implied recognition of Lee. A decade earlier, the United Daughters of the Confederacy had initiated plans to carve likenesses of Lee, Stonewall Jackson, and Jefferson Davis on Stone Mountain in Georgia. In 1923, the work had begun, but the Daughters had not raised much money. To help them, Congress, with very little if any debate, approved the coinage of fifty-cent pieces that could be sold to help finance the project. Perhaps to encourage Republican support, the resolution dedicated the effort to the memory of President Warren G. Harding, who had just died and in whose administration the work at Stone Mountain had begun. Admitting that the coins would be popular primarily in the South, the House committee report compared the legislation to other efforts "to commemorate different national events" and acknowledged that the money raised would be for "a monument to the valor of the soldiers of the South, which was the inspiration of their sons and daughters and grandsons and granddaughters in the Spanish-American and World War." The bill did not specifically mention Lee, but surely legislators realized he would be honored on Stone Mountain, and when they were issued, the coins bore his likeness. Once minted, the coins sold poorly.[8]

A second measure Congress passed in 1924 went further in honoring Lee. A resolution, which began as quoted previously, authorized the restoration of the Lee mansion in Arlington Cemetery. Louis C. Cramton, a Republican representative from Michigan and son of a Union soldier, proposed it. He had visited Arlington many times, and though he was impressed by the exterior, he thought the mansion's interior looked barren. He wanted it restored to the condition it was in when the Lee family lived there. Its restoration, he argued, would re-create the living conditions of the antebellum South. Cramton, who called Lee the greatest of the Confederate generals, also thought the mansion's restoration would honor Lee and serve as a symbol of national reconciliation. It "is unprecedented in history for a nation to have gone through as great a struggle as we did in the Civil War, and so bitter a struggle as that was, and in the lifetime of men then living to see the country so absolutely reunited as our country at this moment." As evidence he pointed to the southerners' role in the Spanish-American War and the World War. Cramton then argued that "no man in the South . . . did more by his precept and example to help bring about that condition than did Robert E. Lee." Congress apparently agreed; Cramton's resolution passed in both houses without debate.[9]

Given that his house had once been seized and that the cemetery was created as a means to punish Lee, Congress's decision seemed particularly significant. Lee had begun to be incorporated into the very symbolic heart of American nationalism. His refurbished home occupied a commanding hill that looked out over the cemetery and then, further out, over the Potomac and a memorial bridge, toward the Lincoln Memorial and the Mall. The Marble Man, many felt, was a national, not just a southern, hero. They stressed his skill as a general, which reflected the increasing militarization of American society, and celebrated his contribution to the restoration of the Union and the implied encouragement of southern military participation in national wars. Lee of the Lost Cause had been replaced by the Lee of national unity.[10]

After the Civil War, the white South sought signs of northern respect while the North looked for evidence of white southern loyalty. Northerners found the first signs of southern loyalty in the late nineteenth century when, white southerners condemned labor and anarchist violence. More important, northerners interpreted white southerners' service in the Spanish-American War and the World War as testimony to their loyalty to the nation. With the inclusion of Lee, the South's leader and hero, in the national cemetery, and the North's embrace of him that this symbolized, Congress and the nation proffered white southerners the respect they had craved since the end of the war.[11]

Not all Americans agreed with making Lee a national hero. "Each year on the 19th of January there is renewed effort to canonize Robert E. Lee, the greatest Confederate general," wrote W. E. B. Du Bois in 1928. "His personal comeliness, his aristocratic birth and his military prowess all call for the verdict of greatness and genius. But one thing—one terrible fact—militates against this and that is the inescapable truth that Robert E. Lee led a bloody war to perpetuate slavery." Du Bois added another reason why Lee should not be a hero. "He followed Virginia not because he particularly loved slavery (although he certainly did not hate it), but because he did not have the moral courage to stand against his family and his clan. . . . It is the punishment of the South that its Robert Lees and Jefferson Davises will always be tall, handsome and well-born. That their courage will be physical and not moral. That their leadership will be weak compliance with public opinion and never costly and unswerving revolt for justice and right."[12]

A year later, the *Chicago Defender*, the nation's leading African American newspaper, criticized an attempt to put Lee's likeness on the memorial bridge across the Potomac. "How people can claim to be patriotic—to love their country, and, at the same time are willing to stand sponsor for a traitor is a baffling mystery. Yet, in numerous spots in this country can be seen monuments and statues to traitors like Robert E. Lee." Three years later, in 1932, The *Defender* responded to a celebration of Lee at New York's Southern Society—which it described as "gentlemen who think so much of their home that they leave it behind to praise it abroad." The editorial summarized the Society's program as proclaiming, "We lost our cause, but we kept our man." After quoting the speeches, the *Defender* called Lee a "DESERTER," claimed he always knew the South would lose, and judged Grant the better general by far. "Robert E. Lee was a great heart, a God-fearing man, but not God-knowing. He put Virginia above the Union and the cause of the loved few above humanity."[13]

Challenges to the Marble Man's stature came not just from African Americans, however. That Congress approved refurbishing the Lee mansion and minting coins with Lee and Jackson on them, along with a few other measures taken by the Coolidge administration that seemed to praise the Confederacy, left Lucy Shelton Stewart all but apoplectic. The daughter of a Union veteran active in the Grand Army of the Republic, Stewart wrote *The Reward of Patri-*

otism, a scathing and skillful critique of the South's role in the Civil War. Published in 1930, it also condemned what Stewart considered a national celebration of Lee, one she found markedly peculiar because it disassociated Lee from the cause for which he fought. "But, if he had been the victor at Appomattox, instead of Grant," she wrote, "'his purity of soul and high sense of personal honor' would not have saved a race from infamous servitude." She accepted the idea that Lee did not like slavery and loved the Union, but still concluded that he had deserted it and plotted to have Virginia secede.[14]

In 1933, British historian J. F. C. Fuller published another attack on a crucial part of the Lee legend: his skill as a general. Fuller admitted that until very recently he had "accepted the conventional point of view that Grant was a butcher and *Lee* one of the greatest generals this world had ever seen." As he wrote *Grant & Lee,* though, he had come to appreciate Grant's genius and to "discover that in several respects [Lee] was one of the most incapable Generals-in-Chief in history." Fuller, though, still offered a surprisingly favorable view of Lee. He argued that Lee was Grant's equal in conceiving a plan of battle but far his inferior in executing it, in large part because he used oral orders and did not exercise enough control over his subordinates. He was, Fuller implied, just too nice. Indeed, Fuller in places praised Lee and offered a most romantic view of his army: "What this bootless, ragged, half-starved army accomplished is one of the miracles of history. It was led by a saint, it was endowed with the sanctity of his cause, and yet had its leader been more of a general and less of a saint, even if this had flinched from it a little of its enthusiasm, its hardship would have been vastly reduced."[15]

In the two years following Fuller's book, Richmond, Virginia, journalist and historian Douglas Southall Freeman published his four-volume biography, *R. E. Lee,* which became and remains for many the culmination of the celebration of the Lee of the Lost Cause, the Lee who offered vindication for the white South. "In his military achievements, Southern people saw the flowering of their racial stock; in his social graces they beheld their ideals embodied; in the honors paid his memory, every one of Lee's former soldiers felt that he had himself received the accolade." Freeman's Lee was a man of unblemished character, deep religious belief, and a commitment to honor and duty. Freeman stressed that Lee's decision to fight for the Confederacy arose not from a commitment to slavery or secession but from loyalty to family and home; it was, he concluded, a decision "he was born to make."

During the war, according to Freeman, Lee proved an amazing leader who commanded his soldiers' intense loyalty throughout the conflict, and a great general, although Freeman offered some criticism of his military leadership and campaigns. Lee did convert to the Confederate cause, Freeman admitted, particularly in his defense of the Confederacy after the war. Yet Freeman's Lee still could be embraced by those who celebrated the Lee of national unity. Freeman praised Lee for his acceptance of defeat and promotion of reunion. "More than any other American, General Lee kept the tragedy of the war from being a continuing national calamity." Freeman's book received high praise, had good sales, and won a Pulitzer Prize.[16]

His view, more than that of Du Bois, Stewart, or Fuller, soon came to dominate the national imagination. Amid the depression, Lee and the Confederacy could be admired as examples of persistence and triumph over adversity. In 1934, Virginia governor George C. Perry evoked that very idea: "Lee's greatness was the greatness that withstood defeat." Perry spoke in the rotunda of the national Capitol, when Virginians dedicated the statues of Lee and George Washington that had stood in Statuary Hall for twenty-five years. Virginia senator Carter Glass presided and noted that earlier opposition to Lee's statue had prevented such a celebration. Various speakers praised Lee's character, military genius, and role in rebuilding the nation. One of them, Senator David L. Walsh of Massachusetts, said that the dedication marked "a final attestation to the entire extinguishment of the passions which once divided our country . . . and which lingered long after all arms had been laid down. . . . We now unite in proclaiming Lee a national hero." Walsh added that it was particularly appropriate that "a successor to Charles Sumner in the Senate . . . stands here to give official expression to this sentiment on behalf of Congress, and, I may be permitted to add, on behalf of the nation."[17]

Congress and the nation still limited their embrace of Lee. Shortly after the dedication ceremony at which Walsh spoke, for example, Congress did not even take up a resolution to erect an equestrian statue to Lee in Arlington Cemetery. But in 1955, Congress went further in honoring Lee by adopting a resolution by Tennessee's Estes Kefauver to dedicate the Lee mansion as "a permanent memorial to Robert E. Lee." Congress did amend the resolution to name the house the Custis-Lee Mansion, but otherwise Kefauver's resolution passed with only limited discussion in both the House and Senate. The resulting law echoed themes in the 1924 resolution that had led to the mansion's restoration. It praised Lee's "high character" as well as his "military genius" and leadership. It celebrated him because "after Appomattox," he fervently "devoted himself to peace, to the reuniting of the Nation, and to the advancement of youth through education." And it expressed Congress's "humble gratitude to a kind Providence for blessing our Nation with leaders of true greatness who, like Robert E. Lee, have been able to see beyond their times, and by whose vision, guidance, and wisdom this Nation has gone forward to a place of world leadership as the unfaltering and powerful champion of peace, liberty, and justice."[18]

The Lee of national unity that now stressed Lee's character, military leadership, and contributions to reunion served the nation's purpose well in the midst of the Cold War. He had become and remained a national hero, a symbol of America's military skill and might. Since shortly after World War I, an army post had borne his name. In the 1930s, he had a tank named for him, and much later a nuclear submarine. President Dwight Eisenhower considered him a great general and American; he hung Lee's picture, along with those of Washington, Benjamin Franklin, and Abraham Lincoln, in the Oval Office. During Eisenhower's tour of the Gettysburg battlefield with Britain's Field Marshall Viscount Montgomery, reporters overheard them questioning Lee's judgment in ordering Pickett's Charge. When that word got out, a penitent president reassured the nation of his admiration for Lee.[19]

Soon thereafter, Lee became, according to historian Thomas L. Connelly, a major figure in the nation's celebration of the Civil War Centennial. The Lee of national unity fit easily into the Centennial's theme. Its leaders, as Robert J. Cook shows in his study of the Centennial, sought to promote unity and patriotism during the Cold War. In a speech to a Washington, D.C., Civil War Roundtable, Bruce Catton, a Civil War historian on the Centennial Commission, pointed out that Lee's home, Arlington, had become a national shrine, connected by a memorial bridge to the Lincoln Memorial, thereby uniting two American heroes. The Centennial celebration, however, soon became embroiled in the controversies that arose as white southerners fought to prevent desegregation and the civil rights movement's attempt to transform the nation. The Marble Man occasionally got caught up in the battles.[20]

As early as 1946, Lucius C. Harper, a columnist for the *Chicago Defender*, argued that after the Civil War the United States should have held the equivalent of the Nuremberg trials and punished Confederate leaders such as Davis and Lee. If it had done so, the "nation today would be far more respectable and honorable in dealing with its citizenry as a whole than is characterized by its social and legal conduct in respect to darker races." In 1957, another *Chicago Defender* piece complained that Lee is celebrated as "'the greatest strategist of his day'" or "described as the 'greatest American.'" "We do not know what sinister influence is behind this wave of admiration," the article continued, arguing that the praise made it seem that the South had won the Civil War and adding that Grant, Sherman, and Sheridan must be turning over in their graves. In 1965, a book review in the *Defender* made a similar complaint: "Go in any book store and one will see biographies of the slaveowners and Confederate Generals by the score." Even as he worked on this review, the author added, my "Sunday paper tells of another biography of Robert E. Lee, the slave men's commander in chief."[21]

In their opposition to African American rights, southern segregationists did in fact employ the Lost Cause and its symbols, including Lee. Communities named streets and schools after the general, and at least some in the Ku Klux Klan claimed that Lee had blessed their organization. Unlike the Confederate flag, though, the Marble Man never became central to the segregationists' battle. A few white liberals, in contrast, tried to use Lee's image on behalf of moderation. The mayor of Atlanta, in criticizing segregationist mobs, observed "that Robert E. Lee wouldn't even spit on the rabble rousers we have today." At a news conference, Minnesota senator Hubert H. Humphrey, fighting for the passage of the Civil Rights Act, urged southerners to act "'like Lee" and "surrender with honor, with the hand of friendship extended and received." Humphrey's evocation of the nationalist memory of Lee, of course, had no impact whatsoever.[22]

If the civil rights movement and the changes it brought did not augur well for the Marble Man, his memory still commanded respect in Congress. In 1972, it voted to change the name Custis-Lee Mansion to Arlington House—the Robert E. Lee Memorial. Three years later, though, the Marble Man became entangled in another battle, rooted not in the 1860s but the 1960s: divisions over the Vietnam War. In 1975, Congress again turned its attention to Lee. The National Archives had rediscovered Lee's request for pardon, which many had assumed had been lost, and which had never been acted upon. With evidence that Lee had fulfilled the requirements, legislators introduced a resolution to restore Lee's citizenship. Two earlier attempts to grant Lee his citizenship, in 1957 and 1970, had failed. This attempt would be different, although it had a similar focus on Lee's image. The 1975 bill's supporters, many but not all from the South, evoked the image of Lee that had dominated since the 1920s. They praised his spotless character, his military genius, and the important role he played in healing the divisions of the war and reuniting the nation. New York's Hamilton Fish went further: "Robert E. Lee . . . is not only a great military hero, but one who can serve as a model today. By his words and his deeds, he set an example that would serve us well to follow in light of some of the bitter divisions that have developed in our country in the recent past based, once again, on war."[23]

Other legislators had that more recent war on their minds and wanted not to refight the Civil War or celebrate national unity but to secure amnesty for Americans who had opposed the Vietnam War. In making their case, they attacked Lee. Philip A. Hart of Michigan compared the Vietnam War resisters favorably to Lee. "What about a lot of young Americans tonight who are underground or semiunderground or uneasy, who may not have been educated at government expense, and certainly never took an oath, except as those who did enter the service? They never took up a weapon against their country. They said, out of central conviction of conscience, that they could not take up a weapon against someone else." Despite Hart's opposition, and after little debate, the Senate passed the resolution unanimously.[24]

In the House, the resolution to restore Lee's citizenship proved more controversial. Opponents even questioned the facts surrounding the document's discovery. Like Hart, though, most challenged the idea of restoring Lee's citizenship but not the freedoms of Vietnam War resisters. New York's Elizabeth Holtzman asked, "General Lee led armies against the country. The Congress is willing to forgive him. What about the young men who refused to bear arms in a war that they thought was unconscionable? Like General Lee, they placed principle above conscription." John Conyers Jr. of Michigan pointed to the irony that "General Lee should be praised for heeding his conscience during the Civil War though his action then had ruinous effects on the Nation, while these young Americans are damned for heeding their consciences, an action which has done no damage to the Nation." In the end, only ten House members voted against the resolution. Their votes probably said more about continued opposition to the Vietnam War than the status of Lee's memory, although the opponents certainly challenged reigning conceptions of him. The Marble Man did not, as Fish had hoped, provide an example for how to heal the divisions over Vietnam.[25]

Congress's restoration of Lee's citizenship may well have marked the pinnacle of Lee's status as a national hero. Even before that, academic attacks on Lee's reputation had begun. In the late 1960s, Civil War historian Thomas L. Connelly and others began to challenge Lee's reputation for military genius. In 1977, only two years after the restoration of Lee's citizenship, Connelly published his study of Lee's image in American society, which argued for a more complex understanding of Lee the man. He wrote that Lee's life was "replete with frustration, self-doubt, and a feeling of failure." Over the next three decades, other historians took up Connelly's critique. Frustrated that "in our collective consciousness [Lee] looms almost as *the* figure of the war, rivaled only by Abraham Lincoln," Alan T. Nolan in 1991 critiqued the mythic Lee that had kept the real Lee from even being "considered." Nolan acknowledged Lee's many merits, explored his complex personal life, and questioned his military genius. More important, he challenged the central assumptions about the Lee of national unity. Nolan argued that Lee supported slavery and secession and questioned Lee's contribution to reunion, pointing to Lee's persistent anger and his commitment to white supremacy. Despite Lee's rhetoric of acceptance and reunion, Nolan concluded, Lee believed that Confederate leaders "should have immunity" and that white southerners "should regain their full power and status immediately and unconditionally," in particular their control over the "status of the freedmen."[26]

In 2000, Michael Fellman published an even more critical biography. In a psychological portrait, Fellman stressed Lee's battle for "self-mastery" and argued, "Only in combat did Lee discover and express a well of anger and desire for action that allowed him to overcome his lifelong habits of self-abnegation and passivity." Fellman agreed with Nolan that Lee supported slavery and secession and went even further in questioning his role in reunion; he proclaimed

Lee a postwar "Southern Nationalist." A later study, Elizabeth R. Varon's *Appomattox*, also challenged the idea, so central to Lee's national reputation, that he accepted defeat, sought reconciliation, and helped remake the nation.[27]

Other biographers offered more positive assessments of Lee. In 1995, Emory M. Thomas published the most admiring biography since Freeman's, though even Thomas was far from uncritical. Writing sixty years after the Richmond editor, Thomas concluded that "Lee was a great human being, perhaps as great as Freeman believed, but not great in the ways that Freeman described. Afflicted with many, though surely not all, of the frustrations and frailties that Connelly and others discerned, Lee was great in his response to his tribulations and to his life in general. He redeemed many moments and brought grace to otherwise grim circumstances." Thomas stressed, "Lee was a great person, not so much because of what he did (though his accomplishments were extraordinary); he was great because of the way he lived, because of what he was."[28]

In 2007, Elizabeth Brown Pryor, a diplomat and scholar, published a more critical study. *Reading the Man* argued that Lee sought to distance himself from slavery and that he only passively accepted secession and followed Virginia's course. She also discussed his limitations as a military leader. After Appomattox, Pryor found, Lee retreated into a private world. In her summary judgment, Pryor challenged Lee's greatness because he did not create anything that "endures" and because his "noble spirit" was subsumed in his society's ignobility. Yet she also observed, "We still recognize importance in Lee because he has left us an enduring example of personal courage against the vagaries of human existence" and an illustration of the fact that "it is possible to fail and yet not be a failure."[29]

If, by the early twentieth-first century, scholars had critically examined Lee's life, accomplishments, and memory, older themes in the Lee mythology persisted in more popular histories. In a 2001 bestseller, *April 1865*, Jay Winik revived the traditional celebration of Lee's contribution to rebuilding the nation. In his decision to surrender at Appomattox, "Robert E. Lee, so revered for his leadership in war, made his most historic contribution—to peace. By this one momentous decision, he spared the country the divisive guerrilla warfare that surely would have followed, a vile and poisonous conflict that would not only have delayed any true national reconciliation for many years to come, but in all probability would have fractured the country for decades into warring military pockets." Winik also credited Lee for not renewing the conflict after Lincoln's assassination and for contributing to reconciliation in the years that followed.[30]

In 2014, best-selling author Michael Korda published yet another biography of Lee, who, he marveled, unlike any other defeated rebel, had become a national hero. Korda's title, *Clouds of Glory,* certainly evoked the celebration of Lee, although he offered various criticisms, particularly of Lee's failures as a general. Korda nevertheless still incorporated aspects of the mythic Lee. He argued that Lee supported a cause he did not embrace and never believed "slavery and secession were necessarily worth fighting for." Although Korda thought Lee should have ended the war two years earlier, he, like so many others, still praised Lee for his decision at Appomattox and, after that, for the example he set for others in submitting to federal authority.[31]

Not long after the publication of Korda's book, public perceptions of Lee appeared to change as cities began to take down Lee monuments. In the 1990s, attacks on Confederate symbolism centered, for the most part, on the Confederate flag rather than Confederate monuments. At that time, calls did arise for the University of Texas to remove six statues, including one of Lee, but the university took no action. Then, in 2015, Dylann Roof murdered nine members of the Emanuel African Methodist Episcopal Church in Charleston, South Carolina. In the wake of that travesty, the demands to remove the monuments to Lee and others recurred in Austin, and two, though not Lee's, came down. Shortly before the murder of the Emanuel Nine, Mayor Mitch Landrieu had begun a campaign to remove four Confederate monuments in New Orleans. Two years later, after much controversy, lawsuits, and difficulties finding contractors willing to take on the project, the city's Lee monument, an early Lost Cause icon, came down.[32]

That same year, 2017, Charlottesville, Virginia, decided to take down its Lee monument. Supporters of the statue held a rally to protest. Representatives of the League of the South attended, and if any group can be said to be still fighting the Civil War, it qualifies. Most who protested taking down Lee's statue were allied with other white supremacist groups and had no ties to the South or the Lost Cause. They espoused an anti-Semitism that had never been a part of the Lost Cause. One protestor from the Midwest murdered a young woman when he drove a vehicle into a crowd that had gathered to oppose the supremacists' presence and to support taking the statue down. President Donald J. Trump declined to condemn the protestors and claimed there were good people on both sides. At about the same time, his chief of staff, John Kelly, called Lee "an honorable man." Two years later, at a campaign rally in Minnesota, the president praised Lee as a great leader and general.[33]

Charlottesville—and probably the president's response—fueled increasing attacks on Confederate monuments and Lee. The University of Texas's Lee finally went to a museum, and the National Park Service rewrote its signage at the Lee mansion in Arlington. Condemnations of the general filled the internet. One, in *The Atlantic,* attacked what its title called "The Myth of the Kindly General Lee." Its author, Adam Serwer, argued that Lee supported slavery and portrayed him as a cruel master. He also challenged the traditional view that Lee promoted reunion and stressed his active support for white supremacy after the war. Two years later, when the murder of George Floyd in Minneapolis led to demonstrations all over the country, protestors quickly turned their ire on Confederate monuments, including another of the icons of the Lost Cause, the Lee monument on Richmond's Monument Avenue. Protestors covered it in graffiti, and Virginia's governor soon called for its removal, although a legal battle ensued. Financier and philanthropist David M. Rubenstein, who a few years before had funded a rehabilitation of the Lee mansion, urged the federal government to "follow suit" and remove Lee's name from the home and instead use "Arlington House, Arlington Cemetery House, Memorial House or any other name that does not offend Americans and helps remind us of the many patriots who have given the last full measure of devotion to their country."[34]

Criticism of Lee continued to escalate. In 2020, Isabel Wilkerson's best-selling *Caste* included in a summary of the fights over monuments to Lee a subtle but damning view of the general himself. That same year, Ty Seidule, a retired general who had long taught at West Point, published *Robert E. Lee and Me,* an anything but subtle critique of Lee's reputation. He told how, growing up in the South and attending Washington and Lee University, he had long considered his hero Lee a great military leader and a saint. As Seidule came to face America's racial past, however, he changed his view. He ended his book with a scathing assessment of Lee. It argued that Lee, unlike many other West Point graduates serving in 1861, left the army, violated his oath to defend the Constitution, chose to defend slavery and commit treason, and then killed American soldiers.[35]

Also in 2020, Virginia chose to replace the Lee statue in the U.S. Capitol with a statue of civil rights activist Barbara Johns, and Congress voted, over President Trump's veto, to rename military posts named after Confederates, including Fort Lee. Court challenges that had delayed taking down Lee monuments in Charlottesville and Richmond were finally settled in 2021, and both came down. In Charlottesville, Lee would be melted down and the material divided among various art projects; in Richmond, he was cut in half and moved to a museum. When the Richmond statue finally came down, not one but two columnists in the *Washington Post* commended the decision and published columns critical of Lee. Other monuments to Lee still stood, though. Washington and Lee University renamed its Lee Chapel and made changes to it. Its recumbent Lee statue remained, and so did Lee as part of the university's name.[36]

Lee still has his defenders. Neo-Confederates, Sons of Confederate Veterans, and many other white southerners—and some northerners—praise Lee. They celebrate his military greatness, leadership, manliness, character, and often his deep Christian faith. Michael Andrew Grissom, in his popular *Southern by the Grace of God*, maintained, "There has never been—nor will there be—a mortal man more admired, more esteemed, or more revered than Robert E. Lee."[37]

Lee even has his academic defenders, though they are more cautious and critical. In a study of the year 1865, published in 2019 even as attacks on Lee intensified, S. C. Gwynne, like Winik before him, praised Lee's decision to surrender at Appomattox, even "going against the spoken wishes of his president and the convictions of many of his officers." In "a long life filled with many achievements, some of them glorious," Gwynne added, "this was perhaps Lee's finest moment." In late 2021, even after the monuments came down, Allen C. Guelzo published yet another biography of Lee. Guelzo did not shrink from calling Lee a traitor and claiming he fought for slavery, but he clearly sought to disassociate Lee from slavery and secession. He focused the book more on understanding Lee's psychology—his attempt to balance "perfection, independence, and security"—than on his politics. The book's conclusion sought to balance what the chapter's title called Lee's "crime" and "glory." The biography's last line read, "Mercy—or at least a nolle prosequi—may, perhaps, be the most appropriate conclusion to the crime—and the glory—of Robert E. Lee after all." A decision to drop the case against Lee, however, hardly seems likely. The criticism will no doubt continue. With African Americans, many historians, and others condemning Lee, the Confederacy, and its monuments, and with white nationalists and a former president rallying to Lee's defense, the Marble Man may remain central in a national debate over racism and white supremacy.[38]

Given a new context of historical memory in which the Marble Man has become an issue, yet another appraisal of Lee's life and career may be helpful. It must evaluate the key components of the national memory of Lee: his spotless character, particularly his religious beliefs; his disassociation from slavery, secession, and the Confederate cause; his military skills; and his efforts after the war to encourage reunion. In doing so, it pays particular attention to Lee's morality, his belief in a personal rather than social ethic, and his nationalism, one resting in an ethnic not civic identity.

CELEBRATIONS OF LEE'S PERSONAL character seem justified. Several biographers have pointed to his frequent flirtations with women other than his wife, although all have concluded he remained a faithful husband. Other than commenting on his attraction to women, however, few have found fault with his personal behavior. Most praise Lee's devotion to duty, honesty, and self-restraint and attribute his character to his deep religious faith. Raised an Episcopalian, Lee actively participated in the church throughout his life, although he was only confirmed at age forty-six. Lee was unquestionably a low-church Episcopalian, and some observers have judged him an evangelical. J. William Jones, the Baptist minister and Confederate chaplain so influential in creating the Lee of the Lost Cause, claimed to have seen Lee's Bible with many passages marked, "especially those teaching the great doctrines of Salvation by Grace, justification by Faith, or those given the more precious promises of the believer."[39]

Lee's letters do reveal a deep and abiding faith, although his expressions of it read less like the exclamations at a revival than the recitations of morning prayer. He wrote little about the necessity of conversion, and as his most recent biographer, Guelzo, notes, said little about either Jesus or the Holy Spirit. Nevertheless, Lee did hold to many aspects of the evangelical faith, although most were common Protestant tenets. He thought the Bible the most important book and read it frequently. He believed in the forgiveness of sins and in the promise of salvation. Upon learning of someone's death, he often wrote of their going to heaven and clearly hoped for his own deliverance there as well. He had, as so many who have studied him point out, a tremendous faith in God's providence. He referred to it often and trusted strongly "that a kind Providence will cause all things to work together for our good." Even in defeat, he advised a cousin and confidant that we must "commit ourselves in adversity to the will of a merciful God as cheerfully as in prosperity. All is done for our good & our faith must continue unshaken."[40]

Central to Lee's faith and life was an emphasis on personal morality. In 1852, he offered one of his sons advice on how to honor him. Lee did not write of taking Jesus as his savior but of the importance of doing right. "Do not be Satisfied with *wishing* & *intending* right, but *do* it. . . . Have the Command of yourself, that will enable you to defy the tempter & scorn the Sinful pleasures he offers. Let your pleasure be in doing good." Lee did write once, in 1857, that God had shown him the "only miracle . . . the power He gives to Truth and Justice to work their way in this wicked world." His letters far more often touted the importance of personal morality—not cussing, keeping the Sabbath, and using alcohol sparingly if at all. Indeed, Lee rarely drank, and he preached temperance, especially to his students at Washington College. (The Kappa Alpha fraternity, which claims Lee as a spiritual father, somehow has overlooked Lee's example here.)[41]

One of Lee's favorite words—"duty"—seems revelatory. It played an important role in three value systems that shaped Lee's life. As an antebellum southern aristocrat, he blended his Christian faith with a sense of honor, and within a culture of honor, one did one's duty. In his career, too, the concept held; a military officer performed his duty. And as a Christian, Lee felt a duty to God. In 1856, he wrote his wife, "We are all in the hands of a kind God, who will do for us what is best, and more than we deserve, and we have only to endeavor to deserve more, and to do our duty to him and to ourselves." For Lee, that duty took the form of right behavior, with his focus not on justice but on righteousness, not on shaping society but on behaving properly.[42]

His conception of morality fit comfortably within the dominant tradition of southern white Protestantism. Influenced by the need to defend slavery, most southern white Protestants' faith emphasized their vertical relationship with God, not a horizontal responsibility for their society. They stressed individual moral behavior, not social justice, and sought to ensure right behavior, not create a righteous social order. Lee conformed to his society rather than transcending it. His working definition of Christian morality contributed to his spotless character but also influenced his attitudes toward slavery, secession, and the Confederacy, issues also central to evaluating the Lee of national unity.[43]

Lee's attitude toward slavery has long been debated. Lee himself held enslaved people, both before and during the war. In his early army career, he had enslaved people who served his personal needs, although at one point he wrote, "I would rather hire a *white* man" than buy a slave. Lee only became a large slaveholder when, as part of his father-in-law's estate, he inherited responsibility for nearly two hundred enslaved people. The will required their emancipation in five years, and when the time came, Lee freed them, although only after consulting his lawyer about the possibility of delay. In the meantime, though, he exploited their labor to help pay the estate's obligations, usually by hiring them out and, in the process, splitting up every family.[44]

Three enslaved people, George Wesley, Mary Norris, and George Parks, frustrated at the delay in their promised emancipation, ran away. In a newspaper story first published in 1859 but which reappeared over the years, including during the most recent attacks on Lee's memory, Wesley told of what happened when he and Norris were captured and returned to Arlington. Lee, they said, ordered them whipped, and at one point he intervened to beat the woman himself. He then insisted that their wounds be washed in brine. Both Freeman and Pryor, one a laudatory the other a critical biographer, raise doubts about whether Lee beat Norris himself, but that he ordered them lashed seems quite likely. When Lee accepted the institution of slavery and his role as master, he inevitably accepted its demands; enslavement required discipline, even by enslavers of spotless character. Lee made that clear in describing what he looked for in an overseer: "I wish to get an energetic honest farmer, who while he will be considerate & kind to the Negroes, will be firm & make them do their duty." "Make" included use of the lash, and in writing of the "duty" of the enslaved, Lee employed his own sense of responsibility to God to describe the responsibility of the enslaved to their enslaver.[45]

Those who see Lee as an opponent of slavery find their best evidence in an 1856 letter to his wife. "In this enlightened age, there are few I believe, but will acknowledge, that slavery as an institution, is a moral & political evil in any country." He thought its evils so obvious that he added, "It is useless to expiate on its disadvantage." Lee quickly followed his antislavery thoughts, though, with observations that echoed aspects of white southerners' defense of the institution. He judged it more of a burden for white than Black people and felt "blacks . . . immeasurably better off here than in Africa, morally, socially, and physically." If he found slavery wrong, Lee left ending it in God's hands. He waited for God's providence to prepare the enslaved "for better things" and to eventually bring emancipation. "While we see the course of the final abolition of human slavery is onward, & we give it the aid of our prayers & all justifiable means in our power, we must leave the progress as well as the result in his hands who sees the end, who chooses to work by slow influences, & with whom two thousand years are but a single day." Lee's religious beliefs often focused on individual rather than corporate sins; hence, before the Civil War, he happily left the righting of what he on some level saw as a social wrong to the Providence of God—and God's own time.[46]

In the meantime, he resented the efforts of anyone who sought to end slavery in the present. As early as 1844, Lee was outraged over resolutions by the American Anti-Slavery Society and thought the society sought "ruin to the present American Church and the destruction of the present Union." Twelve years later, in the same letter in which he expressed his reservations about slavery and written shortly after the 1856 presidential election, the first with a Republican candidate, he criticized "the efforts of certain people of the North" to "interfere with & change the domestic institutions of the South." They must "be aware, that their object is . . . unlawful" and "can only be accomplished by them through the agency of civil & servile war."[47]

Lee's criticism of northern interference with enslavement helps explain his response to secession, which proved far more complex than proponents of the mythic Lee would have it in trying to distance him from the war's issues. In January of 1861 he wrote of his hope that "all honorable means of maintaining the Constitution and the equal rights of the people will be exhausted" and war avoided. Yet he also wrote that month that "a Union that can only be maintained by swords and bayonets, and in which strife and civil war are to take the place of brotherly love and kindness, has no charm for me." He added that "if the Union is dissolved, and the Government disrupted, I shall return to my native State and share the miseries of my people and save in its defense will draw my sword no more." Many of Lee's defenders cite this and similar references to his loyalty to Virginia as evidence of his commitment to states' rights. At least before the war, though, Lee did not justify secession with references to the rights of the states. Rather, he consistently referred to secession as "revolution," one that would lead to war. Lee did not believe secession constitutional, nor did he seek it; indeed, he hoped it could be avoided.[48]

When it came, though, he quickly decided to support it. When he was offered the command of the nation's forces, he said no, not once but twice, in two separate meetings. Two days later he resigned from the army, and only a day later accepted a commission in the Virginia army, and shortly after that, in the Confederate army. Elizabeth Pryor stresses the anguish Lee experienced in reaching that decision, yet he seemed to see it as inevitable. Why did someone who had served the nation faithfully and had only three years before written that he knew "no other Country, no other Government, than the *United States* & their *Constitution*" so readily take up arms against it? Although he did refer frequently to his loyalty to Virginia, his decision inevitably followed from his sense of national identity. After resigning, he wrote to his sister that he had had to decide if he would "take part against my native State," and then explained, "With all my devotion to the Union & the feeling of loyalty & duty of an American citizen, I have not been able to make up my mind to raise my hand against my relatives, my children, my home."[49]

In other letters he phrased the same thought not in terms of his relations but with the simple phrase "my people." Lee's loyalty to Virginia and his decision to fight for the Confederacy rested not on the "duty of an American citizen" or on constitutional issues but simply, as Freeman and Du Bois agreed, on a sense of solidarity with his relatives and his ancestors—his people. He meant, of course, white people, but more than that, people with whom he felt a kinship, a strong sense of identification, one based in "brotherly love." Lee weighed his duty to his people above his duty as an American citizen. Historians Gary Gerstle and Jill Lepore have written of two strands of American nationalism, one based in a civic identity, a commitment to American values and ideals, and the other resting in an ethnic or racial identify. Lee's Americanism, though he had sometimes celebrated its Constitution and ideals, rested more in an ethnic than a civic sense of nationalism. He followed "his people" and became the leading general of the Confederacy.[50]

If Lee proved a reluctant but sure secessionist, he quickly became an equally sure and far more ardent Confederate nationalist. He was an early and bitter critic of the United States, which he termed "their country." Pryor attributes Lee's criticism of that country in large measure to the federal forces' capture and use—Lee would have said abuse—of his home, Arlington. Lee may have seen Arlington's confiscation not just in personal terms but as part of a larger pattern of what he believed to be the northern armies' brutality and savagery. Over the course of the war, in various letters, he condemned what he considered their "ruin & pillage," "malice & revenge," "distress to innocent women and children, occasioned by spiteful excursions . . . unworthy of a civilized nation," as well as "the unchristian & atrocious acts they plot & perpetuate." He blamed the savagery and abuse not just on the Union army but on the nation. "No civilized nation within my knowledge," he charged, "has ever carried on war as the United States government has against us."[51]

Lee's Confederate nationalism also resulted from his fears of what would happen if the Confederacy lost. In a telling letter, written ten days after the Emancipation Proclamation became official, Lee called for greater support for the Confederacy and in the process explained his commitment to the cause: "In view of the vast increase of the forces of the enemy of the savage and brutal policy he has proclaimed, which leave us no alternative but success or degradation worse than death, if we would save the honor of our families from pollution, our social system from destruction, let every effort be made, every means be employed, to fill and maintain the ranks of our arms, until God, in his mercy, shall bless us with the establishment of our independence." Only Confederate victory, he believed, could prevent the end of slavery and what he saw as the racial degradation and pollution of his people—language common in the worst of racist thought. Lee's employment of it made the fact that his loyalty to his people included only whites far more explicit and central than it had seemed before the war.[52]

Two years of hard war later, Lee concluded that independence required the recruitment of Black soldiers and therefore an end to slavery. In making that argument, ironically, he offered his most forthright defense of the institution. "Considering the relation of master and slave, controlled by human laws, and influenced by Christianity and an enlightened public sentiment, as the best that can exist between the white and black races while intermingled as at present in this country, I would deprecate any sudden disturbance of that relation unless it be necessary to avert a great calamity to both." He would prefer to win the war with only white troops, Lee continued, but he thought there were not enough white recruits to prevent the Union army from coming into the South, enlisting Black soldiers, and with their added numbers, defeating the Confederacy and destroying "slavery in a manner most pernicious to the welfare of our people." "Whatever may be the effect of our employing negro troops, it cannot be as mischievous as this." At least if the Confederacy ended slavery, Lee concluded, "we can devise the means of alleviating the evil consequences to both races." Lee clearly intertwined Confederate nationalism and racism and believed that if the Confederacy could not save slavery, it must, at all costs—even the cost of making slaves into soldiers—at least preserve white control of the South's Black population.[53]

Lee also intertwined his Confederate nationalism with his Christian faith, referring often to God's providential relationship with the Confederacy. Lee's letters recounting victories almost always attributed, ever so briefly, Confederate success to God. When the military situation seemed darker, Lee, as so many at the time, adopted a covenantal view. In order to secure victory, Lee believed, Confederates had to prove themselves worthy of God's blessing and support. In early 1862, he wrote his wife that we must "meet with reverses & overcome them," and then he added, "I hope God will at last crown our efforts with success." We "should be humbled & taught to be less boastful, less selfish, & more devoted to right & justice to all the world."[54]

Lee's reference to pursuing "right & justice" proved unusual. As would be expected from someone whose faith focused on personal not social morality, he more often wrote of being less boastful and selfish. A little earlier he had written his wife, "If we can only become sensible of our transgressions, so as to be fully penitent and forgiven, that this heavy punishment under which we labor may with justice be removed from us and the whole nation." In another letter, he expressed his "trust that a merciful God will arouse us to a sense of our danger, bless our honest efforts & drive back our enemies to their homes. Our people have not been earnest enough. Have thought too much of themselves & their ease, & instead of turning out to a man, have been content to nurse themselves & the dimes, & leave the protection of themselves & families to others. To satisfy their consciences, they have been clamorous in criticizing what others have done, & endeavored to prove that they ought to do nothing."[55]

Lee stressed the same themes publicly. In August of 1863, President Jefferson Davis announced one of the many days of prayer and fasting for Confederate victory. Lee's general order in response first stressed doing everything possible to keep the Sabbath. It then went on:

> Soldiers! We have sinned against Almighty God. We have forgotten His signal mercies, and have cultivated a revengeful, haughty, and boastful spirit. We have not remembered that the defenders of a just cause should be pure in His eyes; that 'our times are in His hands,' and we have relied too much on our own arms for the achievement of our independence. God is our only refuge and our strength. Let us humble ourselves before him. Let us confess our many sins, and beseech Him to give us a higher courage, a purer patriotism, and more determined will; that He will convert the hearts of our enemies, that He will hasten the time when war, with its sorrows and sufferings, shall cease, and that He will give us a name and place among the nations of the earth.[56]

In his order, as in the earlier letter, Lee implied that the way to God's favor came through greater support for the Confederate cause. The army's reversals resulted not from anything wrong with Confederate society or much wrong with Confederates—save for that boasting again. Rather, God withheld his favor because of the Confederates' failure to support the Confederate cause strongly enough.

The intensity of Lee's nationalism, his conviction that God favored his cause, his seeing the war as the means to preserve if not enslavement then at least white supremacy, all help explain his behavior as a commanding general committed to prolonging and ultimately winning a war. In celebrating the Marble Man, however, proponents rarely explored and certainly did not emphasize the roots of Lee's Confederate nationalism. Instead, they celebrated Lee as a military genius, as the greatest general, or one of the greatest generals, of the war—if not of all time. Military historians, and perhaps even more, Civil War buffs, take great pleasure in debating a general's successes and failures and then rendering judgment on his relative standing among other military leaders. The traditional view, held by many military historians and the American military, celebrated Lee's military greatness. His critics, who have become slightly more numerous of late, question his tactical or strategic judgment (and sometimes both), his failings in exercising command over his immediate subordinates, and other aspects of his performance.

The possibility of reaching a consensus, much less a definitive judgment, on Lee the general seems highly unlikely—and probably not that important. Virtually no one, however, questions his ability to inspire his troops, who respected him and were devoted to him. Nor has anyone challenged his role as the embodiment of Confederate nationalism. Both made Lee a beloved general during the war, and after it, a force for reunion.

Lee's postwar role, for most who praise it, began with Appomattox and his decision to surrender his army rather than, as other Confederates proposed, resort to a guerilla war. Winik, Gwynne, and some of Lee's biographers make Appomattox Lee's finest moment, and his decision to surrender there formed a key element in the Lee of national unity. Recently, though, historian Elizabeth Varon has challenged that view, subtly arguing that Lee had an agenda at Appomattox, that he sought "a restoration of peace," meaning a return to the old order of aristocratic leadership and Virginia's dominant role in the nation. Caroline Janney's *Ends of War* does not address the issue directly, but her critique of Lee's final order and emphasis on Lee's soldiers going home to continue the fight at least subtly challenges the traditional view.[57]

If Lee had seen his army's surrender as a means to a restoration of the old order, surely he would have justified it in those terms to opponents of surrender, such as E. P. Alexander and President Jefferson Davis, who would have shared that goal. Evidence suggests he did not. As most accounts have it, Lee realized his army had no further options that led to victory and rejected guerilla warfare, which he never particularly favored during the war because he thought it would encourage his soldiers to become outlaws, would needlessly prolong the war, and ultimately would destroy the South. He did not reach that conclusion easily or happily. Varon observes that northerners at Appomattox commented on "Lee's profound sadness and abject powerlessness." No doubt they read him rightly.[58]

Perhaps Lee's decision to meet Ulysses S. Grant at Appomattox can best be explained, strangely enough, by advice he had given his perpetually sick wife many years before. After reminding her that "we must bow with humble resignation to all the chastisements of our heavenly father & submit ourselves entirely to his will," he advised her, "The best course for the recovery of your health, ought therefore to be systematically tried, fairly & patiently. When it is found to fail, try some other, till all reasonable means are exhausted. Then, & not till then, we must be resigned to our fate." That seems an apt summary of Lee' approach to the war. He tried one line of attack, then another, this strategy and that, before concluding on April 9 that he had tried all the reasonable alternatives and had to submit to God's providence.[59]

Other Confederate armies remained in the field, briefly, and Davis still sought to continue the war and preserve the Confederacy. Because of the tremendous love and respect his soldiers and most white southerners had for Lee, when he surrendered, so too for all intents and purposes did the Confederacy. If he had chosen to lead his army to the hills and continue the battle, many of those devoted soldiers probably would have followed. The war may well have continued and exacerbated the divisions it had already created. Supporters of the Lee of national unity and his popular and scholarly defenders are correct: Lee's decision to surrender and to not resort to guerrilla war was probably Lee's most important contribution to the nation. In the years that followed, however, Lee went further in promoting reunion.[60]

General Robert E. Lee on Horseback.
(The Miriam and Ira D. Wallach Division of Art, Prints and Photographs,
Photography Collection, New York Public Library)

After Appomattox, invoking one of his most powerful motivations, Lee claimed that he thought it "the duty of every citizen in the present condition of the country, to do all in his power to aid in the restoration of peace & harmony & in no way to oppose the policy of the State or Genl Governments." He urged former Confederates to remain in the South to work to rebuild the region and restore the nation. He himself did just that. He took the oath of allegiance and applied for pardon. He turned down jobs that might have paid handsomely, assumed the presidency of struggling Washington College, and committed himself to the education of a new generation. Lee rightly claimed to "have done, & continue to do, in my private capacity, all in my power to encourage our people to set more fully to work, to restore the Country, to rebuild their homes & churches, to educate their children, & remain with their States, their friends & Countrymen."[61]

During his presidency of Washington College, the local community of Lexington, Virginia, experienced frequent demonstrations against Reconstruction and in opposition to activities by or in behalf of African Americans, and the college's students often participated. In an early incident, after two days of marches protesting the presence of the military garrison, Lee ordered them stopped. During two more serious disturbances, in which the murder of an African American seemed likely, violence was prevented by the intervention of a student in the first instance and a professor in the second. Both invoked General Lee's opposition to violence. Lee himself probably prevented yet another murder. On still another occasion, local federal officials complained to Lee about his students' confrontation with freedpeople, and Lee again intervened.[62]

Lee expelled or otherwise punished students involved in various racial incidents, although Pryor pointed out that Lee meted out more severe discipline to other students for far less serious shortcomings. And at times, Lee was slow to act; after all, he stopped the marches only on the third day. Certainly, he did not convince the students to abandon such activities, since they recurred. And Lee did not publicly condemn violence against or other attempts to intimidate freedpeople, much less speak in favor of African American rights, though he did discipline students and acted quickly to avoid an open conflict with the army. His mixed record in these incidents epitomized the ambiguities of his behavior after Appomattox. He worked to encourage sectional peace, to avoid confrontations with federal authorities, and to restore the nation, but did little if anything to encourage the white South to confront its racism. He had not abandoned his ethnic definition of nationalism; indeed, it had become far more racial than ethnic.

Although Lee once opposed the erection of a Confederate monument, he also contributed indirectly and directly to the emergence of the Lost Cause narrative. He encouraged Jubal A. Early and others who became central to the South's postwar justification of its actions. He himself promoted some of the central Lost Cause tenets, beginning with his farewell order to his troops, which came to assume mythic importance among postwar white southerners. As Varon and Janney each show, a reference in his farewell order to the North's "overwhelming numbers and resources" helped propagate that false explanation of southern defeat, which became central to the Lost Cause. General Order No. 9 also encouraged the Lost Cause's celebration of Confederate unity and the South's unmatched sacrifice for the cause.[63]

Perhaps Lee, ever loyal to his troops, had to acknowledge the sacrifice and dedication of his army, but the farewell's tone did constitute a reversal of his wartime attitude. Throughout the conflict, Lee had complained about desertions and the lack of public support for the cause. No hint of that appears in his farewell order. Only a few days later, in an interview with a *New York Herald* reporter, he claimed that "the South was never more than half in earnest in this war," but that comment proved an exception, and Lee at that point probably sought to curry northern favor. Lee did not return to that theme during the remainder of his life.[64]

Lee also embraced and promoted the central tenet of the Lost Cause. Before the war, Lee had described secession as revolution; after it, he attributed secession and the cause of the Civil War to states' rights. In that same *New York Herald* interview, Lee claimed that he stood with his state because he was "a firm and honest believer in the doctrine of States' rights," indeed, even in "State sovereignty." On this occasion, Lee's observation came in response to a question about the possibility of convicting Davis of treason. Perhaps he offered a states' rights defense as a means to defend and protect his president—and himself. Yet Lee continued to emphasize states' rights. About a year later, in testimony before the Congressional Committee on Reconstruction, Lee's most public statement after the war, he again made the case for states' rights. He claimed the states had acted legitimately in "merely using the reserved right which they had a right to do so." At about the same time, in a response to an inquiry from a British leader, Lord Acton, Lee offered his most systematic defense of states' rights. His postwar embrace of states' rights had deeper roots than his and Davis's defense, and his conceptions of morality and nationalism again played a role.[65]

Lee's interpretation of the South's actions highlighted that, faced with defeat, Lee never contemplated that he or the South had acted wrongly. In July 1865, he wrote to a relative that he would not flee prosecution because "I am aware of having done nothing wrong." A year later he thanked a friend from Illinois "for doing me the justice to believe that my conduct during the last five eventful years has been governed by my sense of duty. I had no other guide, nor had I any other object than the defense of those principles of American liberty upon which the constitutions of the several States were originally founded, and unless they are strictly observed, I fear there will be an end to republican government in this country." Lee's definition of morality as personal not social, which had limited his covenantal view during the war, played a role here. He was not likely to see defeat as God's judgment on southern society—or as a rebuke for his political choices. Instead, Lee sought to preserve as much of that society as he could.[66]

His new embrace of states' rights was also rooted in his fear of what would follow emancipation; such a theory of government offered the best means to defend the white South from federal efforts to encourage racial equality. Lee readily accepted the death of slavery, but emancipation only heightened his fears about the role of African Americans in society. In the postwar period, the white supremacy inherent in Lee's ethnic definition of nationalism became far more explicit. In his congressional testimony, Lee made his views abundantly clear. He admitted that a few Black people had some potential to acquire "knowledge and skill in their trade or profession"; as a group, though, they were not "as capable of acquiring knowledge as the white man," nor do they have as much "lust of money and property." "The blacks with whom I am acquainted look more to the present than to the future. . . . They are an amiable, social race. They like their ease and comfort, and, I think, look more to their present than to their future condition." Later in his testimony he made it clear he adamantly opposed suffrage for African Americans because "they cannot vote intelligently." When pressed, he went further: "It would be better for Virginia if she could get rid" of Black people. When asked if "Virginia is absolutely injured and its future impaired by the presence of the black population here," Lee answered, "I think it is." So Lee rejected out of hand his fellow Confederate general James Longstreet's suggestion that he join him in working with the Republicans, and in 1868, in his only real political involvement after the war, Lee publicly endorsed the Democratic presidential candidate, who condemned "Black rule" in the South and pledged to end Reconstruction. To ask that Lee support Republican efforts to change the South, much less that he embrace racial equality, is of course to ask much of someone with his attitudes and background. It is not too much to ask of a national hero.[67]

The story of Robert E. Lee provides a perfect example of the perils of setting up marble men, of rendering humans heroes and models for society. All people live ambiguous lives. Lee was a man of unblemished personal morality and a general with uncommon skills. Yet his leadership cannot be disassociated from the cause for which he fought. He supported slavery and secession and became an ardent Confederate nationalist. His decisions then, and even after the war, were shaped by two shortcomings all too common within American society: a definition of morality limited to personal behavior, not social justice, and a definition of citizenship rooted in ethnic and racial identity, not civic ideals. With these fundamental values, Lee proved not exemplary but all too representative, an example not of the strength of his society but of its weakness. Both helped to limit how far Lee would go in adjusting to the loss of the war.

He did do much. Lee deserves great credit, the nation's gratitude, and a place in its history for his decision to surrender and not launch a guerrilla war, and for his postwar advocacy and example in respecting federal authority and seeking reunion. Yet at the same time—these ambiguities always arise—he encouraged southerners who used the Lost Cause to oppose racial change and did nothing to encourage it himself. He had rejoined the nation, but perhaps even more than before he sought to define nationalism in racial terms. He wanted and advocated a white republic.

The Lee of the Lost Cause, a symbol of southern honor and vindication, and later the Lee of national unity, an exemplar of militarism and nationalism, perhaps served a purpose for their times. The pressing issue is no longer sectional reconciliation or the need for solidarity during the Cold War. The necessity of unity persists, but the issue, more than ever, has become a new definition of nationalism based on a civic ideal, one that incorporates all Americans and that confronts racism. The battles of the 1860s formed a part of a far longer confrontation over whether the United States will make the promises of its civic ideals realities for all its people, especially African Americans. That struggle began in 1619, not 1861, and it did not end in 1865 but continues. It was fought not just in the South but throughout the nation. Neither the Marble Man nor the real Lee can serve as a hero in that battle.

The Marble Man, of course, cannot speak, and the real Lee would most likely hold to his views on race. Nevertheless, Lee's observation to Confederate general P. G. T. Beauregard, in a letter urging him to remain in the country and submit to federal authority, seems surprisingly appropriate advice more than a century and a half later. Lee pointed out how George Washington, who had once fought against the French, later came to fight with them. "I need not tell you," Lee wrote, "that true patriotism sometimes requires of men to act exactly contrary, at one period, to that which it does at another, and that the motive which impels them—the desire to do right—is precisely the same."[68]

Perhaps the same could be said of how heroes function. When the nation sought reunion, or even when it sought to promote militarism and nationalism, the Marble Man served some useful function. Today, though, true patriotism calls the nation to finally face its past of racism and inequality even as it embraces a nationalism based on civic identity. Lee made no positive, much less historic, contribution to those causes. If Lee ever merited inclusion in a national pantheon of heroes, he does not in a nation seeking racial reconciliation and an end to white supremacy.

NOTES

1. *Restoration of Lee Mansion: Hearing Before the Joint Committee on the Library*, H.J. Res. 264, 68th Cong., 1st Sess., May 28, 1924 (Washington, D.C.: Government Printing Office, 1925), 1.

2. William A. Blair, *With Malice Toward Some: Treason and Loyalty in the Civil War Era* (Chapel Hill: University of North Carolina Press, 2014), 240–67; John Reeves, *The Lost Indictment of Robert E. Lee: The Forgotten Case Against an American Icon* (New York: Rowan & Littlefield, 2018); Micki McElya, *The Politics of Mourning: Death and Honor in Arlington National Cemetery* (Cambridge, Mass.: Harvard University Press, 2006), esp. 96.

3. Gary W. Gallagher, *The Confederate War: How Popular Will, Nationalism, and Military Strategy Could Not Stave Off Defeat* (Cambridge, Mass.: Harvard University Press, 1997), 63; Douglas

Southall Freeman, *R. E. Lee: A Biography*, 4 vols. (New York: Charles Scribner's Sons, 1934), 3:239.

4. There is a vast literature on Lee's postwar image; see, for example, Thomas L. Connelly, *The Marble Man: Robert E. Lee and His Image in American Society* (New York: Alfred A. Knopf, 1977); Alan T. Nolan, *Lee Considered: General Robert E. Lee and Civil War History* (Chapel Hill: University of North Carolina Press, 1991), 3–8; Gary W. Gallagher, *Lee and His Generals in War and Memory* (Baton Rouge: Louisiana State University Press, 1998).

5. "Robert E. Lee," *New York Age*, May 31, 1890, 2; Elliott Shepard, "Treason Glorified," *Mail and Express* (New York), May 29, 1890, 1.

6. Robert Colby, "Lee Returns to the Capitol: A Case Study in Reconciliation and Its Limits," in *Reconciliation After Civil Wars: Global Perspectives*, ed. Paul Quigley and James Hawdon (New York: Routledge, 2019), 115–129; *Journal of the Forty-Fifth Encampment, Grand Army of the Republic* (Washington, D.C.: Government Printing Office, 1911), 296–316. On ignored proposals for Lee statues, see, for example, H.J. Res. 148, 60th Cong., 1st Sess., March 27, 1908; H.R. 26062, 62nd Cong., July 31, 1912.

7. For a copy of the ad, see Kevin M. Levin, *Searching for Black Confederates: The Civil War's Most Persistent Myth* (Chapel Hill: University of North Carolina Press, 2019), 125–27.

8. Grace Elizabeth Hale, "Granite Stopped Time: Stone Mountain Memorial and the Representation of White Southern Memory," in *Monuments to the Lost Cause: Women, Art, and the Landscapes of Southern Memory*, ed. Cynthia Mills and Pamela H. Simpson (Knoxville: University of Tennessee Press, 2003), 219–33; H.R. 5259, 68th Cong., 1st Sess., January 11, 1924; quote in "Coinage of 50-Cent Pieces in Commemoration of Carving on Stone Mountain, Ga., to Accompany H.R. 5259"; Report No. 277, 68th Cong., 1st Sess.; S. 684, *Congressional Record*, 68th Cong., 1st Sess.; S. 3825, 66th Cong., 2nd Sess., January 31, 1920; Erin L. Thompson, *Smashing Statues: The Rise and Fall of America's Public Monuments* (New York: W. W. Norton, 2022), 84–89. Thompson embeds her account of congressional action in the story of sculptor Gutzon Borglum's fund-raising scams in association with early attempt to carve a monument into Stone Mountain. He got fired and disputes persisted. Carving resumed in the 1960s and the monument was dedicated in 1970.

9. *Restoration of the Lee Mansion*, 7–8; H.J. Res. 264, *Congressional Record*, 68th Cong., 2nd Sess., 1924–25, 244, 4227, 5513. See also McElya, *Politics of Mourning*, 194–97.

10. On militarization, see Thomas J. Brown, *Civil War Monuments and the Militarization of America* (Chapel Hill: University of North Carolina Press, 2019).

11. On the South and unrest, see Gaines M. Foster, *Ghosts of the Confederacy: Defeat, the Lost Cause, and the Emergence of the New South, 1865–1913* (New York: Oxford University Press, 1987), 143–44.

12. Kevin Levin, "W. E. B. Du Bois on Robert E. Lee," *Civil War Memory* blog, May 30, 2017, http://cwmemory.com/2017/05/30/w-e-b-dubois-on-robert-e-lee.

13. "Honoring Rebel Heroes," *Chicago Defender*, November 23, 1929, A2; "The Sublime Figure of Defeat," *Chicago Defender*, January 30, 1932, 14.

14. Lucy Shelton Stewart, *The Reward of Patriotism: A Refutation of the Present-Day Defamation of the Defenders and Preservers of the Union in the Civil War and Exposition of the Cause Which They Overcame* (New York: Walter Neale, 1930), 73.

15. J. F. C. Fuller, *Grant & Lee: A Study in Personality and Generalship* (New York: Charles Scribner's Sons, 1933), 11–12. 117.

16. Freeman, *R. E. Lee*, 1:viii, 431, 4:483.

17. "Acceptance of Statues of George Washington and Robert E. Lee Presented by the State of Virginia," H. Doc. 410, 73rd Cong., 2nd Sess. (SS 9819), June 13, 1934, 28 (Perry), 33–34 (Walsh). For a different view, that the depression diminished the appeal of the Lost Cause, see Nina Silber, *This War Ain't Over: Fighting the Civil War in New Deal America* (Chapel Hill: University of North Carolina Press, 2018), esp. 138.

18. Attempts to put up an equestrian statue to Lee in Arlington did not pass in the 74th, 75th, or 76th Congresses. See H.J. Res. 232, 74th Cong; H.J. Res. 142, 75th Cong.; H.J. Res. 125, 76th Cong. S.J. Res. 62, March 30, 1955, in *Congressional Record*, 84th Cong., 1st Sess., 3983, 3990, 4296, 6936, 7795, 8621.

19. Michael Korda, *Clouds of Glory: The Life and Legend of Robert E. Lee* (New York: Harper Perennial, 2014), 671; Mathew W. Lively, "Dwight D. Eisenhower in Defense of Robert E. Lee," *Civil War Profiles*, blog post, August 10, 2014, http://www.civilwarprofiles.com/dwight-d-eisenhower-in-defense-of-robert-e-lee; British Pathé, "Eisenhower Explains About General Lee (1957)," YouTube, April 13, 2014, https://youtu.be/mOrtOlU8f9Y; Robert G. Nixon, "Ike Says Lee Great, But Still Made Error," *Chicago Daily Defender*, May 16, 1957; "Ike Makes Amends for Gen. Lee Rap," *Chicago Daily Defender*, May 5, 1958, A2.

20. Connelly, *Marble Man*, 157–59; on Catton, see Robert J. Cook, *Troubled Commemoration: The American Civil War Centennial, 1961–1965* (Baton Rouge: Louisiana State University Press, 2007), 62.

21. Lucius C. Harper, "Dustin' off the News: We Should Have Had a Nuremberg After the Civil War," *Chicago Defender*, November 9, 1946, 1; "Reversing the Verdict," *Chicago Daily Defender*, December 19, 1957, 11; Eugene Neter Romany Feldman, "60 Years in Congress and 28 Out," *Chicago Daily Defender*, November 27, 1965, 6.

22. On naming after Lee, see Southern Poverty Law Center, "Whose Heritage? Public Symbols of the Confederacy," February 1, 2019, https://www.splcenter.org/20190201/whose-heritage-public-symbols-confederacy. On Klan story, see Patsy Sims, *The Klan* (New York: Stein and Day, 1978), 44. See also "Sees Peaceful Atlanta Mixing," *Chicago Daily Defender*, April 11, 1961, 2; "Says 'Surrender' in Civil (Rights) War," *Chicago Daily Defender*, November 23, 1963, 6. For another example of evoking Lee on behalf of accepting integration, see Jason Sokol, *There Goes My Everything: White Southerners in the Age of Civil Rights, 1945–1975* (New York: Alfred A. Knopf, 2006), 159.

23. H.R. Res. 10595, 92nd Cong. 2nd Sess., 1972; S.J. Res. 23, 94th Cong., 1st Sess., 1975. Hamilton Fish is quoted in *Congressional Record*, 94th Cong., 1st Sess., July 22, 1975, 23942. Francis MacDonnell provides an excellent overview of earlier attempts to restore Lee's citizenship, although with a slightly different take on the outcome. See MacDonnell, "Reconstruction in the Wake of Vietnam: The Pardoning of Robert E. Lee and Jefferson Davis," *Civil War History* 40 (June 1994): 119–33.

24. *Congressional Record*, 94th Cong., 1st Sess., April 10, 1975, 9877.

25. Ibid., July 22, 1975, 23944–45 (quotes), 23951 (vote).

26. For the debate over Lee's military role, see Gary W. Gallagher, ed., *Lee the Soldier* (Lincoln: University of Nebraska Press, 1996); it includes Connelly's 1969 article questioning Lee's strategic ability. See also Connelly, *Marble Man*; Nolan, *Lee Considered*, 4, 8, 147.

27. Michael Fellman, *The Making of Robert E. Lee* (New York: Random House, 2000), xv, xix,

264; Elizabeth R. Varon, *Appomattox: Victory, Defeat, and Freedom at the End of the Civil War* (New York: Oxford University Press, 2014), 2.

28. Emory M. Thomas, *Robert E. Lee: A Biography* (New York: W. W. Norton, 1995), 14.

29. Elizabeth Brown Pryor, *Reading the Man: A Portrait of Robert E. Lee Through His Private Letters* (New York: Viking, 2007), 472–73.

30. Jay Winik, *April 1865: The Month That Saved America* (New York: Harper Collins, 2001), 166.

31. Korda, *Clouds of Glory*, 163.

32. Brigit Katz, "University of Texas Removes Three Confederate Monuments," *Smithsonian Magazine*, August 21, 2017, https://www.smithsonianmag.com/smart-news/university-texas -austin-removes-confederate-statues-180964578; Mitch Landrieu, *In the Shadow of Statues: A White Southerner Confronts History* (New York: Viking, 2018), 161–200, 217–27; Mary Niall Mitchell, "A Tale of Two Cities: New Orleans and the Fight Over Confederate Monuments," *History*, May 11, 2017 (updated November 28, 2018), https://www.history.com/news/a-tale-of-two-cities-new -orleans-and-the-fight-over-confederate-monuments.

33. "Two Years Ago, They Marched in Charlottesville. Where Are They Now?," ADL, blog, August 8, 2019, https://www.adl.org/blog/two-years-ago-they-marched-in-charlottesville-where-are -they-now; Karma Allen, "Trump Chief of Staff John Kelly Calls Confederate Gen. Robert E. Lee an 'Honorable Man,'" ABC News, October 31, 2019, https://abcnews.go.com/Politics/trump-chief -staff-john-kelly-calls-confederate-gen/story?id=50828711; Andrew Blake, "Donald Trump Praises 'Great General' Robert E. Lee Again: 'He Would Have Won Except for Gettysburg,'" *Washington Times*, September 19, 2020, https://www.washingtontimes.com/news/2020/sep/19/donald-trump -praises-great-general-robert-e-lee-ag.

34. Adam Serwer, "The Myth of the Kindly General Lee," *Atlantic*, June 4, 2017, https://www. theatlantic.com/politics/archive/2017/06/the-myth-of-the-kindly-general-lee/529038; Gregory S. Schneider, "No Longer Untouchable, Lee Statue Becomes Focus of Civic Outpouring in Richmond," *Washington Post*, June 15, 2020, https://www.washingtonpost.com/local/no-longer-untouch able-statue-of-lee-becomes-focus-of-civic-outpouring-in-richmond/2020/06/15/acf6e16e- af11–11ea-856d-5054296735e5_story.html; Russell Berman, "The Nation's Official Memorial to Robert E. Lee Gets a Rewrite," *Atlantic*, August 18, 2017, https://www.theatlantic.com/politics /archive/2017/08/a-national-memorial-to-robert-e-lee-gets-a-rewrite/537237; David M. Rubenstein, "I Funded the Rehabilitation of This Robert E. Lee Memorial. Congress, Please Rename It," *Washington Post*, June 8, 2020, https://www.washingtonpost.com/opinions/2020/06/08/i-funded -rehabilitation-this-robert-e-lee-memorial-congress-please-rename-it. See also Ed Simon, "There Shouldn't Be Any Statues Honoring Robert E. Lee Anywhere," *History News Network*, June 16, 2017, https://historynewsnetwork.org/article/166707; Stan McChrystal, "Good Riddance," *Washington Post*, November 21, 2018, https://historynewsnetwork.org/article/166707; and Colin Woodward, "What Historians Keep Getting Wrong About Robert E. Lee," Lee Family Digital Archive Blog, December 1, 2017, https://leefamilydigitalarchive.wordpress.com/2017/12/01/what-historians -keep-getting-wrong-about-robert-e-lee.

35. Isabel Wilkerson, *Caste: The Origins of Our Discontents* (New York: Random House, 2020), 333–43; Ty Seidule, *Robert E. Lee and Me: A Southerner's Reckoning with the Myth of the Lost Cause* (New York: St. Martin's Press, 2020).

36. Dana Millbank, "Robert E. Lee Was a Stone-Cold Loser," *Washington Post,* September 10, 2021; Eugene Robinson, "Robert E. Lee's Statue Is Gone. Now Can We Dismantle the Myth, Too?," *Washington Post,* September 9, 2021; Johnny Diaz, "Board of Washington and Lee University Votes to Keep Lee's Name," *New York Times,* June 4, 2021; "Frequently Asked Questions," Washington and Lee website, https://www.wlu.edu/the-w-l-story/leadership/board-of-trustees/frequently-asked -questions.

37. Sons of Confederate Veterans, "The Wisdom of General Robert E. Lee," https://www.david rreynolds.org/_forms/LeeWisdom.pdf; "Sons of Confederate Veterans Remember the Life of Gen. Robert E. Lee," *Aiken Standard,* January 5, 2014, https://www.postandcourier.com/aikenstandard /news/sons-of-confederate-veterans-remember-the-life-of-gen-robert-e-lee/article_802bc73f-35d4- 5fcb-a4a3-c9a3cc603168.html; Earl Starbuck, "Robert E. Lee: The Believer," Abbeville Institute Press, April 22, 2021, https://www.abbevilleinstitute.org/robert-e-lee-the-believer; Michael Andrew Grissom, *Southern By the Grace of God* (Gretna, La.: Pelican, 1997), 330.

38. S. C. Gwynne, *Hymns of the Republic: The Story of the Final Year of the American Civil War* (New York: Scribner, 2019), 279–99 at 289; Allen C. Guelzo, *Robert E. Lee: A Life* (New York: Alfred A. Knopf, 2021), 8, 434. George Will wrote an editorial in praise of Guelzo's book for its gentle critique of Lee.

39. J. William Jones, *Life and Letters of Robert Edward Lee: Soldier and Man* (New York: Neale Publishing Company, 1906), 471. For examples of treatment of women, personal morality, and religious beliefs, see Fellman, *Making of Robert E. Lee,* 7–35, 249–53; Pryor, *Reading the Man,* 223–75; Thomas, *Robert E. Lee,* 18–46, 160. The most extensive discussion of Lee's religious life is R. David Cox, *The Religious Life of Robert E. Lee* (Grand Rapids, Mich.: William B. Eerdmans, 2017). Cox stresses that Lee's prewar decision rested on ethical considerations, his postwar commitment to reunion, and reconciliation to a theological belief. Although couched in different terms, it does point to Lee's postwar faith coming closer to the emphasis on a social gospel than is developed here.

40. Guelzo, *Robert E. Lee,* 314–15. On the Bible, see Lee to Martha Custis Williams Carter, December 20, 1865, Lee Family Papers, Lee Family Digital Archive, Stratford Hall, Stratford, Virginia (hereinafter cited as LFPDA). Lee to Jefferson Davis, July 12, 1863, in Clifford Dowdey, ed., *The Wartime Papers of R. E. Lee* (Boston: Little Brown, 1961), 548 (first quote); Lee to Martha Custis Williams Carter, May 2, 1865, LFPDA (second quote). For examples on forgiveness of sins and salvation in the next life, see Lee to Mary Anna Randolph Custis Lee, September 3, 1855, LFPDA; Lee to wife, December 2, 1861, March 27, 1863, and June 26, 1864, all in Dowdey, *Wartime Papers,* 89–90, 419, 808–9.

41. Lee to William Henry Fitzhugh Lee, May 4, 1852, LFPDA. He wrote a similar letter, but added Bible reading, in offering advice to the son of a friend who had died; see Lee to Edward A. Barbour, August 15, 1866, LFPDA. On Lee's own habits and support of temperance, see Jones, *Life and Letters,* 93–94, 441–44; and Fellman, *Making of Robert E. Lee,* 21–22.

42. Lee to wife, April 19, 1857, and Lee to wife, September 1, 1856, both in Jones, *Life and Letters,* 85, 81.

43. Samuel S. Hill Jr. first argued for the emphasis on personal morality in southern white Protestantism. Hill, *Southern Churches in Crisis* (New York: Holt, Rinehart and Winston, 1966), 105–11.

44. Determining when and how many enslaved people Lee held proves more difficult than

one would imagine. See Thomas, *Robert E. Lee*, 72, 179–84, and 211; Pryor, *Reading the Man*, 143–54, 260–75. Quote in Lee to William Henry Fitzhugh Lee, July 9, 1860, LFPDA.

45. A copy of Wesley's charges appears in Pryor, *Reading the Man*, which has a good discussion of the incident, and can also be found at "Testimony of Wesley Norris, National Anti-Slavery Standard, on April 14, 1866," LFPDA. Fellman, *Making of Robert E. Lee*, 67; Pryor, *Reading the Man*, 277. Lee's description of overseer is in Lee to Edward C. Turner, February 13, 1858, LFPDA.

46. Lee to Mary Anna Randolph Custis Lee, December 27, 1856, LFPDA.

47. Lee to Mary L. Custis, April 13, 1844, copy provided by the Virginia Historical Society, Richmond; Lee to Lee, December 27, 1856, LFPDA.

48. Lee to Annette Carter, January 16, 1861, LFPDA; letter, January 23, 1861, in Jones, *Life and Letters*, 120–21. Lee refers to "revolution" in both letters, as he also does in Lee to Ann Kinlock Lee Marshall, April 20, 1861, LFPDA, and Lee to Mary Anna Randolph Custis Lee, January 23, 1861, LFPDA.

49. Pryor, *Reading the Man*, 290–91; Lee to Edward Vernon Childe, January 9, 1857, LFPDA; Lee to Ann Kinlock Lee Marshall, April 20, 1861, LFPDA; Lee to Martha Custis Williams Carter, January 21, 1861, LFPDA.

50. Jill Lepore writes of "ethnic nationalism," Gary Gerstle of "racial," although he also says it includes "ethno-racial terms." Lepore, *This America: The Case for the Nation* (New York: Norton, 2019), 58; Gerstle, *American Crucible: Race and Nation in the Twentieth Century* (Princeton, N.J.: Princeton University Press, 2001), 3–9. Guelzo, *Robert E. Lee*, also stresses Lee's loyalty to family as his motivation (186–89). For an interpretation of Lee's decision that puts it in the context of his politics, see Elizabeth R. Varon, "'Save in Defense of My Native State': A New Look at Robert E. Lee's Decision to Join the Confederacy," in *Secession Winter: When the Union Fell Apart* (Baltimore: Johns Hopkins University Press, 2013), 34–57.

51. For "their country," see Lee to G. W. C. Lee, February 28, 1863, in Dowdey, *Wartime Papers*, 411; Pryor, *Reading the Man*, 306–8. Pryor attributes the new nationalism to what happened at Arlington, not just to Robert but to the Lees. Guelzo, too, stresses personal losses as well as northern behavior in explaining Lee's nationalism. See Guelzo, *Robert E. Lee*, 310. Quotes from Lee to Annie Lee, December 8, 1861, LFPDA; Lee to Judah P. Benjamin, December 20, 1861, in Dowdey, *Wartime Papers*, 92–93; Lee to James A. Seddon, July 18, 1864, LFPDA; Lee to James A. Seddon, June 13, 1863, LFPDA; Lee to Seddon, March 6, 1864, in Dowdey, *Wartime Papers*, 678–79; Lee to G. H. C. Lee, January 19, 1862, in Dowdey, *Wartime Papers*, 106.

52. Lee to James A. Seddon, January 10, 1863, in Dowdey, *Wartime Papers*, 390. Guelzo, *Robert E. Lee*, also points to Lee's view of Confederates' failures as a lack of dedication to the cause (315).

53. Lee to Andrew Hunter, January 11, 1865, LFPDA.

54. For examples of giving God credit for victories, see Lee to Jefferson Davis, June 27, 1862, and Lee to Anne Carter Lee and Eleanor Agnes Lee, September 30, 1862, LFPDA; General Orders No. 5, May 7, 1863, in Jones, *Life and Letters*, 243–44; telegram, Lee to Jefferson Davis, June 15, 1863, in Dowdey, *Wartime Papers*, 515. Quote from Lee to Mary Anna Randolph Custis Lee, February 8, 1862, LFPDA.

55. Lee to Mary Custis Lee, December 25, 1861, in Captain Robert E. Lee, *Recollections and Letters of General Robert E. Lee* (Garden City, N.Y.: Garden City Publishing, 1904), 58–59; Lee to Anne Carter Lee, March 2, 1862, LFPDA.

56. Headquarters Order, August 13, 1863, in Lee, *Recollections and Letters*, 105–6.

57. Varon, *Appomattox*, 36–39, 63; Caroline E. Janney, *Ends of War: The Unfinished Fight of Lee's Army after Appomattox* (Chapel Hill: University of North Carolina Press, 2021), 56–57. Varon makes much of Lee's use of the phrase "restoration of peace"; Lincoln, too, used the phrase to talk about ending the war.

58. Aaron Sheehan-Dean, *The Calculus of Violence: How Americans Fought the Civil War* (Cambridge, Mass.: Harvard University Press, 2018), 79, 96, 328–30, 345–47. See also E. P. Alexander, *Military Memoirs of a Confederate: A Critical Narrative* (1907; Dayton, Ohio: Press of Morningside Bookshop, 1977), 600–617; A. L. Long, *Memoirs of Robert E. Lee* (New York: J. M. Stoddard, 1886), 409–27; James Longstreet, *From Manassas to Appomattox: Memoirs of the Civil War in America* (Philadelphia: J. B. Lippincott, 1896), 618–31; Lee to Jefferson Davis, April 12, 1865, LFPDA; Lee to Davis, April 20, 1865, in Dowdey, *Wartime Papers*, 938–39.

59. Lee to Mary Anna Custis Lee, January 9, 1856, LFPDA.

60. On Davis's continued determination, see William J. Cooper Jr., *Jefferson Davis, American* (New York: Alfred A. Knopf, 2000), 525–32.

61. Lee to Gentlemen [Board of Washington College], August 24, 1865, LFPDA; Lee to John B. Brockenbrough, January 23, 1866, Robert E. Lee Papers, Digital Archive, Washington and Lee University Library. For other examples of Lee urging people to stay and work, or of conciliatory policies, see Lee to John Letcher, August 28, 1865, LFPDA; Lee to Josiah Tatnall, September 7, 1865, LFPDA; Lee to Mathew F. Maury, September 8,1865, LFPDA; Lee to Mrs. Jefferson Davis, February 23, 1866, and Lee to Fitzhugh Lee, June 8, 1867, both in Lee, *Recollections and Letters*, 223–24, 259–61.

62. Fellman, *Making of Robert E. Lee*, 258–63; Pryor, *Reading the Man*, 454–56. For a different interpretation of these events, see John M. McClure, "The Freedmen's Bureau School in Lexington Versus 'General Lee's Boys,'" in *Virginia's Civil War*, ed. Peter Wallenstein and Bertram Wyatt-Brown (Charlottesville: University of Virginia Press, 2009), 189–200.

63. On the statue, see Lee to Thomas L. Rosser, December 13, 1866, LFPDA. For other examples of encouraging the development of the Lost Cause, see Lee to Edward Pollard, October 12, 1865, Lee Papers, Washington and Lee University Library, Lexington, Virginia; Lee to Walter H. Taylor, July 31, 1866, LFPDA; Lee to Cassius F. Lee, June 6, 1870, LFPDA; Thomas M. Cook, "The Rebellion: View of General Lee," *New York Herald*, April 29, 1865, 1. See also Varon, *Appomattox*, 68–71; Janney, *Ends of War*. Gary W. Gallagher minimized Lee's own involvement in and acceptance of the general order, which was written by Lee's aide Walter H. Taylor. Gallagher, "Proximity and Numbers: Walter H. Taylor Shapes Confederate History and Memory," in *Civil War Witnesses and Their Books*, ed. Gary W. Gallagher and Stephen Cushman (Baton Rouge: Louisiana State University Press, 2021), 261–90.

64. For examples of wartime laments about lack of support, see Lee to Jefferson Davis, September 21, 1862, and August 17, 1863, LFPDA; Lee to James Longstreet, November 28, 1862, LFPDA; Lee to Jefferson Davis, June 10, 1863, and April 20, 1865, both in Dowdey, *Wartime Papers*, 507–9, 938–39.

65. Cook, "Rebellion," 5; *Report of the Joint Committee on Reconstruction at the First Session, Thirty-Ninth Congress* (Washington, D.C.: Government Printing Office, 1866), 2:133; Lee to Sir John Acton, December 15, 1866, LFPDA.

66. Lee to Martha Custis Williams Carter, June 20, 1865, LFPDA; Lee to James May, July 9, 1866, in Jones, *Life and Letters,* 391.

67. *Report of the Joint Committee on Reconstruction,* 2:130, 134–36; Lee to Longstreet, October 29, 1867, in Jones, *Life and Letters,* 393–94; Pryor, *Reading the Man,* 451–52.

68. Lee to P. G. T. Beauregard, October 3, 1865, LFPDA.

— 7 —

THE SOLID SOUTH AND
THE NATION-STATE

T HE LOST CAUSE PROCLAIMED that Confederates fought for states' rights,
not slavery, and made that doctrine central to its view of the national government. In 1920, Mildred Lewis Rutherford, one of the most influential
leaders of the United Daughters of the Confederacy, not only proclaimed states'
rights as the South's cause but insisted that "the people must not surrender this
power to direct their local affairs to the Government." If the Lost Cause had a
continuing and powerful hold over white southerners' attitudes—and particularly if they were still fighting the Civil War—they should have consistently
championed the rights of the states and fought against the creation of the powerful national government that had emerged in the United States by World War II.[1]

The South, and the West for that matter, have most often benefited from
the national government's financial aid and assistance, and yet today they are
home to many people hostile to the federal government—and to groups determined to subvert it. Many, even many white southerners, assume that the
white South's opposition to federal power has existed since the Civil War and
has never waned. Arlie Russell Hochschild's widely read *Strangers in Their Own
Land*, for example, attributes South Louisianans' unwillingness to face environ-
mental problems and their embrace of the Tea Party, in part, to the persistence
of "grooves of history" cut by the 1860s.[2]

Historians, too, stress the South's consistent support for states' rights and
opposition to federal power. The title of Glenn Feldman's collection of essays,
Nation Within a Nation: The American South and the Federal Government, presents
the argument in its most emphatic form. Feldman's introduction acknowledges
that the South took federal aid, but he still puts the matter only slightly less

dramatically than the book's title: "Sectional resentment of the central government as something wholly separate, alien, even hostile, . . . has persisted and, one might argue, grown over time." The essays in the volume, however, go on to describe a somewhat more complex relationship between the South and the national government. Even historians who admit that complexity nonetheless still tend to treat a strong, consistent opposition to federal power as a fundamental element in the white South's politics. Often, they attribute that commitment to states' rights to the power of the Lost Cause.[3]

Since Appomattox, as historians have rightly stressed, white southerners' determination to preserve white supremacy has impelled them to fight federal intervention in southern race relations. In the 1890s and early 1900s, to preserve white supremacy, the southern states disfranchised almost all African Americans, and many poor whites as well. A smaller electorate facilitated the dominance of the region by a white elite committed to a hierarchical society built on white supremacy and with a rigid class and gender structure, a society promoted by the Lost Cause at the turn of the twentieth century.

Even more, disfranchisement made possible the total dominance of the Democratic Party within the region and the one-party system that came be called the Solid South. Historians of the Solid South, though, did not always assume its hostility to all forms of federal power. Indeed, some have shown the South's important role in the expansion of the nation-state. Recent historiographical trends have led historians closer to Feldman's case for persistent opposition to the nation-state, yet a case can be made from existing studies that between the end of the nineteenth century and the end of World War II, the white South played an important role in an expansion of many of the major functions of the federal government.

HISTORIANS OF THE SOLID SOUTH often attribute its loyalty to the Democratic Party, the very reason for the term "Solid South," to the continuing influence of the Civil War. Southerners, they pithily put it, voted as they shot. "In the haze of the Southern memory," David M. Potter observes of the early twentieth-century South, "the Democratic Party was becoming indistinguishable from the Lost Cause, and equally sacred." In the series of lectures in which he tied the party to the Lost Cause, delivered in 1968, Potter actually offered a better explanation of the South's loyalty, one rooted in present utility rather than past loyalties. Potter argues that southern Democrats had tremendous influence in Congress at a time when Republicans dominated national politics, because the white South had eliminated Black, and many white, voters without having its representation in Congress commensurately reduced, because of its one-party system, and because of its senators' and congressmen's resulting seniority and their skillful manipulation of the rules of Congress. The South thereby formed, as Potter succinctly phrased it, a "majority within a minority party," which gave them the power to block many measures, particularly those on behalf of civil rights for African Americans or that in any way threatened the South's repressive racial and social order. As a result, Potter concludes, the South had finally achieved what John C. Calhoun sought in the 1830s, a system in which the South served as a concurrent majority. During President Woodrow Wilson's administration, as Potter mentions almost in passing, southern support contributed to the creation of important new federal agencies. Although Potter does not make the point, his interpretation certainly implies that the South expressed its concurrence not just in stopping interference in race relations but also in creating many other forms of federal power—and not just during Wilson's administration.[4]

Potter delivered his lectures toward the end of an era in which southern historians often stressed or at least assumed the South's Americanness, and many historians examined the region's contribution to the two major reform movements of the first half of the twentieth century, the Progressive Era and the New Deal. As early as 1951, Arthur S. Link credited southern congressmen with pushing Wilson to a more radical reform agenda, and in 1963, before she became the founding mother of southern women's history, Ann Firor Scott wrote of a "Progressive Wind from the South" and made a case for southern congressmen's support for the expansion of the federal government's role. Frank Freidel, perhaps his generation's most distinguished student of the New Deal, pointed to divisions among southerners over the possible expansion of federal power but still concluded, "It was Southern leadership in Congress that enacted the New Deal program and subsequently supplied the president the requisite margin of victory to pass defense measures in the late thirties and early forties."[5]

As late as 1987, a distinguished volume of historiographical essays, *Interpreting Southern History*, included one on southern political history from Populism to the New Deal. In it, Richard L. Watson Jr. referred to southern influence in Congress at certain times and not at others, but he also showed southern Democrats' role in Progressive Era legislation and the New Deal before 1937. The next year, Dewey W. Grantham, very influential among the post–World War II generation of historians of the South, published an overview of politics in the Solid South. It highlighted divisions within the region's congressional delegations, and like Freidel's work, it stressed their continued conservatism. In the end, though, Grantham argued that the South played a key role in passing Progressive Era laws and supported the New Deal's expansion of federal power. Like many historians who acknowledge the South's role in shaping the New Deal, Grantham seemed at pains to explain that support, in part because he assumed that most southern congressmen were conservatives and that southern conservatives were "still addicted to the rhetoric and thought patterns of the 'lost cause.'" He and others who shared his hesitancy about southern support for federal power therefore pointed to such factors as white southerners' "traditional attachment to the Democratic party, pride in the party's national victories, the influential position of southern congressmen in Washington, Roosevelt's remarkable popularity, and their desperate need of economic relief." Yet Grantham also admitted that southern legislators overcame their doubts about the early New Deal because it enjoyed tremendous support in the South.[6]

Most recent studies, though, have less to say about the South's role in the expansion of the federal government's power than those of Grantham or Freidel. David M. Kennedy's Pulitzer Prize–winning 1999 contribution to the Oxford History of America series, *Freedom from Fear,* discusses the New Deal's achievements with little if any reference to the southerners' involvement in passing early New Deal legislation, and certainly not with the emphasis that Freidel put on their importance. Kennedy refers explicitly to southern Democrats' suspicion of "all forms of social insurance" and brings in the South primarily when its representatives abandoned Roosevelt after 1937. In a more recent history of the Democratic Party, Michael Kazin points to the fact that from the time of the rise of William Jennings Bryan, many white southerners embraced the Democrats' liberal vision. He acknowledges that southern congressman played an important role in the Progressive Era but says almost nothing about the early New Deal. Kazin focuses on Roosevelt's second term and emphasizes the enhanced role and power of organized labor, Democratic support for an antilynching bill, and the emergence of a new urban liberal wing of the party—all of which led many white southerners to rethink their loyalty to the party. Having been all but ignored in his discussion of the New Deal, white southerners became an important and conservative force in his next chapter on the post–World War II era.[7]

At least three historiographical trends have altered approaches to the issue of the Solid South's relationship with the nation-state. Two of those trends, New Left historiography and the cultural turn, both of which developed long ago but remain influential, did not lead to an examination of the Solid South's role in the creation of the nation-state. New Left scholarship minimized the accomplishments of reform and subsumed both Progressivism and the New Deal under the concept of "corporate liberalism," which attributed "reform" to the efforts of the corporate and business elite. That interpretation left a limited role for the South. The second trend, the new cultural history, all but turned away from the study of politics and state formation. *Reinterpreting Southern Histories,* a 2020 volume of historiographical essays intended to supplant the earlier *Interpreting Southern History,* does not, unlike its predecessor, have an essay on politics from Populism to the New Deal. The essays it does include make little mention of Progressive reform or the New Deal. Its editors stress the influence of postmodernism on southern historiography. Whether because of its influence or other factors, historians do spend more time on culture, or the stories people tell themselves, than on politics and government, or the state people create. Such an approach would certainly fit well with an emphasis on the power of the stories and symbols of the Lost Cause and leads logically to seeing their continuing influence.[8]

In a third trend, southern historians often stress southern distinctiveness, rather than its Americanness, as an earlier generation of historians had. In a 2018 collection of historiographical essays on the New South, Stephanie A. Carpenter's "The Great Depression and the New South" does mention southern support for the New Deal but devotes much more attention to the impact of the New Deal on the South. In doing so, it accurately reflects a dominant trend in the literature. Southern historians who now focus on the South's failings and distinctiveness choose to explore how the New Deal changed or, as they more often conclude, did not change the South, particularly its race relations. The emphasis on persistent racism also leads, as in Kennedy, to a focus on southern Democrats' opposition to Roosevelt during his second term and the resulting formation of a conservative coalition of Midwestern Republicans and southern Democrats, a story first told in James Patterson's *Congressional Conservatism and the New Deal*. A focus on the late 1930s leads logically to the white South's opposition to the civil rights movement, a central theme of the historiography of the post–World War II South, and to the white South's growing conservatism and influence, a focus of recent political commentary.[9]

SOUTHERN HISTORIANS' JUSTIFIABLE emphasis on racism and conservatism, like their stress on the Lost Cause and its stories, has contributed to the assumption that the Solid South always opposed the expansion of federal power. Yet an exploration of an existing and expanding literature, not just among historians but also among scholars in other disciplines interested in the creation of the American state, demonstrates not the Solid South's invariable support for states' rights but instead the important role the South played in the creation of an expanded, powerful nation-state. This work conceptualizes the dispute over the powers of the nation-state not as a continuation of the Civil War but as a confrontation between the nation's core and its periphery.

At least one of these studies of state formation, though, fits neatly into a narrative that stresses continued divisions between the sections and southern opposition to federal power. In *Yankee Leviathan: The Origins of Central State Authority in America, 1859–1877*, political scientist Richard Bensel argues for the role of the North in the expansion of the national administrative structure and stresses that sectionalism overrode class divisions, prevented the formation of a social democratic party, and hindered the development of social welfare functions within the national government. He goes further: "The United States in the late nineteenth century was really two separate nations joined together by force of arms," and he ends the book by declaring that "the continuing dilemma of southern separatism, not social dislocation associated with industrialization, would be the major problem facing late-nineteenth-century state builders." Bensel's South is not too far from Feldman's nation within a nation.[10]

In an earlier book on a later period, *Sectionalism and American Political Development, 1880–1980*, Bensel conceptualized the battle over the nation-state rather differently. He grounded "sectional competition . . . in a geographical division of labor between the economically advanced northern core and the underdeveloped southern and western periphery," a sectional division that "has been and remains the dominate influence on the American political system." A modernizing industrial society began in the core and generated opposition in the agrarian periphery, which then led to "a basic incompatibility between the economies of the industrial core and the agrarian periphery, an incompatibility that has its origins in the radically different orientation of the two regions toward the world-economy." Bensel still concluded, as he would in his later book, that the core played the central role in the expansion of the national government because the periphery viewed the nation-state "with some suspicion," although he admits "major exceptions to this pattern, such as the Wilson administration and the early years of the New Deal." Some might object that his two exceptions played a central role in the expansion of federal power.[11]

Two other major studies by political scientists share Bensel's conception of the battle as between core and periphery but do not agree with him that the northeastern core shaped the nation-state. In 1999, Elizabeth Sanders's *Roots of Reform: Farmers, Workers, and the American State, 1877–1917* challenged the corporate liberalism thesis. Like Bensel's earlier book, it places the emergence of the state in the context of a confrontation between core and periphery, but unlike Bensel, Sanders concludes that "the dynamic stimulus for Populist and Progressive Era state expansion was the periphery agrarians' desire to establish public control over a rampaging capitalism." The South, she contends, proved "the most cohesive of the periphery component regions" and "almost inevitably led the periphery's voting bloc in Congress."[12]

Where Sanders focuses on the Progressive Era, in *Fear Itself,* Ira Katznelson provides an overview of the New Deal and World War II. Katznelson makes an even stronger case than Potter for southern Democrats in Congress using their power to block any challenge to the South's system of white supremacy; like so many since Patterson, he also shows the South's growing conservatism in Roosevelt's second term. Whereas Potter had talked of a concurrent majority, Katznelson writes of the representatives of the former slave South as "the most important 'veto players' in American politics." "Both the content and the moral tenor of the New Deal were profoundly affected. Setting terms not just for their constituencies but for the country as a whole, these members of Congress reduced the full repertoire of possibilities for policy to a narrower set of feasible options that met their approval or at least their forbearance." Unlike Potter, who said little about the South's positive role, Katznelson makes the

South central to the passage of most important New Deal legislation, but that argument seems to have attracted less attention than his stress on how the South's determination to preserve white supremacy restricted the powers of the national government.[13]

In any case, Katznelson emphasizes the South's contribution to the creation of federal power perhaps more than any scholar before him. Southern Democrats in Congress, he writes, constituted "the pivotal bloc in the national legislature." "Although they—and the institutions in Washington they knew most intimately—did not make the key difference at every turn, the South's capacity to veto what the region did not want and its ability to promote, as a pivotal actor, the policies it did favor matter regularly and insistently over the course of the Roosevelt and Truman years." Katznelson concludes that "we live in a different country, different from what might have been without the exercise of power by southern members within America's uniquely capable national legislation." But Katznelson makes clear, "Without the South, there could have been no New Deal."[14]

A recent politics dissertation by Sean P. Beienburg attempts to revive the states' rights tradition on behalf of modern conservatism by freeing it from its close association with racism. He reminds historians of the seemingly obvious reality that the federal system was built on a widespread acceptance of the role of the states. Beienburg makes the important point that assertions of the rights of the states and opposition to an expansion of federal power often came from regions other than the South. Beienburg then goes even further than Sanders or Katznelson, saying, "Contrary to our perception of states' rights and antifederal politics being the purview of southern Democrats, between Reconstruction and the New Deal states of the South rarely raised such claims on issues that did not have a clear racial element. Instead, . . . the general rule was for the former Confederacy to aggressively champion federal expansion—to the bewilderment of contemporary observers who repeatedly but inaccurately misunderstood the nation's constitutional fault line as a continuation of the Civil War."[15]

Sanders and Beienburg show how the formation of the nation-state after the Civil War owed less to divisions rooted in that conflict than in the division between core and periphery based on their disparate responses to industrialization, economic concentration, and the expansion of a national market economy. They, along with Katznelson, also provide a powerful challenge to the ideas that the white South's commitment to the Lost Cause involved sustained support for states' rights or that southern Democrats consistently fought against federal power. They certainly did not argue that the South constituted a nation within a nation. Indeed, they make the case for the Solid South's essential role in expanding the power of the nation-state during the crucial period of its formation. A wide array of scholarship in both history and public administration allows a closer look at the South's role in the creation of the nation-state by focusing on the expansion of several key aspects of the new federal power: the income tax, moral legislation, economic regulation, social welfare policy, and defense.[16]

"THE MODERN DEMOCRATIC social service state," wrote historian George E. Mowry long ago, "probably rests more on the income tax than upon any other single legislative act." Political scientist Kimberly Johnson, in her later study of the rise of the national administrative state, makes the same point more emphatically: "The introduction of a national income tax was an important institutional and state-building change for the national state. With its own independent and non-diminishing source of revenue, the national government was now relatively independent of state-level interests," which enabled "the growth of a larger centralized state." If so, the South played an important role in providing the primary tool for the construction of the powerful nation-state, despite the tax opponents' appeal to the Lost Cause and the memory of the Civil War.[17]

Historian John D. Buenker's 1985 study *The Income Tax and the Progressive Era* acknowledges the South's role in passing the income tax. White southerners, he explains, favored it as a welcome alternative to the tariff that treated their region unfairly. They also believed an income tax would encourage greater economic equality among the states and undermine what they interpreted as the Northeast's economic colonialism of their region. In addition, loyalty to the Democratic Party contributed to southern congressmen's consistent support for submitting the amendment to the states for ratification. Yet Buenker still makes much of southern opposition to the amendment. He stresses that it "experienced highly effective opposition in all but a handful of southern legislatures, with two states refusing ratification and three others granting it only on the second try." He then ties that opposition to the "hallowed tradition of states' rights." Many southerners, he adds, "coupled their arguments with emotional appeals to the Lost Cause, conjuring visions of a new invasion of the South by an array of federal tax collectors, while others pleaded for state income tax or warned of the threat to the ability of the state to sell its bonds."[18]

Charles V. Stewart's earlier study of the income tax debates in Congress, however, documents southern support and shows that on the floor several southern representatives spoke in favor of the amendment and none opposed it. More recently, Robin L. Einhorn acknowledges the southern opposition that Buenker highlighted. The amendment, she admits, faced opposition in most state legislatures, and two southern states, Virginia and Florida, along with four states outside the region, refused to ratify it. Yet Einhorn counters Buenker's emphasis on the two states where ratification failed with the simple statement that "seven of the first nine states to ratify had been slave states during the Civil War." She offers her own interpretation of the reasons for southern support, finding that southern enthusiasm for a national income tax grew out of its opposition to the tariff, as Buenker had said, and out of its expectation that an income tax would bring economic benefits. But unlike Buenker, she does not find the Lost Cause so powerful. "Southern opponents of the income tax evoked their memories of the Civil War and Reconstruction," she admits, but its far more numerous "supporters believed that times had changed." To help make her point, she quotes the response of a member of the Virginia convention to someone who had called for those who had stood with Lee to stand against the amendment: "'The war is over, and for God's sake let us not bring these things into the practical problems of the day. We must look to the future, and not to the past.'" Einhorn makes the case for widespread southern advocacy of the federal income tax and the central role the region played in its passage. She highlights her conclusion that most opponents rejected appeals to the Lost Cause with an apt title for her essay: "Look Away Dixieland."[19]

If Einhorn is right about southern support and Mowry and Johnson are right about the centrality of the income tax to state building, then the South helped to make possible the powerful nation-state that would emerge by World War II. As Stewart points out, the tax's advocates did not necessarily seek to increase the power of the state, but clearly its potential to strengthen the nation-state did not frighten them. Southern Democrats soon did much more to expand national power in moral legislation and other forms of federal intervention.

During the antebellum era, white southerners had uniformly opposed federal moral legislation because they feared that if the national government had the authority to legislate morality, it could employ that power to attack slavery. After the Civil War, southern Democrats continued to fear federal regulation of morality. Most of the Christian lobbyists who campaigned for federal moral legislation came from outside the South, and northern Republicans passed much of the early moral legislation, such as the Comstock Law to keep pornography and information about birth control out of the mails. The slightly later Edmund–Tucker Act attacking polygamy, however, had a southern sponsor and some southern support. As the nineteenth century ended, more southern representatives became proponents of moral legislation; they even campaigned for and supported a law, modeled on the Comstock Law, to limit gambling information in the mails. In stark contrast to their former attitudes, they thereby asked the federal government to outlaw a state institution they saw as immoral, the Louisiana Lottery.[20]

Southern support for moral legislation continued to grow; in the years from 1907 to 1921, southerners introduced more bills to regulate morality than did representatives from any other region. They did not always embrace moral legislation, however. When Congress debated legislation to outlaw white slavery, or the interstate transportation of prostitutes and women for immoral purposes, some southern Democrats opposed the bill because they, as political scientist James A. Morone's phrases it, "immediately fretted about states' rights." If this becomes law, Morone quotes Representative William Richardson from Alabama saying, "there are no limits to which the Federal government might go . . . to regulate the morals of the states." But even as Richardson and other southerners invoked states' rights in opposing passage of the Mann Act, other of the region's representatives spoke in its favor.[21]

The most dramatic expansion of federal power over morality came with prohibition, leading to what Morone calls "American government's overlooked growth spurt." He explains, "Government officials tried to stamp out a major industry and an everyday form of leisure. Reformers used the state to redeem the citizens and their society. Did the New Dealers ever try anything quite as ambitious?" A few southerners did oppose prohibition, often invoking states' rights. And no doubt, as Morone's and other recent studies of prohibition stress, it appealed to white southerners in part because they saw it as a means to control African Americans, the reverse of what they had generally feared about federal intervention. Nevertheless, white southern Democrats did enthusiastically call and vote for such a dramatic expansion of federal power. Two of them, Richmond P. Hobson, a hero of the Spanish-American War linked to his father, a Confederate soldier, and Morris Sheppard, a Texan who often championed the Lost Cause, played central roles in passing the amendment in Congress. In the House, almost 80 percent of southerners voted to send the amendment to the states, and every southern state ratified the amendment, nine of them by margins of more than 2 to 1 in both houses of their legislatures.[22]

In "Beyond Parochialism: Southern Progressivism, Prohibition, and State-Building," Ann-Marie Szymanski points not only to the South's support for the prohibition amendment but also to its support for its enforcement. Two recent book-length studies of prohibition, Lisa McGirr's *The War on Alcohol: Prohibition and the Rise of the American State* and a book by Beienburg that builds on his dissertation, also stress that the South held fast to its support for prohibition until after its repeal. Like Morone, they stress that prohibition constituted a dramatic expansion of federal power—and not just over alcohol. McGirr stresses that prohibition played a "critical role in the building of the modern American state," particularly in the enforcement of antidrug laws, and fostering "new appetites for the possible uses of such power." Beienburg agrees, contending that "Prohibition's creation of a national law enforcement regime altered not only the relationship between the states and the federal government but also that between the government and the individual."[23]

Southern Democrats not only contributed to the adoption of the income tax and the establishment of federal power over morality but also helped to expand the nation-state's role in economic regulation. In no aspect of the economy did its support for federal regulation prove more uniform or the powers created more expansive than in agriculture. Just as in legislating morality, though, the South initially took no part in the expansion of federal involvement. It began during the Civil War, with the South out of the Union. Northern Republicans passed the Morrill Act for agricultural education and established the Department of Agriculture. In 1884, Congress created, within the department, the Bureau of Animal Industry, charged with controlling infectious diseases that threatened meat production. Southern Democrats in Congress opposed creation of the bureau and subsequent attempts at "arresting contagion," to use the title of Alan L. Olmstead's and Paul W. Rhode's book on the subject. Texans seeking to protect their state's cattle industry in particular fought such legislation; economic interests proved as important as states' rights in explaining the South's continued opposition to federal involvement in meat production. Many southerners in Congress even voted against the Meat Inspection Act in 1907.[24]

Nevertheless, in the late nineteenth century, southern attitudes toward federal involvement in agriculture began to change. Only three years after opposing the creation of the Bureau of Animal Industry, southern Democrats supported the 1887 Hatch Act that provided for agricultural extension agencies run by land grant colleges. During the Progressive Era, southern Democrats, often led by Sheppard, who had championed prohibition, pushed for an expanded federal role in agricultural policy. "Despite their states-rights tradition and instinctive distrust of federal activism," Dewey Grantham concluded long ago, southern congressmen "provided large majorities for long-term rural credits, a federal warehouse statute, an agricultural extension program, vocational education, and more effective regulation of commodity exchanges." Sanders reaches a similar conclusion. Southern Democrats "had not completely abandoned the defense of states' rights. When the race issue emerged in the debate over the extension bill, they insisted on the states' authority in social matters." Overwhelmingly, though, both southern congressmen and white southern farmers supported new federal agricultural programs during the Progressive Era.[25]

During an agricultural depression in the 1920s, southern Democrats advocated the McNary–Haugen bill, which proposed federal regulatory intervention in the agricultural market. During the New Deal years, southern Democrats gave overwhelming support to the passage of the Agricultural Adjustment Act, a central part of the New Deal, passed in 1933, that did intervene in the market to raise crop prices. In the Senate, only two southerners voted against it, and just four opposed it in the House. When the Supreme Court declared it unconstitutional, southern Democrats supported legislation that continued to provide for federal intervention to maintain agricultural prices. The program's success, Kenneth Finegold and Theda Skocpol argue, owed much to the existing government infrastructure that the South had helped create during the Progressive Era. That administrative structure included "experts in Washington who shaped the direction of policy, then overseen by local committees, in the south often made up of large cotton farmers." Other analyses of New Deal farm policy stress instead the role of those local committees, but overall, the national government's involvement in agriculture constituted a dramatic shift toward a greater federal role and authority.[26]

As Anthony J. Badger summarizes it, New Deal agricultural policy brought a "combination of production controls, government payments, and price supports"—policies that persisted until the 1970s. "The New Deal as a result regulated the daily economic lives of millions of farmers to an unprecedented degree—destroying some of their crops, telling them what they could and could not grow, providing an alternative source of credit." Or as Pete Daniel puts it, "More thoroughly than Sherman's army, the New Deal troops marched through the southern countryside and reconfigured it; the old declined, and in its place emerged a rural South modeled on the long-held dream of the United States Department of Agriculture of large farms, plentiful implements, and scientific farming." Yet, Daniel adds, southern rural people had tremendous enthusiasm for federal intervention and worshipped President Franklin Roosevelt for providing it. Most indicative of southern rural thought was the fact that 95 percent of farmers in the flue-cured tobacco regions and 75 percent of cotton growers participated in federal agricultural programs. Even planters in the Mississippi Delta, "the most Southern place on earth," James C. Cobb shows, embraced federal benefits.[27]

In fact, economic need rather than political theory probably explained southern support for agricultural policy. The complexities of a modern economy and the prospect of greater profits overcame any traditional states' rights ideology or any reflexive opposition to the federal government inculcated by the Lost Cause. With largely successful efforts to guarantee prices, New Deal agricultural policy involved a more dramatic expansion of federal involvement in the economy than in any other industry save electric power—and both had tremendous support from the South.

Southern Democrats also supported other aspects of federal economic regulation, though with somewhat less enthusiasm and consistency than they did in agriculture, and in some instances they opposed it. For example, Kimberly Johnson maintains that in the case of Progressive Era attempts to regulate food and drugs, the South, "where whiskey and other liquor distillers, as well as the proprietary medicine manufacturers and distributors, were located," was notable for "a complete absence of popular or official agitation for legislation, beyond a token pure food law." In 1906, when the Pure Food and Drug Act passed overwhelmingly, many House members abstained. Southerners cast sixteen of the seventeen negative votes, though. Jerome M. Clubb and Howard W. Allen also question southern Democratic loyalty in the Progressive Era Senate. They determined that senators from the South Atlantic states proved very supportive of the party's reform agenda, whereas those from the West South Central states were significantly less supportive. Yet even Clubb and Allen found substantial southern support for banking, and even business, regulation.[28]

The crafting and horse-trading needed to create and pass the Interstate Commerce Commission, the Federal Trade Commission, and the Federal Reserve System proved incredibly complex, and in each case the final legislation resulted from intense negotiations among competing perspectives shaped by the dynamics of party politics, regional economic interests, and attitudes toward government. In the end, though, southern Democrats played a significant role in the creation of these three key regulatory agencies that expanded the national government's presence and power in the economy.

In the long fight over the Interstate Commerce Commission, an early expansion of government regulation passed in 1887, John Reagan, the former postmaster general of the Confederacy and later frequent participant in Lost Cause celebrations, took the lead in the Senate. Political scientist Stephen Skowronek carefully traces the contested views and compromises that shaped railroad regulation, including Reagan's own. In the end, he concludes, the "most solid support in both houses" came from "the South, the Midwest, and the West," pretty much in that order. Two later articles, both by Keith T. Poole and Howard Rosenthal, convincingly demonstrate the South's central role in the passage of the Interstate Commerce Act. Another political scientist, Scott James, also credits the South with helping to establish the regulatory agency the act created. Southern support for such regulation may have waned with time; Skowronek finds decreased southern support for Progressive Era legislation to strengthen the Interstate Commerce Commission's regulatory powers.[29]

With Wilson, a Democrat, in the presidency, southerners in Congress helped create two more of the most important federal agencies, intended to provide government oversight of the economy, the Federal Reserve System in 1913 and the Federal Trade Commission in 1914. In each case, though, the final legislation creating them resulted from compromises among competing interests and the differing goals of the core and the periphery. In their accounts of the creation of the Federal Reserve, both Sanders and Roger Lowenstein, in *America's Bank*, argue that going back to the days of Andrew Jackson, many southerners and other farmers feared a central bank. Carter Glass, the Virginia Democrat who guided the bill to passage, claimed that Jackson haunted him throughout the process. Glass's caution in creating the bank, according to Lowenstein, was largely owing to his fears of federal interference in southern race relations and his ardent states' rights views, tied to his father's service in the Confederate army and his memory of the Civil War. In the end, Lowenstein argues, Glass helped push through the bill to fulfill his political ambitions, and after compromises to make more radical southerners happy, southern votes helped to ensure its passage. In part because of the compromises, Lowenstein contends, the Federal Reserve would be an unusual central bank. "Power would be shared between the center and the periphery, between the federal government and the private banks that it was designed to serve. If the establishment of the Fed constituted a landmark moment, when the direction of society veered from laissez-faire toward government control, it was nonetheless intended to be a compromise."[30]

With the passage of the Federal Trade Act and the Clayton Anti-Trust Act, Sanders sees another compromise between the core's desire for a strong, autonomous commission and the periphery's call for strict legal standards governing corporate behavior. James's account of the passage of the Clayton Act and the creation of the Federal Trade Commission challenges both the corporate liberalism thesis and Sanders's emphasis on agrarian opposition to corporate power. James instead stresses Democrats' need to build their party through an appeal to progressive voters. He therefore highlights the irony that "the party of limited government and states' rights . . . would preside over major extensions in the reach of the American state." The paradox may not be as great as James suggests, because the southern Democrats' commitment to states' rights might not have been as strong as he assumes.[31]

The early New Deal further extended the national government's involvement in the economy, and one of its more radical interventions came in the electric industry. The New Deal created, through the Tennessee Valley Authority and the Rural Electrification Administration, alternatives to private companies, in each case with significant southern support. Two other major additions to the regulatory state, which sought to restore faith in private economic institutions, were the Securities and Exchange Commission and the Federal Deposit Insurance Corporation, each of which met with southern approval. Jordan A. Schwarz has shown that Jesse H. Jones, a Texan who headed the Reconstruction Finance Corporation, played an important role in the creation of the FDIC. "Jones himself," Schwartz says, "had favored the concept ever since he heard William Jennings Bryan espouse it in 1908." The combination of Progressive and New Deal Era reforms had expanded the government's involvement in regulating agriculture, industry, and finance.[32]

Roosevelt's expansion of federal power proved even more dramatic in yet another function of government, social welfare legislation—and southern support for it is more surprising. Before the New Deal, two of the largest federal social welfare programs, the Freedmen's Bureau and the pension system for Union veterans and their dependents, met with not just southern opposition but also outright hostility. The Freedmen's Bureau challenged southern whites' control of their states' African American populations, and the pension system, for the most part, excluded the southern states. The South proved a little more open to a third early social welfare program, the 1921 Sheppard-Towner Act, a short-lived but innovative program to establish clinics for mothers and their babies. The Children's Bureau, which had been established in 1912, and various women's groups pushed for its adoption. Theda Skocpol, however, shows that few women's groups in the South joined that campaign. Even so, at the request of female reformers, Sheppard once more sponsored legislation to extend federal involvement. Despite the opposition of the American Medical Association, the vote on his bill to create the clinics gained overwhelming support because, most scholars agree, legislators feared newly enfranchised women. Most of the opposition within Congress came from southern Democrats and northeastern, particularly New York, Republican; both groups claimed the bill threatened states' rights. After enactment, however, every southern state participated in the program, although Louisiana and Texas did so only after much debate. Massachusetts, Connecticut, and Illinois never participated.[33]

The New Deal's major expansion in the field of social welfare policy, which proved a model of a new federal function of establishing basic standards of living, was of course the Social Security Act. Southern Democrats supported its passage and, according to Katznelson, played a key role in bringing it about.

The retirement system's initial exclusion of farm and domestic workers from coverage made white southern support easier, but recent studies suggest southerners were not the driving force behind their exclusion. Southern Democrats did in other ways work to limit the federal government's power to shape policies within their states but also sought to ensure that their states always qualified for federal funding.[34]

Expanding federal involvement in social welfare policy proved less popular than the other expansions among southern representatives, who perceived its potential to undermine the rigid social and racial order of the Solid South. For the same reason, federal support for organized labor generated even more southern Democratic opposition. Northern, urban Democrats' new focus on such issues and their advocacy of a federal antilynching bill hardened southern Democrats' opposition and, most historians agree, even led some to consider abandoning their party. Changes within the Democratic Party, as James Patterson shows, did contribute to the formation of a conservative coalition of southern Democrats and Midwestern Republicans that opposed any expansion of the New Deal. In his description of that growing split within the Democratic Party, Jason Morgan Ward stresses the role of race but adds, "As the anti–New Deal movement gained steam, southern conservatives linked recent history to the enduring lessons of the Lost Cause." Patterson's earlier study, however, points out that the "chasm" that was emerging "was not simply sectional." Half of the conservative coalition came from outside the South, Patterson argues, and southern Democratic support for Roosevelt's administration remained higher than in the "East or the Midwest, sections with larger numbers of Republicans." Patterson notes that the most significant factor in explaining whether representatives joined the new conservative coalition was whether they represented rural districts, an observation that seems almost prophetic in relation to the social basis of the early twenty-first-century conservative movement.[35]

Even after the formation of the conservative coalition, the Solid South contributed to one other aspect of federal power: the military establishment. Like support for moral legislation, strengthening the national military would seem to be one of the last things a South still remembering, much less fighting, the Civil War would support. Indeed, as Skowronek emphasizes, late nineteenth- and early twentieth-century attempts to modernize the military originated with military professionals, and these efforts were opposed by white southerners who instead advocated lower military spending and reliance on a strong national guard. Bensel, too, finds southern and periphery "resistance to military preparedness measures" in the years leading up to World War I and considers that resistance to be "consistent with earlier opposition to Reconstruction and the 1890 Force Bill. The South continued to see military power in the hands of the central government as a threat to 'republican liberty,' by which they meant regional political autonomy." Some historians argue that opposition persisted into the twentieth century. Jeanette Keith, for example, makes a case for southern opposition to World War I, particularly among rural southerners. She relates that opposition to southerners' persistent hostility toward the federal government and resentment of northern capital.[36]

In an earlier study, Anthony Gaughan acknowledges southern opposition to both preparedness and intervention. But, he concludes, once the war began and President Woodrow Wilson made support for the war a question of loyalty to the nation, southerners responded by embracing the cause. They even delighted in pointing out how much more patriotic they were than their northern counterparts. Three articles in a recent collection of essays on the South and World War I support Gaughan's view. James Hall discusses early southern opposition to the war but shows how in North Carolina enthusiasm for the cause and a willingness to serve in it quickly increased. Fritz Hamer chronicles how South Carolina's leaders suppressed disloyalty and thereby had "an opportunity . . . to align themselves with national policy." And Kathelene McCarty Smith and Keith Phelan Gorman recount how both faculty and students in North Carolina's women's college supported the war.[37]

"Since the end of World War I," Gaughan also observes, "no other region of the country has supported the use of American military force abroad more consistently than the South." World War I brought a greater federal presence into the region, in the form of new military posts and the veterans' hospital system, without much opposition. Naming some of those new military posts after Confederate leaders, Jennifer Keene argues, helped make Confederate identity patriotic and loyal. Post names may have contributed in some minor way to the South's growing support for the military. By the late 1930s, as even those historians who stress the South's growing conservatism and opposition to the expansion of the New Deal agree, southern Democrats in Congress proved the most loyal block of support for Roosevelt's intervention in World War II and his expansion of the military. Long ago, Freidel wrote that southern Democrats "supplied [Roosevelt] the requisite margin of votes to pass defense measures in the late thirties and early forties." Taking matters further, Katznelson argues that the South played a leading role in the expansion of the federal military establishment.[38]

The Solid South's contribution to the expansion of the military came late but proved important. By the years around World War II, though, it had already supported other dramatic expansions in federal power, by providing funding for that expansion through the income tax; by helping to establish as never before a role for the federal government in controlling morality; by pushing for one of its most radical expansions, intervention in the market to support agricultural production and prosperity; by leading the fight for central agencies to regulate aspects of the economy; and more tentatively, by voting to expand federal social welfare activity. In some cases, as Sanders, Livingston, Katznelson, and other scholars show, southern Democrats—though not only southern Democrats—created an unusual nation-state by preserving some of the prerogatives of the states. These scholars, however, still stress the new authority of the nation-state.

Throughout that expansion, some conservative southern congressmen opposed individual aspects of the expansion, or even all of it, often fearful that increased federal power might be used against the South's rigid racial and social order. Opposition outside of Congress began to grow as well. As the decade progressed, as Katherine Rye Jewell explains in her study of the Southern States Industrial Council, southern industrialists subtly challenged the New Deal and developed a new justification for opposing federal regulation: an emphasis on free enterprise. That approach helped shape the region's post–World War II conservatism. Nonetheless, during the New Deal, southern Democrats in Congress voted for, and often proposed and led the fight for, new federal powers. Most white southerners seemed to agree, as overwhelming southern votes for Roosevelt testify.[39]

The Solid South's solid support for federal power hardly seems surprising in a narrative of the growth of the administrative state that conceptualizes the fight for such a state not as a continuation of the divisions over the Civil War but as a battle between the core and the periphery—the South, parts of the Midwest, and the West. Calls for a more active federal government came from the periphery's position within a modernizing economy. Some scholars, in a similar interpretation, point to a split between urban and rural areas. Explaining divisions over the extent of federal power as division between the core and the periphery or the city and the countryside not only shifts attention away from the idea of a continuing Civil War but also anticipates the basis of the twenty-first-century culture war, with support for the conservative revolt based not just in the South but also in the Midwest and West—everywhere but the urban areas of the East and West Coasts, or as some might say, in the periphery but not the core.

After World War II, almost every historian agrees, the conservative coalition that had formed in the late 1930s became stronger. The Democratic Party's increased support for civil rights and African Americans' demands for racial change challenged white southerners' old assumptions. They lost confidence that their influence within the Democratic Party would prevent federal intervention in race relations, no longer assumed that white northerners agreed with them on matters of race, and had to face the fact that Black people could not simply be ignored or suppressed.

In the 1950s and 1960s, in their attempt to do just that, to perpetuate the oppression, segregationist leaders appealed to Lost Cause themes, naming schools and streets after Confederate leaders and waving the Confederate flag. Yet their appeals to the Lost Cause, as historian Robert J. Cook concludes, failed to fully mobilize white southern opposition. Perhaps the Solid South's limited embrace of the states' rights tradition and its long support for expanded federal power contributed to that failure—and to a surprising twist in the segregationists' fight. After a long, determined, violent campaign to preserve segregation, the opposition collapsed surprisingly quickly when defeat ultimately came. In an "ironic turn," as Katznelson wisely observes, during the Depression southern politicians "helped save liberal democracy so successfully that they ultimately undermined the presuppositions of white supremacy"—and, he could have added, the weak federal government that served to support it. The white South had helped to create the very federal power that later undermined its racial order.[40]

Because of the changes brought by the civil rights movement, the Civil Rights and Voting Rights Acts, and federal intervention in southern race relations, many white southerners came to resent and rail against the power of the new national government. The conservative surge in southern politics that began in the late 1930s and intensified in the 1950s and 1960s became more extreme in the decades after 1980, and it no doubt contributed to why so many assume the white South had always opposed the expansion of federal power. Yet early twenty-first-century southern conservatism owes more to the years after 1945 than to those after 1865, which also helps explain why the lines of division in the late twentieth and early twenty-first centuries do not really follow those of the Civil War. The South may still be more conservative than much of the country, but racial politics and antigovernment sentiments clearly extend well beyond the Mason–Dixon Line.

NOTES

1. Mildred Lewis Rutherford, *Truths of History: A Fair, Unbiased, Impartial, Unprejudiced and Conscientious Study of History* (Athens, Ga.: 1920), ix.

2. Arlie Russell Hochschild, *Strangers in Their Own Land: Anger and Mourning on the America Right* (New York: Free Press, 2016), 207–10.

3. Glenn Feldman, ed., *Nation Within a Nation: The American South and the Federal Government* (Gainesville: University of Florida Press, 2014), 2.

4. David M. Potter, *The South and the Concurrent Majority,* ed. Don E. Fehrenbacher and Carl N. Degler (Baton Rouge: Louisiana State University Press, 1972), 37, 59.

5. Arthur S. Link, "The South and the 'New Freedom': An Interpretation," *American Scholar* 20 (Summer 1951): 314–24; Anne Firor Scott, "A Progressive Wind from the South, 1906–1913," *Journal of Southern History* 29 (February 1963): 53–70; Frank Freidel, *FDR and the South* (Baton Rouge: Louisiana State University Press, 1965), 2.

6. Richard L. Watson Jr., "From Populism Through the New Deal: Southern Political History," in *Interpreting Southern History: Historiographical Essays in Honor of Sanford W. Higginbotham,* ed. John B. Boles and Evelyn Thomas Nolen (Baton Rouge: Louisiana State University Press, 1987), 308–89; Dewey W. Grantham, *The Life and Death of the Solid South: A Political History* (Lexington: University Press of Kentucky, 1988), 66, 103. More recently, Eric Rauchway has also pointed to the strength of southern support. See Rauchway, *The Great Depression & The New Deal: A Very Short Introduction* (New York: Oxford University Press, 2008), 88.

7. David M. Kennedy, *Freedom from Fear: The American People in Depression and War, 1929–1945* (New York: Oxford University Press, 1999), 262; Michael Kazin, *What It Took to Win: A History of the Democratic Party* (New York: Farrar, Straus and Giroux, 2022).

8. For an introduction to the corporate liberalism interpretation, the New Left, and the cultural turn, see Peter Novick, *That Noble Dream: The "Objectivity Question" and the American Historical Profession* (Cambridge: Cambridge University Press, 1988), 439–40 and passim; Craig Thompson Friend and Lorri Glover, *Reinterpreting Southern Histories: Essays in Historiography* (Baton Rouge: Louisiana State University Press, 2020).

9. Stephanie A. Carpenter, "The Great Depression and the New South," in *The New South*, ed. James S. Humphreys (Kent, Ohio: Kent State University Press, 2018), 150–72; James T. Patterson, *Congressional Conservatism and the New Deal: The Growth of the Conservative Coalition in Congress, 1933–1939* (Lexington: University of Kentucky Press, 1967).

10. Richard Franklin Bensel, *Yankee Leviathan: The Origins of Central State Authority in America, 1859–1877* (New York: Cambridge University Press, 1990), 425, 436.

11. Richard Franklin Bensel, *Sectionalism and American Political Development, 1880–1980* (Madison: University of Wisconsin Press, 1984), xix, 23, 52.

12. Elizabeth Sanders, *Roots of Reform: Farmers, Workers, and the American State, 1877–1917* (Chicago: University of Chicago Press, 1999), 3–4, 27.

13. Ida Katznelson, *Fear Itself: The New Deal and the Origins of Our Time* (New York: Liveright, 2013), 15–16.

14. Ibid., 21.

15. Sean Patrick Beienburg, "Constitutional Resistance in the States Between Reconstruction and the New Deal" (PhD diss., Princeton University, 2015), 239–40.

16. My categories here are generic but I hope still useful. For more extensive categories, see Ballard C. Campbell, *The Growth of American Government: Governance from the Cleveland Era to the Present*, revised and updated (Bloomington: Indiana University Press, 2015), esp. 38. Campbell has little to say about the role of the South during the period discussed here beyond its push for an income tax (209) and its opposition to civil rights legislation (187–88). See also his later book, *The Paradox of Power: Statebuilding in America, 1754–1920* (Lawrence: University of Kansas Press, 2021).

17. George E. Mowry, *The Era of Theodore Roosevelt and the Birth of Modern America, 1900–1912* (1958; New York: Harper Torchbooks, 1962), 263; Kimberley S. Johnson, *Governing the American State: Congress and the New Federalism, 1877–1929* (Princeton, N.J.: Princeton University Press, 2007), 31–32.

18. John D. Buenker, *The Income Tax and the Progressive Era* (New York: Garland, 1985), 190, 236.

19. Charles V. Stewart, "The Formation of Tax Policy in America, 1893–1913" (PhD diss., University of North Carolina at Chapel Hill, 1974), 86, 97,104, 110; Robin L. Einhorn, "Look Away Dixieland: The South and the Federal Income Tax," *Northwestern University Law Review* 108 (January 2014): 773–97, quotations at 793, 795–96.

20. The argument here about the expansion of federal power over morality rests primarily on Gaines M. Foster, *Moral Reconstruction: Christian Lobbyists and the Federal Legislation of Morality, 1865–1920* (Chapel Hill: University of North Carolina Press, 2002).

21. James A. Morone, *Hellfire Nation: The Politics of Sin in American History* (New Haven, Conn.: Yale University Press, 2003), 257–77 at 265.

22. Morone, *Hellfire Nation*, 283; Foster, *Moral Reconstruction*.

23. Ann-Marie Szymanski, "Beyond Parochialism: Southern Progressivism, Prohibition, and State-Building," *Journal of Southern History* 69 (February 2003): 107–36. In an argument similar to Beienburg's contention that a commitment to states' rights existed outside of and not just in the South, Szymanski also stresses that a tension between localism and nationalism was not unique to the South but was common throughout the country. Lisa McGirr, *The War on Alcohol: Prohibition and the Rise of the American State* (New York: W. W. Norton, 2015), esp. xvi and 246; Sean Beienburg, *Prohibition, the Constitution, and States' Rights* (Chicago: University of Chicago Press, 2019),

3. See also Daniel Okrent, *Last Call: The Rise and Fall of Prohibition* (New York: Scribner, 2010); and Joe L. Coker, *Liquor in the Land of the Lost Cause: Southern White Evangelicals and the Prohibition Movement* (Lexington: University Press of Kentucky, 2007).

24. Alan L. Olmstead and Paul W. Rhode, *Arresting Contagion: Science, Policy, and Conflicts Over Animal Disease Control* (Cambridge, Mass.: Harvard University Press, 2015).

25. Sanders, *Roots of Reform*, 314–39, quotation at 334; Grantham, *Life and Death of the Solid South*, 66.

26. Kenneth Finegold and Theda Skocpol, *State and Party in America's New Deal* (Madison: University of Wisconsin Press, 1995).

27. Anthony J. Badger, *The New Deal: The Depression Years, 1933–40* (New York: Hill and Wang, 1989), 147, 159; Pete Daniel, "The New Deal, Southern Agriculture, and Economic Change," in *The New Deal and the South*, ed. James C. Cobb and Michael V. Namorato (Jackson: University Press of Mississippi, 1984), 42; James C. Cobb, *The Most Southern Place on Earth: The Mississippi Delta and the Roots of Regional Identity* (New York: Oxford University Press, 1992).

28. Johnson, *Governing the American State*, 93, 106; Jerome M. Clubb and Howard W. Allen, "Party Loyalty in the Progressive Years: The Senate, 1909–1915," *Journal of Politics* 29 (August 1967): 567–84.

29. Stephen Skowronek, *Building a New American State: The Expansion of National Administrative Capabilities, 1877–1920* (New York: Cambridge University Press, 1982), 135–50, 273–74, quote on 149; Keith T. Poole and Howard Rosenthal, "The Enduring Nineteenth-Century Battle for Economic Regulation: The Interstate Commerce Act Revisited," *Journal of Law and Economics* 36 (October 1993): 837–60; Poole and Rosenthal, "Congress and Railroad Regulation: 1874 to 1887," in *The Regulated Economy: A Historical Approach to Political Economy*, ed. Claudia Golden and Gary D. Libecap (Chicago: University of Chicago Press, 1994), 81–120; Scott C. James, *Presidents, Parties and the State: A Party System Perspective on Democratic Regulatory Choices, 1884–1936* (New York: Cambridge University Press, 2000), esp. 104.

30. Sanders, *Roots of Reform*, 232–59; Roger Lowenstein, *America's Bank: The Epic Struggle to Create the Federal Reserve* (New York: Penguin, 2015), 7–8.

31. Sanders, *Roots of Reform*, 267–97; Scott C. James, "Building a Democratic Majority: The Progressive Vote and the Federal Trade Commission," *Studies in American Political Development* 9 (Fall 1995): 331–85.

32. Katznelson, *Fear Itself*, 252–57; Roger Biles, *A New Deal for the American People* (DeKalb: Northern Illinois University Press, 1991), 74; Jordan A. Schwarz, *The New Dealers: Power Politics in the Age of Roosevelt* (New York: Vintage, 1994), 73.

33. Joseph Benedict Chepaitis, "The First Federal Social Welfare Measure: The Sheppard-Towner Maternity and Infancy Act, 1918–1932" (PhD diss., Georgetown University, 1968); Carolyn M. Moehling and Melissa A. Thomasson, "The Political Economy of Saving Mothers and Babies: The Politics of State Participation in the Sheppard-Towner Program," *Journal of Economic History* 72 (March 2012): 75–103; Theda Skocpol, *Protecting Soldiers and Mothers: The Political Origins of Social Welfare Policy in the United States* (Cambridge, Mass.: Harvard University Press, 1992), appendix 2.

34. Katznelson, *Fear Itself*, 258–60; Daniel Beland, *Social Security: History and Politics from the New Deal to the Privatization Debate* (Lawrence: University Press of Kansas, 2005), 87–99.

35. Jason Morgan Ward, "'Negroes, the New Deal, and . . . Karl Marx': Southern Antistatism in Depression and War," in *Nation Within a Nation*, ed. Glenn Feldman (Gainesville: University of Florida Press, 2014), 112; Patterson, *Congressional Conservatism and the New Deal*, 160, 323, 329–31. For more on the use of urban–rural tensions, see Charles W. Eagles, "Urban–Rural Conflict in the 1920s: A Historiographical Assessment," *Historian* 49 (November 1986): 26–48.

36. Skowronek, *Building a New American State*, 212–47; Bensel, *Sectionalism and American Political Development*, 127; Jeanette Keith, *Rich Man's War, Poor Man's Fight: Race, Class, and Power in the Rural South During the First World War* (Chapel Hill: University of North Carolina Press, 2004).

37. Anthony Gaughan, "Woodrow Wilson and the Rise of Militant Interventionism in the South," *Journal of Southern History* 65 (November 1999): 771–808; James Hall, "Manhood, Duty, and Service: Conscription in North Carolina During the First World War," in *The American South and the Great War, 1914–1924*, ed. Matthew L. Downs and M. Ryan Floyd (Baton Rouge: Louisiana State University Press, 2018), 41–60; Fritz Hamer, "World War I and South Carolina's Council of Defense: Its Campaign to Root Out Disloyalty, 1917–1918," in Downs and Floyd, *American South*, 61–88; and Kathelene McCarty Smith and Keith Phelan Gorman, "The Call to Duty in the Old North State: Patriotism, Service, and North Carolina Women's Colleges During the Great War," in Downs and Floyd, *American South*, 116–34.

38. Gaughan, "Woodrow Wilson," 771; Keene quoted in John M. Giggie and Andrew J. Huebner, eds., *Dixie's Great War* (Tuscaloosa: University of Alabama Press, 2020), 22; Freidel, *FDR and the South,* 2; Katznelson, *Fear Itself,* 276–363.

39. Katherine Rye Jewell, *Dollars for Dixie: Business and the Transformation of Conservatism in the Twentieth Century* (Cambridge: Cambridge University Press, 2017).

40. Robert J. Cook, *Troubled Commemoration: The American Civil War Centennial, 1961–1965* (Baton Rouge: Louisiana State University Press, 2007), 325–26; Katznelson, *Fear Itself,* 23.

— 8 —

THE CONFEDERATE FLAG, THE LOST CAUSE, AND A CONTINUING CIVIL WAR?

O N JUNE 17, 2015, Dylann Roof murdered nine people in the Emanuel African Methodist Episcopal Church in Charleston, South Carolina.
Searches for information on Roof quickly led to a website that included
pictures of him holding a Confederate battle flag. African Americans in South
Carolina soon called for removal of the Confederate flag from a flagpole beside
the Confederate monument on the state capitol grounds. Governor Nikki Haley
and much of the state's Republican establishment, worried in part about how its
continued presence might discourage outside investment and undermine economic development, endorsed taking down the flag. Later that summer, after a
contentious debate in the South Carolina House, the legislature voted to remove
the flag. By then, attacks on the flag had spread to other states, and the governor
of Alabama ordered the battle flag removed from its capitol grounds. Two years
later, after demonstrations in Charlottesville, Virginia, over taking down a Robert E. Lee monument and the murder of George Floyd in Minneapolis, public
debates over Confederate monuments became more common than fights over
Confederate flags. Focus on the flag revived a bit in 2021, after a few people in
the mob that attacked the United States Capitol on January 6 carried Confederate flags; a picture of one of them inside the Capitol drew much attention.[1]

People who saw Roof with the Confederate flag, or the flag in the United
States Capitol, often linked the flag's display to the Lost Cause and to a continuing Civil War. Yet those who fly or defend the Confederate flag may act out of
different, more complex motives. Understanding their motivation begins with
a historical overview of the flag's public display, a survey of its changing role,
and the story of flag fights, particularly in the 1990s. By the early 2000s, various

compromises were reached to reduce its official use, and though many people had changed their attitudes about the flag, other had not. Americans remain divided over the issue. The factors that shape that division, deduced from the debates over the southern states' official use of the flag and from polling data, prove complex and diverse.[2]

An understanding of persistent loyalties to the flag should acknowledge the influence of the Lost Cause; a few white southerners still cite their ancestors when they explain their love of the flag, or they manifest a persistent defensiveness about attacks on it or on the South. Other factors, though, are more central to the defense of the flag. It has become a symbol of white supremacy, pure and simple, but also a means to display white racial grievance. That sense of grievance involves more than race, has spread outside the South, and has become politicized. This has made the lines of division over recent flag disputes very different from those of the Civil War or the Lost Cause. The sense of grievance among flag supporters, rooted in part in the fear that white people are losing their influence and their opportunities in a changing America, helps to explain why, by 2016, the division between opponents and proponents of the Confederate flag so closely resembles the country's current political and cultural divide, why the debate over the flag has become partisan, and why the greatest support for the flag comes from Republicans.

IN THE DECADES AFTER the Civil War, white southerners revered the battle flag, along with the three other primary flags of the Confederacy. Some still honored the Stars and Bars and the two subsequent official flags of the Confederacy. Southerners generally flew these flags, most often the battle flag, only on Confederate memorial days, during veterans' reunions, and on other ceremonial occasions. In the late 1930s, flying of the battle flag expanded as white southern fears of federal intervention in southern race relations increased, after only a southern filibuster prevented passage of a federal antilynching bill and southern Democrats began to break with the New Deal. In 1948, the battle flag's use by the Dixiecrats—the segregationist, independent southern Democratic Party that ran South Carolina's J. Strom Thurmond for president—spurred the flag's popularity. By the 1950s, it had become an ornament of popular culture, with Confederate flags flown in a multitude of contexts and featured on coffee mugs, T-shirts, beach towels, bikinis, and many other items. Flag defenders who claim it just represents southern pride often cite such uses to defend their position. At the same time, and not unrelated to its prominence in southern popular culture, the Confederate battle flag's use as the banner of the Ku Klux Klan, the Citizens' Councils, segregationist mobs, and others opposed to the civil rights movement and racial change cemented its association with white supremacy. In 1956, Georgia adopted a new state flag that featured the battle flag, and in the early 1960s, both Alabama and South Carolina began to fly the battle flag over their statehouses.[3]

Throughout these years, African Americans opposed flying the Confederate flag. The memory of the Civil War may be more central to African American attitudes than to those of most white southerners. Since the Civil War, African Americans have embraced what David W. Blight terms an "emancipationist memory" of the war; it stressed that the South seceded and the Confederacy fought to preserve slavery and thus made ending slavery and achieving equality the war's primary purpose. For African Americans, the Confederate flag therefore symbolized an attempt to preserve slavery. Yet in forging the flag's association with white supremacy, the segregationist use of the flag in the battles of the 1960s may have been as important, if not more important, than the memory of the battles of the 1860s. Since the civil rights era, the battle flag has become for African Americans a symbol of segregation and other forms of racial oppression as well as of slavery and the Confederacy.

After the victories of the civil rights movement, African Americans gained the public voice and power to demand an end to the flag's official display. At first, public controversies centered on the flag's use by colleges and high schools. In the 1970s and 1980s, a few legislators proposed removing the Confederate flag from the Alabama State Capitol, or adopting a new Georgia state flag, but these efforts failed. So, too, did the NAACP's demand for the flag's removal from atop the South Carolina State House dome; the NAACP then called for an economic boycott of the state until the flag came down.

Only in the 1990s did the fate of the Confederate flag generate an intense public debate. In 1993, after a moving speech by Illinois senator Carol Moseley-Braun, the nation's first Black female senator, the United States Senate denied the United Daughters of the Confederacy a patent renewal because its seal included the Stars and Bars, the first official flag of the Confederacy. At about the same time, disputes about the battle flag began in earnest in five southern states. In Alabama, the fight began in 1987, when the flag was removed from the state capitol building as part of a construction project. African American lawyers filed suit to prevent its return, and based on an 1895 law that said only the American flag would fly above the capitol, they won their case. The state's Republican governor appealed the decision, but when Democrat James Folsom Jr. replaced him, Folsom dropped the appeal, and in early 1993 he announced that the flag would not return. Outcries against his decision forced him to fly the flag near a monument on the capitol grounds. In Florida, where a Confederate battle flag flew as part of a flag display on that state's capitol grounds, two African American legislators in 1996 entered legislation to remove it. Their bill did not pass, but the state later temporarily moved the display as part of a remodeling project. In 2001, after other states had removed their flags, Governor Jeb Bush decided not to reinstall the display and instead placed the flag in a nearby museum.[4]

The most bitter fights occurred in South Carolina, Georgia, and Mississippi. In the early 1990s, Kay Patterson and other African American legislators in South Carolina called for the flag's removal from atop the capitol dome. The flag then became an issue in the 1994 election when Republican gubernatorial candidate David Beasley campaigned to keep it flying. Two years later, to the surprise of many, then-Governor Beasley called for taking the battle flag off the capitol dome; his attempt failed and may have contributed to his defeat in the next election. The fight raged on until, in 2000, his Democratic successor supported, and the legislature passed, a compromise, one opposed both by the flag's staunchest supporters as well as by the NAACP and most Black legislators. It removed the flag from above the capitol dome and placed it on a flagpole erected next to the Confederate monument on the South Carolina State House grounds.[5]

In Georgia, in 1992 and 1993, Governor Zell Miller attempted unsuccessfully to change the existing state flag, which incorporated the battle flag. The attempt's failure may have contributed to his reelection defeat. Seven years later, in 2000, another Democratic governor, Roy Barnes, and the legislature reached a compromise on a new flag. Opposition to it quickly developed and may have contributed to Barnes's defeat. His successor, Republican Sonny Perdue, pushed for and secured a referendum, and in 2004 Georgians rejected both the new flag and the current one. They voted to return to the pre-1956 flag, one without the battle flag though with stripes similar to those of the first official flag of the Confederacy. Only in Mississippi, where a referendum led to a resounding rejection of a new flag design, did no compromise occur. As it had since 1894 and would until 2021, the Mississippi state flag continued to include the Confederate battle flag.[6]

The compromises achieved by the early 2000s—taking down the Confederate flag in three states and redesigning the state flag in another—demonstrated changes in attitudes toward the official display of the Confederate battle flag. Polling data confirms the changes over the past three decades. Sociologist John Shelton Reed, in his 1982 *Southerners,* reported that, when asked about the use of Confederate flags in public schools, then more of an issue than its display on state capitols or incorporation into state flags, most white southerners approved. Only 23 percent of whites who identified themselves as southerners, and only 38 percent of those who lived in the South but did not identify as southern, opposed its use in schools. Among African Americans, 45 percent objected. By 1994, only a small shift in public attitudes had occurred. That year, a Southern Focus Poll conducted by the University of North Carolina's Center for the Study of the American South showed that only 33.5 percent of southerners and 37.1 percent of northerners opposed the flag's public display. At the climax of the crucial debates of the 1990s, more people opposed public use, but still not a majority. Two of three polls taken in 2000 showed that more people opposed its official display than supported it, 49 to 41 percent in one and 45 to 42 percent in the other. The third poll found that more people, 46 percent, wanted it to continue to fly than wanted it to come down, 44 percent.[7]

In the aftermath of the 2015 Charleston murders, two national polls asked Americans about flying the flag over government buildings or property and a third asked whether South Carolina had made the right decision. All three found support for removal had risen, in one to 57 percent, in another to 55 percent, but in a third only to 49 percent. Over a roughly thirty-year period, support for ending official use of the flag had risen significantly, at the very least by 14 and perhaps by 20 percentage points. The shift in public attitudes no doubt in part reflects a generational change, although surely some people had changed their minds. Many had not, however, and no consensus had emerged.[8]

The Charlottesville protests in 2017 and George Floyd's murder and the widespread protests that followed it in 2020 again forced Americans to face their nation's history of racial oppression. In 2021, Mississippi finally replaced its state flag that incorporated the battle flag and adopted a new one. With that change, official display of the flag had ended, and even private use had declined dramatically, though some groups and individuals still fly and promote it. Public opinion polls also indicated a continuing shift in attitudes about the flag. One taken in 2020 suggested that 55 percent of southerners and 56 percent of people nationally considered the battle flag a symbol of racism.[9]

Two other polls that year, though, showed that more people thought it a symbol of southern pride. Most important, both polls found Americans almost equally divided in their view of the Confederate flag. Also in 2020, after an African American stock car driver found what appeared to be a noose in his car's work area, NASCAR banned flying the flag at its racetracks. President Donald Trump objected on the grounds of free speech and in a later interview called the flag a source of pride for southerners. Trump's comments, according to one account, led to an 8 percent increase in Democrats calling the flag racist. The debate over the flag since the 1990s has become politicized and tied to a deep cultural divide within the nation.[10]

IN 2015, POLLS SHOWED, not surprisingly, white southerners to be among the strongest supporters of the Confederate flag's official use, and earlier studies demonstrate a statistically significant relationship between being a southerner and supporting the flag. Many white southerners who champion the flag explain their support as an act of loyalty to their Confederate forebears. During the 2000 debate about flying the Confederate flag over the South Carolina State House, for example, a few lawmakers who opposed its removal delivered impassioned speeches replete with references to their Confederate ancestors. Senator Glenn McConnell mentioned that another senator's "great-great-grandfather and my great-great-grandfather were in the same prison" during the war, and in another speech, he said taking down the flag was "an emotional issue, , , , one of love for our ancestors." Senator Addison (Joe) Wilson, another flag defender (better known for later shouting "You lie!" during President Barack Obama's State of the Union address), also called the fight "very, very personal. And it's personal because it's my family. For me it began very early in that I was named for a Confederate General." Wilson then went into considerable detail about his own ancestor's service during the Civil War. McConnell's, Wilson's, and similar appeals suggest that heritage, which pro-flag white southerners frequently juxtapose against racism as the reason they fly the flag, plays a role in support for the flag. A similar but slightly different way to define the role of heritage would be as the influence of the Lost Cause. The war's memory clearly did influence McConnell, Wilson, and no doubt other flag supporters.[11]

But by the 1990s, polls suggest, the Lost Cause had little influence on most white southerners. In the 1994 Southern Focus Poll, only 30.7 percent of southerners said they had an ancestor in the Confederate army. Another 7.6 percent had ancestors on both sides, and 7.7 percent claimed a Union ancestor. The rest did not know. In other words, unlike McConnell and Wilson, almost two-thirds of southerners either did not have a Confederate ancestor or did not know if they did. More than 40 percent of the same poll's sample could not name a Civil War battle. Only 32.7 percent could name one other than Gettysburg, which had been the title of a motion picture the year before. Almost half agreed with the statement "It's important to remember our history, but the Civil War doesn't mean much to me personally." Slightly more northerners than southerners (48.5 to 44.8 percent) said the war was important to them. More northerners than southerners disagreed with the statement "We would be better off if we paid less attention to history and put the past behind us." Almost 40 percent of southerners favored putting the past behind us, while only 27 percent of northerners did. Nor did shibboleths or symbols often tied to the Lost Cause seem to be widely embraced. In the poll, only 6.5 percent of southerners responded that they used the term "War Between the States," sometimes considered a marker of loyalty to the Lost Cause. A different poll, taken the year before, found only 13 percent of white southerners owned a Confederate flag; the only group that exceeded that average by much were eighteen- to twenty-four-year-olds, which may reflect the flag's presence in country music more than its relation to the Lost Cause.[12]

A majority of white southerners, it seems, did not know whether they had a Confederate ancestor, knew little about Civil War history, and cared relatively little about their Confederate past. Interest in or knowledge about the war—in other words, what might be termed the content of the Lost Cause—seems to have diminishing influence on attitudes toward the flag. In his analysis of an earlier 1982 poll with similar results, Reed perceived little relationship between knowing one had a Confederate ancestor or having an interest in southern history and a high degree of regional identification. He did not totally deny what he called the "historical connection," or what might be called the Lost Cause, as a factor in southern regional identity. But Reed did observe that "if regional identification depends upon a conscious and literal inheritance of the Confederate tradition, . . . it is in a great deal of trouble."[13]

In the fights over flying the flag and in answers to pollsters' questions, white southerners still do display a persistent pride in the Confederacy. In that same 1994 Southern Focus Poll, 86.7 percent of southerners agreed that if they had had an ancestor who fought for the Confederacy, they would feel proud of him. A similar percentage of northerners, asked the same question about a Confederate ancestor, also responded that they would be proud of him, which suggests that a national and not just a regional respect for military service may explain the pride. In answers to a somewhat different question in a 2011 poll, however, regional differences did emerge. Only 32 percent of non-southerners believed it appropriate for politicians to praise Confederate leaders; 52 percent of southerners said it was appropriate.[14]

Even in the absence of ancestral ties or much knowledge of the Civil War, southern respect for Confederate soldiers and leaders testifies to some sense of identification with the Confederacy. Indeed, according to Senator Arthur Ravenel Jr., one of the flag's most ardent defenders during South Carolina's fight in 2000, if the flag came down, "the children of South Carolina will be taught, in the name of political correctness, to be ashamed of their state's history." He clearly wanted to preserve their pride. Responses like Ravenel's reveal a sense among some white southerners that an attack on the flag constitutes an attack on them.[15]

Southern defensiveness has its roots in the defense of slavery, the Civil War, and the Lost Cause. In contemporary debates over the Confederate flag or monuments, critics of celebrating the Confederacy justly emphasize the ties between the Lost Cause and the perpetuation of white supremacy. The Lost Cause did indeed celebrate a fixed social order built on white supremacy, but other factors also shaped the Lost Cause. Defeat in the Civil War left many white southerners, Confederate soldiers most of all, defensive. In a culture shaped by honor, late nineteenth-century white southerners feared that defeat on the battlefield had resulted in a loss of honor and manhood. They therefore needed both their fellow southerners and their former foes to acknowledge their heroism, manliness, and military skills and to admit the cause's legitimacy. The Lost Cause encouraged a vindication of both the soldiers and the Confederacy, but it had more success in the case of the soldiers than of the cause. White northerners acknowledged Confederate valor, sacrifice, and military skill, but most did not change their minds on the South's responsibility for the war and its attempt to destroy the Union. In subsequent decades, northerners frequently criticized the South and looked down upon southerners, pointing to the region's poverty, backwardness, religiosity, racism, and other failings. As white southerners continued to feel under attack, their defensiveness persisted. During the recent flag fights, some white southerners saw attacks on it as yet another attempt to criticize and dishonor them, and they therefore support flying it.[16]

People who live outside the South and have no sense of attachment to the region have no reason to feel defensive about the flag or the Confederacy. As the debate over the battle flag and its association with white supremacy raged in the 1990s, and particularly after the Charleston murders, regional attitudes toward the flag shifted. Whereas northern whites once had supported flying the battle flag at rates similar to those in the South, by 2015, opposition to the public use of the flag had increased in other regions, particularly the Northeast. People who lived outside the South more easily changed their minds. Unlike Ravenel, they did not have to worry about what condemning the flag implied about their state's history, their ancestors, or themselves. They could dismiss the flag and its historical associations as yet another sign of southern failings. And the fight itself could be portrayed as a continuation of the Civil War, thereby equating racial repression with support for the Confederacy. Yet focusing the debate on southern shortcomings has its costs. It fails to explain support for the flag among whites in other regions, and more important, obscures or ignores national failings in matters of race.[17]

ANCESTRAL TIES, PRIDE IN the Confederacy, and a persistent defensiveness play a part in white southern loyalty to the flag, but these are not the central factors in the defense of the flag. Polling data consistently shows a stark difference in the attitudes of white and Black people toward the flag, although that gap had narrowed by 2015. And studies of individual Confederate flag fights have repeatedly demonstrated a statistically significant relationship between flag support and racism.[18]

Although he is in no way a typical flag supporter, Dylann Roof, whose murders set off the recent disputes over the battle flag, provides an example of the blatant form racism can take and serves as evidence of how loyalty to the Confederate flag is often the result of contemporary concerns rather than historical loyalties. Seeing Roof's picture with a Confederate flag, some observers quickly labeled him a die-hard Confederate. Although much remains unknown about Roof's motives and beliefs, what is known so far does not reveal a deep interest in Confederate history, although he does have a Confederate ancestor. Stirred by the murder of Trayvon Martin, a young Black man shot while walking peacefully through a predominantly white neighborhood, Roof embraced a radical white supremacy, railed about Black crime, and believed African Americans had taken over. His cause became a race war and the restoration of white supremacy. He initially found sustenance for his racist views on the website of the Council of Concerned Citizens, which has neo-Confederate ties and whose South Carolina chapter helped lead the fight to keep the flag flying over the South Carolina capitol.[19]

On a pre-massacre journey around South Carolina, Roof had his picture taken not only with Confederate flags but also at Confederate historical sites. In an insightful analysis of that tour, two *Washington Post* reporters noted that in Charleston, Roof did not appear to have visited Fort Sumter. They found it "odd for someone who drives a car with a Confederate license plate to ignore the place where the Confederacy began. But when the totality of pictures on his Web site, and the manifesto he posted there, are considered, it becomes apparent that the only part of the Confederacy that interested him was slavery. There are no pictures of Civil War battlefields, no screeds about the heroic Robert E. Lee, George Pickett's charge at Gettysburg, no Lost Cause ideology." Roof found inspiration not in the Confederacy, but as historian Edward Ball, who covered Roof's trial, observed, in Nazi Germany. If he thought anyone a saint, it was Hitler, not Lee. Roof embraced the Confederate flag, but in his Facebook profile picture he wore a jacket that had on it the flags of South Africa and Rhodesia. Any flag associated with white supremacy, it seemed, would do.[20]

Roof was not alone in his embrace of the flag as a symbol of white supremacy. Shortly after the Emanuel Nine murders, several flag-wielding whites in Georgia formed a caravan of pickup trucks that descended on a Black child's birthday party. They got out, according to a press account, "and unleashed a storm of death threats and anti-Black slurs, and pointed a shotgun" at the children, an attack for which they were convicted of terrorism. The next year, in

Houston, a group calling itself White Lives Matter went to an African American neighborhood, stood outside the local NAACP headquarters, and waved various Confederate flags. They claimed to protest attacks on white police officers and to denounce the NAACP for not responding to them. For them and many of its supporters, the battle flag serves primarily as a symbol of white supremacy; racism's association with the flag is central, surprisingly obvious and matter-of-fact, and most important, purposeful.[21]

Their racism, though, may not stem from the Lost Cause. In 2017, a few of the individuals or groups involved in the events in Charlottesville, such as Michael Hill and the League of the South, had direct ties to the Lost Cause, talk of secession, and dream of independence. Like Roof, most white nationalists in Charlottesville, many from outside the South, embraced the flag simply as a symbol of white supremacy and racial purity. The use of the flag by the Ku Klux Klan and neo-Nazis in the 1950s and 1960s not only had cemented its ties to white supremacy but also had associated it with a virulent form of anti-Semitism, never a theme in the Lost Cause but on display in Charlottesville. Also like Roof, white nationalists and neo-Nazis display the battle flag along with a host of other racist and neo-Nazi symbols. Their ideological racism owes more to Nazism and a nativist strain of white Protestant nationalism, promoted by the film *Birth of a Nation* and epitomized by the Ku Klux Klan of the 1920s, than to the Lost Cause.

MANY WHO WOULD NEVER think of joining a neo-Nazi group still defend the flag out of a racism intensified by a sense of racial grievance. In most states, African Americans instigated the campaigns against the flag, and the NAACP played a central role. Many white southerners defend the flag because they see taking it down as a concession to African Americans. During a 1994 protest over the flag on the South Carolina State House, for instance, a white woman there to support the flag shouted at a Black counterprotestor, "We've given you everything you've asked for! We're tired of it!" In the midst of the South Carolina debate in 2000, Senator Ravenel claimed, "The flag is a lot stronger now with a boycott a-goin' on than it was before. You don't really think the General Assembly of South Carolina is gonna knuckle under to the N-A-A-C-P, headquartered in . . . wherever the hell they are—where is it, New York?"[22]

Flag advocates often added that if the state took the flag down or removed it from the state flag, Black protestors would only ask for more. This argument sometimes just offered a way to dismiss as unreasonable the demand to remove the flag. In a letter to a newspaper, one Mississippi woman complained that "too many concessions" to African Americans had been made already, and she added that if Mississippi adopted a new state flag, "They'll want us to change the state flower because they don't like the smell." Most often, flag defenders referred vaguely to future demands concerning symbols or monuments. References to concessions, though, reflected more than fears for the loss of symbols. They also emerged from a more profound form of racist politics, one that intertwines the rhetoric of concessions with sanitized interpretations of history.[23]

During recent debates, the fear may well be that admitting the flag's ties to racial oppression in the past will lead to a major "concession"—doing something to address historic discrimination. Dylann Roof again provides a surprising example. In a little-noticed section of the racist screed that he prepared before the murders, he wrote, "I wish with a passion that n——s were treated terribly throughout history by Whites, that every White person had an ancestor who owned slaves, that segregation was an evil oppressive institution, and so on. Because if it was all true, it would make it so much easier for me to accept our current situation," by which he meant the loss of white supremacy. "But it isnt [sic] true. None of it is. We are told to accept what is happening to us because of ancestors [sic] wrongdoing, but it is all based on historical lies, exaggerations and myths." Roof's formulation wrongly assumes a world of African American domination, but his reasoning nonetheless implies a realization that if history did show that white people had oppressed Black people for centuries, actions to help African Americans might be justified.[24]

Refusal to confront just that conclusion, polling data suggests, relates to support for the flag. After South Carolina's 2015 fight over the flag, a Winthrop University poll asked, "Do you feel that generations of slavery and discrimination do or do not make it difficult for Blacks to work their way out of the lower class?" Of those South Carolinians who believed that history did make it hard for African Americans to succeed, 71 percent disapproved of flying the flag on the capitol grounds, but among those who thought history did not make it hard for African Americans to get ahead, only 30 percent said that they disapproved. Denying America's racial history eliminates one justification for attempts, such as affirmative action or social welfare programs, to help African Americans.[25]

The flag's ties to racism, in sum, helps to explain white supremacists' embrace of it and much of the support for flying the flag. Many also oppose ending its public use because they do not want to admit the nation's racial past and thereby open the possibility of addressing it in the present. To defend the flag allows them to deny that history.

THE ROLE OF RACISM and racial grievance in support for the flag helps to explain how the fight over the flag has become intertwined with current cultural and political divisions. The demographic divides over the flag point to the centrality of those current divisions rather than the persistent influence of the Lost Cause. A 2015 CNN national poll revealed differences in support for the flag—a difference of 16 percentage points between those who had not attended college and those who had, and a 14 percentage point difference between those who made under $50,000 and those who made more. A still larger difference existed between rural and urban support; 60 percent of the nation's rural residents favored keeping the flag up, whereas only 36 percent of city dwellers did. The largest difference revealed in the poll, however, was between members of the two political parties. Seventy percent of Democrats agreed that the flag should come down from government buildings, but only 39 percent of Republicans did. Sixty percent of Republicans supported the continued flying of the flag, a higher percentage than any other group except rural residents, who matched it. No stark North-South division emerged, however, because attitudes in the Midwest resembled those in the South. The 2015 CNN poll did show a 7 percent higher opposition in the Midwest to the display of the flag compared to in the South, but two other polls that year and another in 2000 suggested little difference in attitudes between the two regions; in one poll, support for the Confederate flag in the Midwest even exceeded that in the South. If the lower numbers for the Midwest are accurate, then the demographic pattern of support for the flag in 2015 looks much like the divide revealed in the 2016 presidential election, with support for the flag primarily in the South and Midwest and opposition to it in the urban areas of the Northeast and West Coasts, and with rural residents, the working class, and the less educated more likely favoring its official display than urban dwellers, the wealthy, and the more educated.[26]

The battle flag has become enmeshed in the nation's larger cultural and political divide. The dynamics of the flag fight since the 1990s helps explain that new role. A major reason Democratic governor Zell Miller campaigned to change the Georgia state flag was the Atlanta business community's fear that the flag would make attracting industry more difficult and that it would make Georgia a less welcoming place for the international community during the 1996 Olympics in Atlanta. In 2000 and 2001, the same commercial motives arose in other states. During the Mississippi referendum, wrote John Shelton Reed, the new state flag "was endorsed by nearly every Mississippian that any-one ever heard of." The campaign to eliminate the battle flag from the existing state flag, he continued, drew support from "a truly remarkable coalition of historic adversaries: civil rights activists and country-club Republicans, stu-dent newspapers and university presidents, casino managers and fundamen-talist ministers, trial lawyers and industrialists, college professors and football coaches." A remarkable coalition, indeed, but one that drew heavily from a local elite with national and international ties. In South Carolina, another "di-verse confederation of business, civil, educational, government and religious interests," as one study put it, led the fight to take the flag off the capitol build-ing. It included "at least 25 business groups, seven civic groups, 17 educational institutions, 17 government bodies, 26 government officials, and 18 religious organizations." Again, the elite and the establishment, worrying about national and international hostility to the flag, fought to take it down. Whereas at the turn of the twentieth century the southern elite promoted the Lost Cause, at the turn of the twenty-first century, as historian Thomas J. Brown rightly ob-served, much of the white South's elite led the campaign to remove the flag.[27]

While established leaders and a wealthy business elite, both in the South and in the rest of the nation, campaigned to take down the Confederate flag, persistent support for the flag came from the heartland and from among the less educated and less wealthy, the same groups that provided many members to the Tea Party movement after 2009 and many of Donald Trump's most ar-dent supporters in 2016. A poll taken during the 2016 South Carolina primary confirmed that confluence: only among those who planned to vote for Ted Cruz or Trump did support for the flag exceed 50 percent, with 70 percent of Trump voters arguing that the flag should continue to fly.[28]

Tea Party and flag supporters shared more than demographic characteris-tics, however. In her study of Tea Party members in South Louisiana, sociologist Arlie Russell Hochschild found that their political beliefs grew out of what she calls their "deep story," their contention that people helped by the government break in line in front of hardworking folks like themselves, who have played by the rules and now stand in line, waiting for the benefits of the American dream. In explaining their resulting resentment, Hochschild does not emphasize the role of race, but it is certainly an important factor—Tea Party supporters often see African Americans as the line breakers. In 2000, a national poll asked whether "the government in Washington is paying too much, not enough, or about the right amount of attention to the needs and problems of blacks and other minorities." Of those who thought the government paid too much attention, 74 percent wanted the Confederate flag to continue to fly over the South Carolina State House; among those who thought it did *not* pay enough attention, only 22 percent favored flying the flag, a difference of 52 percentage points, a far larger split over displaying the flag than was evident in race, region, education, wealth, or any demographic category in a 2015 poll. Taking down the flag then becomes yet another concession to "them," and honoring the flag represents a denial of America's racial past, which makes it easier to dismiss programs designed for "line breakers."[29]

Some of the flag's supporters embrace it as a way to express their sense of grievance, not just against the Black "line breakers" but also against an elite establishment that they believe to be out of touch with their values and obsessed with what they dismiss as "political correctness," including opposition to the Confederate flag. The Lost Cause helped make the battle flag a symbol of grievance, although country music and southern rock, which used it as a symbol of alienation and defiance, contributed as well. It now represents less the content of the Lost Cause, a memory and knowledge of the Confederacy, and more a sense of grievance about society today.[30]

It may also have become a symbol of traditional values. Psychologist Jonathan Haidt has written of various mental triggers that help shape modern American political divisions, triggers tied to a traditional view of society associated with rural America. Among them he includes loyalty, or strong ties to one's group; authority, or an "urge to respect hierarchical relationships"; and sanctity, or an emphasis on purity that also "makes it possible for people to invest objects with irrational and extreme values—both positive and negative—which are important for binding groups together." Perhaps authority, but certainly loyalty and sanctity, play a role in opposition to demands that the Confederate flag

come down. White southerners may be particularly susceptible to these triggers because of the indirect influence of the Lost Cause. At its height in the late
nineteenth and early twentieth centuries, the Lost Cause offered a model of the
good society as one built not just on white supremacy but on deference to aristocratic leaders and loyalty to the social order. The social vision of the Lost Cause
and the emphasis on conformity and order necessary to sustain a rigid, repressive racial and class system helped to render white southerners particularly
given to tribalism and hierarchy and invested in symbols that supported both.[31]

In evoking such values, the battle flag represents less the Confederacy than
a vision of an unchanged America, or perhaps only a vision of an America some
believe once existed. In 1951, a store owner in Knoxville, Tennessee, maintained, "The Southerner loves his country, his women, his church, and his
whiskey. The flag is a symbol of all these things so dear to his life." Forty-five
years later, a letter to the editor of a Birmingham, Alabama, newspaper explained, "As a Southern-American, I am tired of being told by others what the
Confederate flag means to me. . . . Speaking for myself, Southern heritage represents a way of life. . . . It represents a time when you could walk the streets
without fear. A time when the little man had a chance to make a life for his
family. A time when God's law was above all else." These definitions of Southern heritage and the meaning of the flag could just as easily define a conservative Republican vision of America, one shared in the heartland, not just in
the South. Indeed, most of the flag's proponents tie those values to the United
States, not to the Confederacy, which helps to explain the initially seemingly
paradoxical fact that the region with the strongest ties to the Confederate flag is
also the region with the largest percentage of people who think it is important
for the Pledge of Allegiance to be repeated in schools and who see America as
a great country. Rallying around the Confederate flag may be, in the minds of
many of its proponents, much more about preserving a conservative, traditional
vision of a white America than about perpetuating the memory of the Confederacy, much less reviving it.[32]

Opposition to further programs to aid minorities; a sense of grievance
against African Americans but also against cultural, business, and governmental elites; a strong sense of group loyalty; and an attachment to symbols lead the
flag's defenders to the Republican Party, which they think shares their concerns

and which, according to Haidt, has proved far more adept than Democrats at crafting messages to appeal to the triggers of loyalty and sanctity. Many Republicans do champion the flag as another way to appeal to such voters. Since the mid-1990s, the battle over the flag has become increasingly partisan. With three exceptions—Beasley, Bush, and Haley—it was Democratic governors who led the campaigns to end public use of the Confederate flag. In 1994, for the first time, South Carolina Democrats included in their platform a call to take the flag down. That same year, the South Carolina Republican primary ballot included a nonbinding referendum on the flag, and 75 percent of voters said to keep it flying. Two years later, during a primary fight, Republican presidential candidate Patrick Buchanan defended flying the flag over the South Carolina capitol building. He proclaimed, "Everyone should stand up for their heritage," mentioned his own Confederate great-grandfather, and disassociated the flag from slavery by claiming, "It did not fly over slave quarters, it flew over battlefields." In 2000, a renewed legislative debate over the flag coincided with another presidential primary. Democratic candidates quickly called for the flag's removal, and Republicans John McCain and George Bush said the decision should be left to South Carolina.[33]

That same year, conservative Republican polemicist Ann Coulter, a native of Connecticut and graduate of Cornell, came to the defense of the battle flag. It has "nothing to do with race," she stated categorically. "It stands for a romantic image of a chivalric, honor-based culture that was driven down by the brute force of crass Yankee capitalism, which was better at manufacturing weapons than using them, and that shortly thereafter gave us the Grant administration and the Gilded Age." Over the next few years, Coulter continued to defend the flag. In a 2004 book, she blamed the Democrats for the controversy, challenged what she called "revisionist history written by liberal know nothings," and claimed that the "Civil War did not pit pure-of-heart Yankees against a mob of violent racist Southerners." She dismissed the idea that the battle flag "represents admiration for slavery" as "a vicious slander against the South." She admitted slavery was "among the ugliest chapters in this nation's history—the ugliest after abortion, which the Democrats will get around to opposing in the year 3093." Pointing out that the pre–Civil War Democratic Party defended slavery, Coulter maintained that she would "start believing the Confederate battle flag hurts somebody's feelings as soon as the existence of the Democratic Party hurts their feelings, too." Trump was not the only Republican to embrace the flag.[34]

The stark partisan division, along with the equally dramatic rural–urban and heartland–coastal divides, shows that though white southern ties to the past and defensiveness may contribute to support for the flag, racism and an interrelated sense of cultural grievance are more important in explaining the twenty-first-century embrace of the flag. The Lost Cause played a role originally, but in the recent fights, loyalty to it is far less important. A sense of white racial and cultural grievance leads to support of the flag and the Lost Cause more than the other way around.

THE FIGHT OVER THE Confederate battle flag, like so many other disputes over historical symbols and memory, is less about the past than about the present and even the future. The controversy over the flag has been incorporated into a current partisan and cultural divide, with the demographic divisions over the flag being very similar to those that shape contemporary politics. To call that divide a continuation of the Civil War dramatically overstates the case. Although the white nationalists currently flying the flag may seek a new civil war, theirs would look very different from the last one, with a very different geographic divide. Even among Americans who consider the views of neo-Nazi and white nationalists extreme, deep and significant divisions do exist, particularly between the two parties. Attitudes toward the battle flag have become another sign of that divide.

Nevertheless, after the decades-long fight over the Confederate battle flag, its official use has ended, and attitudes toward it may be changing. One 2020 poll indicated that 56 percent of Americans, and even 55 percent of southerners, say the flag is a symbol of racism, although other polls found that far fewer Americans agreed with that. Whatever shift has occurred, whether it has been accompanied by a better understanding of history remains far from clear. A 2015 poll found that 53 percent of Americans believe slavery led to the Civil War. Yet an earlier poll, taken in 2011, gave people a choice of slavery or states' rights, and only 37 percent replied slavery; 53 percent chose states' rights. The fight over the Confederate battle flag has probably done more to change attitudes toward the flag than to deepen public understanding of fundamental historical questions concerning slavery and racism.[35]

Changes in the use of and attitudes toward the Confederate flag nevertheless remain important. The removal of a symbol so closely associated with white supremacy is good in and of itself—and even more so if the battle flag actually stimulates racism, as one experimental study by psychologists has suggested to be the case. If the flag debate serves as a prelude to a more fundamental discussion of the heritage of slavery, segregation, and racial oppression, and of the persistence of white supremacy in American society, it will become even more important. But the lag in changes in historical views and the persistent divisions over the flag suggest that a fight over symbolism, though important, is inevitably incomplete; it may lead to compromise over symbols but not to a conversion in attitudes toward substance, in this case race. Insofar as the public discussion frames the issue as a continuation of the Civil War, it may divert attention from addressing African American grievances against contemporary American society, but also the sense of grievance on the part of at least some of the flag's supporters. The long and continuing battles over Confederate symbolism reveals a serious and troubling divide within American society today. Framing it as a continuation of the Civil War or the persistence of the Lost Cause emphasizes the failings of the white South and thereby obscures the racist heritage and racial problems of the country as a whole.[36]

APPENDIX 1

2000 and 2015 Polls on Public Use of the Confederate Flag

2000 Gallup/CNN Poll, Flying the Flag on Southern State Capitols

OPINION	NATIONAL	EAST	SOUTH	MIDWEST	WEST
Stop the practice	44	50	43	40	45
All right to fly	46	42	48	50	45

2000 CBS Poll, Flag Flying on South Carolina State Capitol

OPINION	NATIONAL	EAST	SOUTH	NORTH CENTRAL	WEST
Remove	45	44	42	48	49
Remain	42	45	46	37	37

2000 NBC Poll, Flag Flying on South Carolina State Capitol

OPINION	PERCENTAGE
Should remove	49
Should remain	41

2015 CNN Poll, Removing the Flag from Government Property Other Than Museum

OPINION	NATIONAL	EAST	SOUTH	MIDWEST	WEST
Support	55	63	49	56	54
Oppose	43	35	50	40	43

2015 Pew Poll, South Carolina Taking Down the Flag

OPINION	NATIONAL	EAST	SOUTH	MIDWEST	WEST
Right to do	57	65	54	53	61
Wrong to do	34	26	38	40	27

2015 "A Nation Still Divided: The Confederate Flag,"
McClatchy-Marist Poll, Taking Down the Flag from Public Places

OPINION	NATIONAL	EAST	SOUTH	MIDWEST	WEST
Favor	49	57	46	43	55
Oppose	43	35	48	49	37

Note: In listing the results of "A Nation Still Divided," I combined the categories of "Strongly favor" with "Favor," and "Strongly oppose" with "Oppose." In all other polls, such answers as "Don't know" are not listed.

APPENDIX 2

Relationship between Demographic Characteristics
and Attitudes about the Confederate Flag

These tables provide a rough measure of the importance of various demographic characteristics in shaping attitudes about the Confederate flag. Using the 2015 CNN/ORC International poll, I compiled the percentage-point difference for those supporting the public use of the Confederate flag within each demographic group. For example, for gender, I subtracted female support for the official use of the flag (52%) from that for males (58%) to get 6 percentage points. I have listed resulting differences in percentage points for each demographic category in ascending order of difference.

2015 CNN Poll

CATEGORY	TOTAL DIFFERENCE
Age (4 categories)	1 to 9 points
Gender	6 points
Region (East, Midwest, South, West)	7 to 15 points
Race (white/Black)	11 points
Wealth	16 points
Education	18 points
Rural/urban	24 points
Party (Democrat/Republican)	32 points

Source: CNN/ORC International Poll, July 2, 2015, https://i2.cdn.turner.com/cnn/2015/images/07/01/confederate.flag.pdf.

I compiled the same information from the 1994 Southern Focus Poll, which reported only southern responses, so the comparison is far from exact, but it does suggest that over the course of the past decades the demographic basis of support for the flag has changed. Differences by region and education increased slightly, but there was a dramatic increase in divergence along wealth, rural-urban, and party lines.

1994 Southern Focus Poll

CATEGORY	TOTAL DIFFERENCE
Metropolitan/Non-metropolitan	0.1 points
Region (North/South)	1.3 points
Age	1.3 to 6 points
Gender	7.1 points
Party (Democrat/Republican)	10.2 points
Wealth	2.6 to 10.6 points
Education	9.2 to 17.7 points
Race (white/Black)	21.7 points

NOTES

1. "Secessionist Group to Launch 'Operation Retaliation,'" *Post and Courier* (Charleston, S.C.), July 29, 2016; Kevin M. Levin, "For the Virginia Flaggers, It's Hate, Not Heritage," *Daily Beast*, September 21, 2016 (updated April 13, 2017), https://www.thedailybeast.com/for-the-virginia-flaggers-its-hate-not-heritage; Graham Moomaw, "Anti-establishment GOP Candidate in Virginia Governor's Race Looks to Ride Confederate Nostalgia to Richmond," *Richmond Times-Dispatch*, March 28, 2017; Dan Mangan, "Kevin Seefried, Who Carried Confederate Flag into the Capitol During Trump-Fueled Riot, Arrested with Son," CBNC, January 14, 2021, https://www.cnbc.com/2021/01/14/kevin-seefried-who-carried-confederate-flag-into-the-capitol-arrested.html.

2. After the Roof murders, for example, Mason Adams termed Roof "obsessed with the Civil War." Adams, "How the Rebel Flag Rose Again—and Is Helping Trump," *Politico*, June 16, 2016, http://politico.com/magazine/story/2016/06/2016-donald-trump-south-confederate-flag-racism-charleston-shooting-213954. See also Adams, "Dylann Roof's Rebel Yell: How the Persistence of the Confederacy Led to the Charleston Slaughter," *Politico*, June 20, 2015, https://www.politico.com/magazine/story/2015/06/dylann-roofs-rebel-yell-119249.

3. On the history of the flag and its use see, John M. Coski, *The Confederate Battle Flag: America's Most Embattled Emblem* (Cambridge, Mass.: Harvard University Press, 2005); Patrick M. McElroy, "The Confederate Battle Flag: Social History and Cultural Contribution" (master's thesis, University of Alabama, 1995). For pictures of the various Confederate flags, see illustration in "The Fiery Cross and the Confederate Flag," p. 139.

4. Laura R. Wollver, Angela D. Ledford, and Chris J. Dolan found that the Columbia, South Carolina, *State* averaged eighteen articles per month on this subjecct in the 1960s, five in the 1970s, and three in the 1980s, before rising to twenty-five in the 1990s. Wollver, Ledford, and Dolan, "The South Carolina Confederate Flag: The Politics of Race and Citizenship," *Politics & Policy* 29 (December 2001): 719. A ProQuest-generated chart of coverage in the *New York Times* shows a similar pattern by decade. Coski, *Confederate Battle Flag*; Jonathan I. Leib, Gerald R. Webster, and Robert H. Webster, "Rebel with a Cause? Iconography and Public Memory in the Southern United States," *GeoJournal*, 52 (2000): 303–10.

5. In addition to Coski and to Leib, Webster, and Webster, see K. Michael Prince, *Rally 'Round the Flag, Boys! South Carolina and the Confederate Flag* (Columbia: University of South Carolina Press, 2004).

6. J. Michael Martinez, "The Georgia Confederate Flag Dispute," *Georgia Historical Quarterly* 92 (Summer 2008): 200–28.

7. John Shelton Reed, *Southerners: The Social Psychology of Sectionalism* (Chapel Hill: University of North Carolina Press, 1983), 140; Center for the Study of the American South, "Southern Focus Poll, Fall 1994," question 101, http://hdl.handle.net/1902.29/D-30614, accessed June 7, 2023; NBC News/*Wall Street Journal* poll, January 2000; CBS News poll, February 2000; and Gallup/CNN/*USA Today* poll, May 2000. See appendix 1 for a table of the various polls.

8. CNN/ORC International poll, July 2, 2015; "Across Racial Lines, More Say Nation Needs to Make Changes to Achieve Racial Equality," Pew Research Center, August 5, 2015, https://www.pewresearch.org/politics/2015/08/05/across-racial-lines-more-say-nation-needs-to-make-changes-to-achieve-racial-equality; "8/6: A Nation Still Divided: The Confederate Flag," McClatchy–

Marist Poll, Marist Institute for Public Opinion, August 6, 2015, https://maristpoll.marist.edu /polls/86-a-nation-still-divided-the-confederate-flag.

9. Nicholas Reimann, "Majority of Southerners Now View the Confederate Flag as a Racist Symbol, Poll Finds," *Forbes*, July 15, 2020; "Dueling Realities: Amid Multiple Crises, Trump and Biden Supporters See Different Priorities and Futures for the Nation," PRRI, October 2020, https:// www.prri.org/wp-content/uploads/2020/10/PRRI-Oct_2020_AVS.pdf; Linley Sanders, "What the Confederate Flag Means in America Today," YouGov, January 13, 2020, https://today.yougov.com /topics/politics/articles-reports/2020/01/13/what-confederate-flag-means-america-today.

10. Libby Cathey and Louis Martinez, "Trump Declares U.S. in 'Culture War,' Calls Flying Confederate Flag 'Freedom of Speech,'" ABC News, July 8, 2020, https://abcnews.go.com/Politics /trump-declares-us-culture-war-flying-confederate-flag/story?id=71656456; Doina Chiacu, "Trump Says Confederate Flag Proud Symbol of U.S. South," Reuters, July 19, 2020, https://www .reuters.com/article/us-usa-trump-confederate/trump-says-confederate-flag-proud-symbol-of-u-s -south-idUSKCN24K0I0; Cameron Easley, "As Trump Defends Confederate Flag, Democratic Voters Increasingly Say It's Racist," *Morning Consult,* July 22, 2020, https://morningconsult.com /2020/07/22/conferederate-flag-racism-southern-pride-polling.

11. CNN/ORC international poll, July 2, 2015; "Across Racial Lines"; "8/6: A Nation Still Divided"; Beth Reingold and Richard S. Wike, "Confederate Symbols, Southern Identity, and Racial Attitudes: The Case of the Georgia State Flag," *Social Science Quarterly* 79 (September 1998): 568–80; Christopher A. Cooper and H. Gibbs Knotts, "Region, Race, and Support for the South Carolina Confederate Flag," *Social Science Quarterly* 87 (March 2006): 142–54; "Secessionist Group to Launch 'Operation Retaliation'"; *South Carolina Senate Journal,* April 5 and 12, 2000 (McConnell quote), and April 13, 2000 (Wilson quote).

12. "Southern Focus Poll, Fall 1994," questions 44, 92, 93, 100, 103, 105. John Shelton Reed, "An Embattled Emblem," *Southern Cultures* 1 (Spring 1995): 396. See also "Civil War at 150: Still Relevant, Still Divisive," Pew Research Center, April 8, 2011, https://www.pewresearch.org/politics /2011/04/08/civil-war-at-150-still-relevant-still-divisive. Pew states that 8 percent of Americans displayed the Confederate flag. Kathleen Weldon reported that 14 percent of southerners "displayed the Confederate flag in their home or office or on their car or clothing." Weldon, "Public Opinion on the Confederate Flag and the Civil War," *HuffPost*, December 6, 2017, https://www.huffpost.com /entry/public-opinion-on-the-confederate_b_7796458.

13. Reed, *Southerners,* 85.

14. "Southern Focus Poll, Fall 1994," question 97; "Civil War at 150."

15. Prince, *Rally 'Round the Flag,* 185.

16. Here and throughout, the interpretation of the Lost Cause rests on Gaines M. Foster, *Ghosts of the Confederacy: Defeat, the Lost Cause, and the Emergence of the New South, 1865–1912* (New York: Oxford University Press, 1987). Much subsequent scholarship has emphasized continued northern criticism of Confederate soldiers and their cause. See John R. Neff, *Honoring the Civil War Dead: Commemoration and the Problem of Reconciliation* (Lawrence: University Press of Kansas, 2005); Barbara A. Gannon, *The Won Cause: Black and White Comradeship in the Grand Army of the Republic* (Chapel Hill: University of North Carolina Press, 2011); Carolina E. Janney, *Remembering the Civil War: Reunion and the Limits of Reconciliation* (Chapel Hill: University of North Carolina Press, 2013). On attacks on the South in the twentieth century, see Natalie J. Ring, *The Problem*

South: Region, Empire, and the New Liberal State, 1880–1930 (Athens: University of Georgia Press, 2012); Angie Maxwell, *The Indicted South: Public Criticism, Southern Inferiority, and the Politics of Whiteness* (Chapel Hill: University of North Carolina Press, 2014); Reed, *Southerners.*

17. "Southern Focus Poll, Fall 1994," questions 97, 101; CNN/ORC International poll, July 2, 2015.

18. John A. Clark, "Explaining Elite Attitudes on the Georgia Flag," *American Politics Quarterly* 25 (October 1997): 482–96; Reingold and Wike, "Confederate Symbols"; Gerald R. Webster and Jonathan I. Leib, "Whose South Is It Anyway? Race and the Confederate Battle Flag in South Carolina," *Political Geography* 20, no. 3 (March 2001): 271–99; Gerald R. Webster and Jonathan I. Leib, "Political Culture, Religion, and the Confederate Battle Flag Debate in Alabama," *Journal of Cultural Geography* 20, no. 1 (2002) 1–26; Byron D'Andra Orey, "White Racial Attitudes and Support for the Mississippi State Flag," *American Politics Research* 32 (January 2004): 1–18; Cooper and Knotts, "Region, Race, and Support"; Logan Strother, Spencer Piston, and Thomas Ogorzalek, "Pride or Prejudice? Racial Prejudices, Southern Heritage, and White Support for the Confederate Flag," *Du Bois Review* 14 (Spring 2017): 295–323; Ryan D. Talbert and Evelyn J. Patters, "Racial Stratification and the Confederate Flag: Comparing Four Perspective to Explain Flag Support," *Race and Social Problems* 12 (2020): 233–45.

19. On the South Carolina chapter of Council of Conservative Citizens, see Wollver, Ledford, and Dolan, "South Carolina Confederate Flag," 714.

20. Neely Tucker and Peter Holley, "Dylann Roof's Eerie Tour of American Slavery at its Beginning, Middle and End," *Washington Post*, July 1, 2015; Edward Ball, "United States v. Dylann Roof," *New York Review of Books*, March 9, 2017. See also Rachel Karadzi Ghansah, "A Most American Terrorist," *GQ*, August 21, 2017. At one point after his arrest, Roof made a list of his favorite movies. *Gone With the Wind* didn't make it but *Twelve Years a Slave* did. He thought it anti-white but well made. The list of movies appears in the document he wrote in prison, available at "Dylann Roof's Jail Journal," Age of Treason blog, January 9, 2017, http://age-of-treason.com/2017/01/09/dylann-roofs-jail-journal.

21. Ben Guarino, "They Waved the Confederate Flag and a Shotgun at a Black Child's Party. Now They're Headed to Prison on Terrorism Charges," *Washington Post*, February 28, 2017; Michael E. Miller, "Armed, Confederate Flag–Waving White Lives Matter Protesters Rally Outside Houston NAACP," *Washington Post*, August 22, 2016.

22. Woman quoted in "Confederate Flag Argument Heard in S.C. State Legislature," *Jet*, May 16, 1994, 17; Ravenel quoted in Prince, *Rally 'Round the Flag*, 203.

23. John Shelton Reed, "The Banner That Won't Stay Furled," *Southern Cultures* 8 (Spring 2002): 86.

24. Roof's manifesto appeared online at http://lastrhodeisan.com/data/documents/5t/88.txt. Copy in the author's possession.

25. "Winthrop Poll: Majority of S.C. Support Confederate Flag Removal," September 30, 2015. Copy in author's possession. For a news story on the poll, see "Winthrop Polls Looks at Race Relations After Flag Removal," WLTX, April 28, 2016, https://www.wltx.com/article/news/winthrop-polls-looks-at-race-relations-after-flag-removal/101-157481935.

26. On regional divides, see Gallup/CNN/*USA Today* poll, May 2000; CNN/ORC Interna-

tional poll, July 2, 2015; "Across Racial Lines"; "8/6: A Nation Still Divided." Other percentages are from the CNN/ORC International poll, 2015. See appendix 2 for poll numbers.

27. Leib, Webster, and Webster, "Rebel with a Cause?," 306; Reed, "Banner That Won't Stay Furled," 78–79; Wollver, Ledford, and Dolan, "South Carolina Confederate Flag," 716; Thomas J. Brown, *Civil War Canon: Sites of Confederate Memory in South Carolina* (Chapel Hill: University of North Carolina Press, 2015), 222–23.

28. "Trump, Clinton Still Have Big S.C. Leads," Public Policy Polling, February 16, 2016, https://www.publicpolicypolling.com/polls/trump-clinton-still-have-big-sc-leads.

29. Arlie Russell Hochschild, *Strangers in Their Own Land: Anger and Mourning on the American Right* (New York: Free Press, 2016). Hochschild ties such views to honor and to the Lost Cause—the latter much more directly than it is tied in here. CBS News Poll #2000–02A: Race, February 6–10, 2000, available through the Roper Center for Public Opinion Research, Cornell University.

30. Jason T. Eastman and Douglas T. Schrock, "Southern Rock Musicians' Construction of White Trash," *Jean Ait Belkir: Race, Gender & Class Journal* 15 (2008): 205–19.

31. Jonathan Haidt, *The Righteous Mind: Why Good People Are Divided by Politics and Religion* (New York: Vintage, 2012), 150–79 at 165 and 179.

32. McElory, "Confederate Battle Flag," 51 (Knoxville man quote); Webster and Leib, "Whose South Is It Anyway?," 273 (letter to the editor); Leo Ray, "A Tale of Two Flags" (undergraduate paper, Louisiana State University, 2017), copy in possession of author; Art Swift, "Smaller Majority 'Extremely Proud' to Be an American," Gallup poll, July 2, 2015. Clark, "Explaining Elite," also ties the flag to traditionalism.

33. Prince, *Rally 'Round the Flag,* 161, 168; "Debate Issues Dear to Southern Hearts," *Atlanta Journal,* March 1, 1996, A13; Leib, Webster, and Webster, "Rebel with a Cause?," 309.

34. Ann Coulter, "A Confederacy of Dunces," *Jewish World Review,* February 1, 2000; Coulter, "The Battle Flag," in *How to Talk to a Liberal (If You Must)* (New York: Crown Forum, 2004), 170–76.

35. Reimann, "Majority of Southerners"; "As Trump Defends Confederate Flag"; "8/6: A Nation Still Divided"; *60 Minutes/Vanity Fair* poll, April 2011, available through the Roper Center for Public Opinion Research, Cornell University.

36. Joyce Ehrlinger et al., "How Exposure to the Confederate Flag Affects Willingness to Vote for Barack Obama," *Political Psychology* 32, no. 1 (2011): 131–46.

CONCLUSION

ONFEDERATE FLAGS AT THE national Capitol and bitter disputes over taking down Confederate monuments readily evoke the idea of a continuing Civil War. As with the defense of the flag, a persistent identity rooted at least in part in the Lost Cause obviously plays a role, at least for some. A very few neo-Confederates may even still dream of secession and an independent southern nation. Yet to interpret current debates as Americans still fighting the Civil War, no matter how inviting it may be, should be avoided and the limits of the Lost Cause understood.[1]

The vast majority of white southerners do not dream of secession or revel in the memory of the Civil War; indeed, many of them know little about the war or their ancestors' roles in it. Fewer than 10 percent still hold to the old Lost Cause shibboleth of calling the Civil War the War Between the States. The Lost Cause did not create a persistent nationalism or ideology; it only yielded symbols than can be invoked on behalf of various causes, none more often and logically than white supremacy, given the defense of slavery mounted by the Confederacy and Lost Cause ideology. And as the essays here have shown, in the twentieth century, the white South embraced sectional reconciliation and came to see the region as part of one nation.

The nation's adoption of Civil War as the name for the conflict, a name chosen because it avoided any reference to the war's issues, testified to reconciliation, and D. W. Griffith's wildly popular movie *The Birth of a Nation* incorporated its blatant racism into a vision of a reunited nation. The southern representatives in Congress who played a crucial role in expanding the federal government's power certainly embraced that nationalism. When white southerners feared that the national government or other forces threatened white control of their society, whether in the 1960s or the 2010s, they sought not to secede from but to maintain control over a nation they saw as theirs.

People from outside the region sometimes take up Confederate symbols for the same reasons white southerners do. White nationalists came to Charlottesville, Virginia, to rally around a Lee statue and a president called those protestors "fine people" and commended flying the Confederate flag. Donald Trump hardly seems to have been shaped by the Lost Cause—or, for that matter, by any knowledge of the war at all. It is hard to imagine anyone more different from the Lost Cause's central figure, Robert E. Lee, than Trump. Trump's loyalists rally behind a leader who was a tycoon and showman and hails from New York City; he promoted the slogan "Make *America* Great Again." His followers, even the white southerners among them, hardly seem imbued with the Lost Cause. They see themselves not as establishing a new nation or reviving a failed one but as taking back *their* nation, a nation many of them, at least, see as a white Protestant nation. This is a vision more like that of the 1920s Ku Klux Klan—a national organization employing symbols that Thomas Dixon and W. D. Griffith had consciously associated with the nation, not just with the South—than of the Lost Cause.

A resentment of African American progress since the civil rights movement and opposition to government aid for African Americans contribute to many of Trump's followers' perception that they have lost status in a changing nation and to their resentment of economic and, especially, cultural elites. Their fears and resentments are also rooted in economic and cultural divisions between the coasts and the heartland—a division not unlike that which characterized the early twentieth-century debate between core and periphery over federal power. The recent battle over the Confederate flag unfolded along similar lines. An analysis of that fight suggests that one's political party, one's residence in either a rural or an urban area, and one's wealth and education, more than the continuing power of the Lost Cause, shape loyalty to Confederate symbols.

The Lost Cause, of course, played a role in creating the current division. The hierarchical southern society it helped to create left the South underdeveloped—an area of the periphery least transformed by the economic changes and a society most given to tribalism. In perhaps its most significant contribution to fostering the current debate, the Lost Cause denied that a determination to preserve slavery led to secession, which made it far easier for the white South to ignore its racism. The Confederate celebration at the turn of the twentieth century then went further and provided white southerners with rituals and a view of history that promoted a sense of vindication and virtual victory, not an identity shaped by guilt and defeat, as C. Vann Woodward argued.

The South and the nation would be much better off today if more white southerners had responded to Woodward's call for a deeper understanding of their past, especially an appreciation of the evils of slavery and secession. Interpreting current divisions as simply a continuation of the Civil War, though, does little to help overcome that failure. It evokes not the current demographic divides but simply a North-South split and therefore implies that the South alone still fights to preserve white supremacy. It falsely suggests that racism is a southern and not a national phenomenon, and it makes it far too easy for white northerners to hold to their "Treasury of Virtue," as Robert Penn Warren put it, and to ignore their own involvement with slavery, long history of racial discrimination, and persistent mistreatment of African Americans. Portraying today's battles over white supremacy as a continuation of the Civil War also minimizes the historical depth of American racism. It did not begin with the Confederacy, or even in 1619. It arrived in the minds of the English people who settled America, and it helps explain their decision to establish a slave society. The following two centuries of slavery then intensified it.[2]

Americans in the twenty-first century need to address not just the memory of the Civil War but also the national legacy of slavery and racism. They need to understand not just the racial but also the social, economic, and cultural divisions in the nation today. Understanding the history of the Lost Cause helps by showing how it shaped the modern South. But so too does understanding the extent of reunion and sectional reconciliation as well as the limits of the Lost Cause's power as time has passed. To argue that white southerners are still fighting the Civil War obscures far more than it illuminates and does not help Americans to address the deep divisions that threaten their nation.

NOTES

1. On neo-Confederate, see Evan Hague, Heidi Beirich, and Edward H. Sebesta, eds., *Neo-Confederacy: A Critical Introduction* (Austin: University of Texas Press, 2008).

2. Robert Penn Warren, *The Legacy of the Civil War: Meditations on the Centennial* (New York: Alfred A. Knopf, 1961); Winthrop D. Jordan, *White Over Black: American Attitudes Toward the Negro, 1550–1812* (Chapel Hill: University of North Carolina Press, 1968).

INDEX